THE HUMAN COST OF A MANAGEMENT FAILURE

THE HUMAN COST OF A MANAGEMENT FAILURE

Organizational Downsizing at General Hospital

SETH ALLCORN
HOWELL S. BAUM
MICHAEL A. DIAMOND
HOWARD F. STEIN
FOREWORD BY RODERICK W. GILKEY
AND GARY R. LIEBERMAN

QUORUM BOOKS
Westport, Connecticut • London

Library of Congress Cataloging-in-Publication Data

The human cost of a management failure : organizational downsizing at
   General Hospital / Seth Allcorn . . . [et al.].
         p.   cm.
      Includes bibliographical references and index.
      ISBN 1–56720–002–8 (alk. paper)
         1. Hospitals—Administration—Case studies.   2. Downsizing of
      organizations—Case studies.   3. Corporate reorganization—Case
      studies.   4. Reengineering (Management)—Case studies.
      5. Hospitals—Administration—Psychological aspects.   I. Allcorn,
      Seth.
      RA971.H766   1996
      362.1´1´068—dc20   95–37482

British Library Cataloguing in Publication Data is available.

Library of Congress Catalog Card Number: 95–37482
ISBN: 1–56720–002–8

First published in 1996

Quorum Books, 88 Post Road West, Westport, CT 06881
An imprint of Greenwood Publishing Group, Inc.

Printed in the United States of America

The paper used in this book complies with the
Permanent Paper Standard issued by the National
Information Standards Organization (Z39.48–1984).
10   9   8   7   6   5   4   3   2   1

» «
======

Contents

» «

Foreword

Roderick W. Gilkey and Gary R. Lieberman

Soren Kierkegaard once observed that the problem with life is that we live it forwards but understand it backwards. Nowhere is this truth more evident than when dealing with the realities of managing large-scale organizational change. This book provides all of us who are involved with such daunting challenges the kind of retrospective wisdom that can help us "live forward" with greater sensitivity and effectiveness. The story that Allcorn and his colleagues tell is not merely a cautionary tale warning us of the perils and pitfalls of leading organizational change, it also contains affirmative and positive lessons about what we need to do to provide constructive leadership and facilitate generative change.

Among the lessons learned are these:

- Organizations cannot downsize their way to excellence. In theory, reengineering and downsizing eliminate unnecessary work; in practice these responses eliminate people, implicitly defining them as unwarranted costs and underperforming expenditures. Downsizing is not a strategy, it is a tactic necessitated by a lack of a strategy. It is also a belated attempt to correct errors based on lack of insight and anticipation on the part of top leaders. Similarly, downsizing is not a positive vision; it is the expression of a lack of one. Such failures are based on an inability to anticipate the need for change, which always diminishes options and erodes opportunities; in this case the opportunity to redeploy people in new roles and promote organizational growth. In failing to anticipate the future, leaders are frequently overcome by it. Their belated and ineffective responses to change are painfully well documented in this book. If the present provides us with an unfolding context in which to view the future, we must ask why it is that we have such difficulty using it to envision the future and anticipate the challenges it brings. The failure lies in ourselves. It is for this reason that the authors' psychoanalytic perspective offers us so much. For it is, more specifically, in our unconscious that the limitations reside.

- The psychological defenses that allow us to maintain a coherent, stable sense of ourselves and our world can operate at the expense of seeing the new and threatening realities to which we must eventually accommodate. The paradox that emerges here is that in providing seeming clarity and precision, our view of the world can become fixed and defensive, screening out information about new realities that eventually descend on us and can disrupt and even destroy us. Paradoxically, we are more likely to hold on to outmoded views of the world if it has afforded us success. The philosopher Emile Cartier put the matter succinctly, "There is nothing more dangerous than an idea if it is the only one you have" (Langer, 1957). When it is a leader that holds on to his or her view of how to operate in the present, he or she imperils the future. This is the story you as the reader have before you. It tells of how, through our own psychological dynamics and defenses, we endanger the organizations and people to whom we are closest.

- The consequences of these dynamics are well documented by the authors, who write, "It is perhaps an understatement to say that the top-down handling of the restructuring process has left all levels of management feeling vulnerable, disrespected, worthless, ineffective, and unwanted. It is also noteworthy that the experience at General Hospital is not unique and, in fact, has been played out in many organizations throughout the United States."

- The critical factors in organizations are the human ones: To ignore them is to imperil the entire organization. This book is compelling, in part because of the authors' willingness to move beyond the academic safety of being observers to become participant observers, experiencing and communicating their emotional reactions. This makes their observations vivid and profound, because they come from the depths of suffering they are willing to experience, not merely observe. It will be important for the non-psychoanalytically trained reader to understand that the authors' propensity to share their own emotional reactions reflects neither the loss of critical objective distance nor self-indulgent catharsis and self-revelation. It is rather the responsible use of one's inner reactions as a form of important data about the realities one encounters in dealing with the human situation. It is particularly useful when trying to understand intense emotional situations, where our tendency is to avoid distressing effects and their significance and meaning. Of all the competencies required of managers and leaders, emotional competence may be the least understood and most important. From this perspective, the authors' insights and active participation provide a sounding board and stimulus for our own thoughts, emotions, and opinions, further enhancing our understanding.

- Leadership that fails to deal with the human factor will always be misguided and ineffective. In reality, the most difficult human forces for leaders to manage are those within themselves. How easy it is to deal with the complexities and paradoxes of organizations by creating simplistic plans and schemes that violate the complex realities of the organizations and the people in them. How easy it is to see dysfunction as residing in "others" who are then seen as redundant and expendable. How easy it is to see crisis as a function of external "industry turmoil" rather than as our own failure to anticipate, learn, and act effectively. Leaders are prone to yield to these psychological seductions, because doing so obscures their own responsibility for setbacks and reversals of fortune. Beyond that, they provide face-saving rationalizations and comforting activities to remove the "badness" that has descended on their world. Unfortunately, when this "badness"—understood as unwarranted costs and excessive capacity—is human, the reverberating and long-term costs can become tragic for everyone. Human capital is the most critical ingredient in organizational success. When human capital is suddenly viewed as an expendable commodity, it is discounted and devalued and will soon underperform.

- Arrogance is antithetical to leadership; it is a symptom of the inability to overcome the predictable uncertainties and anxieties associated with leading change. If that arrogance expresses itself by disenfranchising the people who helped build the organization, the changes can destroy it. Using external consultants to displace internal human resources is also counterproductive and destructive. As the authors state, "What these interviews show most clearly is how organizational change that does not involve participation of staff members can have harmful, personal psychological consequences that will cripple virtually any structural design."

- Expert consultants who are insensitive to human (process) issues provide little useable, effective expertise. Calling in specialized expert consultants presumes a correct diagnosis of the organization's problems. If this diagnosis is not consensually validated, it is likely to be a political response serving the interests of the politically empowered. If the diagnosis is not accurately defined, the use of the consultants' solutions is, again, likely to produce the organization's biggest problems.

- Leadership calls for humility and openness. Without those qualities it is very difficult to survive transition—the moment of chaos between no longer and not yet. In some ways we could say that the psychological contribution of this book is to document how unchecked narcissistic pathology in leaders wreaks havoc on their organizations. In that sense, the book is both a rich documentary and a valuable cautionary tale.

- While leadership requires belief in oneself, confidence in one's decision making, and willingness to take calculated risks, successful execution requires openness and active listening. In the context of change management, a leader should look for and insist upon open discussion and debate among the people affected. Hearing the reactions of others and taking advantage of the opportunity to incorporate their ideas will help move the organization most positively through the change and into the future. Such openness is as difficult to exercise as it is necessary, since the temptation is to make decisions on behalf of the organization—because one is the leader. This story illustrates, however, what can occur when leaders become myopic and fearful of the organization and exercise their power out of anxiety rather than shared aspirations.

While these lessons have great value, to focus on them as the principal accomplishment of the book and its authors is to miss the richer, more subtle insights offered here. As they state, "The purpose of the book is to add to the research and understanding of organizational change in the form of downsizing, restructuring, and reengineering by providing an in-depth look at the lives of an organization's members undergoing these types of management responses to change." It is from the rich field interviews that we gain the most compelling understanding of the effects of leadership decisions. The authors effectively force us out of the safe haven of management jargon, where we talk about structures, systems, redesign, and restructuring, as we are forced to deal with the human realities of pain, suffering, anxiety, and guilt. They force us to see the moral ambiguities inherent in the exercise of power and the destructive consequences endemic to the management of change.

As a result of the interviews, the reader is able to follow the negative effects of a lack of communication coupled with an exclusionary, forced change process. Over the course of the year, the authors have vividly documented the change process as experienced by the recipients. The increasing levels of frustration, anger, and anxiety on the part of the employees is very clear. Thus, while a successful change process moves through different stages, if the downsizing and reengineering is viewed purely in a short-term, bottom-line perspective, the initiative never moves beyond the chaotic intermediate stages toward real improvement. This book helps us understand and prepare for the typical reactions of those the decisions affect most, the people within the organization.

The authors teach us an invaluable lesson about leadership and change. They do so in a remarkable series of first-person essays that capture their individual perspectives on what they have observed. It is worth mentioning that while the lessons they share are drawn from the healthcare industry, the insights they share are universal. In its ultimate form, organizational change is a personal choice. Either we confront ourselves and our limited view of the present and change, or we fail to see the need to change in time and risk destruction. As individuals, failing to see the need for change and avoiding painful truths can hurt us and those around us. As leaders, responsible for ensuring the future of our organizations, we can—as this book demonstrates so convincingly—inflict irreparable damage when we fail to see the truth.

» «
═══════════

Preface

During the past thirty years, American industry has witnessed phenomenal change—driven by international competition, swings in economic cycles, and changes in government policy ranging from protectionism to the promotion of competition and free trade. Change is just about the only thing that is assured (Vaill, 1989).

During these times, executives, consultants, researchers, and students of management have witnessed the coming and going of many ways to manage change—to gain and keep a competitive edge. Management by objectives (MBO) and a myriad of Japanese-like approaches have come and gone. In their place are management techniques that promise to have more staying power because they represent cultural change, such as total quality management (TQM), or they promise broad systemic solutions that revolutionize work, such as organizational restructuring and business process reengineering (BPR). Yet another popular approach to managing change that sounds good enough to help manage stock values is downsizing.

Announcements of downsizing, restructuring, and reengineering have become an everyday occurrence during the past decade. Some large organizations have announced personnel cuts as high as 50,000, although few details and time frames are provided. Blue-collar and, more recently, white-collar jobs are being eliminated in the seemingly endless pursuit of becoming "lean and mean."

Downsizing and restructuring seldom occur by themselves. If an organization is to have fewer employees who accomplish more work and assume a customer focus, they must work better and smarter, and thus enters BPR, which restructures work. It is critical to rethink how work is performed as attrition, layoffs, early retirements, consolidations of departments and roles, and the elimination of layers of management occur. Those who remain are usually hard pressed to get the job done, especially when they have to spend considerably more time in meetings creating and implementing change and dealing with its negative side effects. Salaried executives and managers find that they have to increase the hours that they work. At the same time, hourly employees lose overtime and may have to go home without pay if there is no work to do. These kinds of changes make it easy to see how costs are held down. But everyone also seems to lose—including, it is being discovered, the stockholders—because downsizing, restructuring, and reengineering often fail to deliver on their promise of creating a more productive and profitable organization. In fact, sometimes these methods for managing change actually detract from organizational competitiveness.

Anyone who has been through a downsizing, restructuring, and reengineering knows exactly what happens if it is not carefully handled. Morale, organizational loyalty, and trust in top management vanishes. Employees become angry, fearful, and paranoid. Their lives are put on hold, like a deer transfixed in the center of a highway by the headlights of a speeding truck. Roadkill is all too common on the downsizing and reengineering superhighway. Those who are left are traumatized by the near miss and feel guilty about surviving. They must also mourn their many losses of colleagues and, perhaps more profoundly, their fantasies about themselves as valued human beings with promising careers. Survivors become exceptionally anxious about their being next. The rumor mill flourishes and is often fed by "top management–speak," which seldom answers the one important question, "What about me?" Employees, it is said, must adjust. As a result, employees direct their efforts at personal survival, which translates into withdrawing from each other, not speaking up in meetings, avoiding taking risks, and keeping an eye out for a new job.

The question is, "Why does top management, so often and with seemingly such a cavalier attitude, select downsizing, restructuring, and reengineering as strategies for coping with change when research indicates that they are all too often poor choices?" Three explanations seem likely. The first explanation lies in top management disbelieving or ignoring (denying and rationalizing) information that downsizing, restructuring, and reengineering can be extraordinarily devastating to organizations, including their own. They may think, "If everyone else is doing it, we must be behind the power curve." Consultants often become the "hired guns" who assuage management anxieties by providing reassuring strategies and soothing statistics as well as performing the important ritualistic role of becoming the expendable scapegoat.

Another explanation is that CEOs and others in their inner circle seize upon downsizing, restructuring, and reengineering as highly observable actions on their part that make it appear as though they are taking charge of a dire situation. Announcing downsizing makes them look good (especially turnaround executives), and it often favorably affects public perceptions and industry analysts and, by extension, stock prices. Never mind that the same executives who led the organization into harms way now plan on leading it out. Never mind that their poor leadership methods may contribute to creating an even more devastating organizational experience as downsizing and reengineering ensues.

A third explanation that might account for selecting such brutal responses to change lies in the existence of deeply embedded, sadistic personality tendencies which come forward (but which still remain out of consciousness) when one or more senior executives (they often seem to be more alike than different) feel that it is the organization, middle management, and employees who are bad and must be punished for creating poor productivity and profitability. Downsizing may then be viewed as giving everyone a "wake-up call." Executives who are anxious about their abilities and the survival of their organization find that "the enemy is not us but them," the members of their organization, which permits the executives to emotionally distance themselves from their employees and unwittingly take out their bad feelings and hostility on them. In effect, the employees deserve what they get.

These are three less than rational explanations for choosing organizational downsizing, restructuring, and reengineering when research has demonstrated them to be questionable and often destructive strategies for coping with change (Cameron, 1994; Filipowski, 1993; Roth, 1993). It is no wonder that outsiders, such as turnaround specialists and consultants, are often hired to do the "dirty work" which carries with it much deeper symbolic meaning, not unlike an organizational holocaust.

Understanding organizational change in the form of downsizing, business process reengineering, and organizational restructuring is critical if they are to be used properly (Cameron, 1994; Filipowski, 1993; Roth, 1993). Research regarding their effects and efficacy have, thus far, focused on surveys and one-time interviews. This research has raised fundamental questions about the validity of these approaches and, in particular, downsizing. There is yet another way to understand the nature and impact of these types of organizational change. The powerful lens of an in-depth longitudinal case study provides much greater insight about how exactly these types of change affect organization members; their thoughts, feelings, and behavior; and organizational effectiveness.

This book is based upon a longitudinal case study of organizational change that includes three sets of interviews with twenty-three senior and mid-level hospital administrators that were collected over a period of one year. The case materials are independently evaluated by three psychoanalytically informed organizational consultants. The case interpretations open for examination how organizational life can be understood using a psychoanalytically informed perspective.

This book illuminates exactly what happens to people when downsizing, restructuring, and reengineering are imposed upon the management and employees of an organization. The reader is invited to join the intimate experience of those interviewed in the hope that reading their story will create greater insight and sensitivity to changing organizations through downsizing, restructuring, and reengineering. In particular, the story of General Hospital provides the reader a fuller appreciation of the organizational devastation that is played out when downsizing, restructuring, and reengineering become the principal tools for adjusting to change.

ACKNOWLEDGMENTS

We wish to acknowledge the participation and courage of the twenty-three hospital administrators who made this book possible. We also thank those who contributed their time to proofreading and commenting on the manuscript. Thanks are also owed to our wives and family members, who supported the writing of this book by tolerating our absences "at General Hospital." Last, a special acknowledgment is owed to Lt. Savik for her many hours of steadfast companionship during this project.

» «

Introduction

This book is for healthcare and physician executives, consultants, human resource professionals, students, and researchers who want to understand how change in the form of downsizing, restructuring, and reengineering affects those who manage large complex organizations. The method used in this book is a longitudinal case study that spans one year in the lives of twenty-three healthcare administrators faced with the need to downsize, restructure, and reengineer their hospital. The interviews were conducted at four-month intervals and, when taken together, tell the reader an intense story about General Hospital (all names are changed throughout the book) and how those who managed it experienced and dealt with change.

The story is an intimate one. The thoughts and feelings of those going through the change are shared with the reader. These are, it is worth noting, very likely similar to the thoughts and feelings of those in thousands of other organizations undergoing the same types of change. Downsizing, restructuring, and reengineering have become popular responses to the need for change. These management strategies have become the bread and butter of many consulting companies, and they seem to be liked by top management, perhaps because they rely upon traditional management tools such as redrawing organization charts, recasting job descriptions, redesigning work, and analyzing numbers to determine efficiency. Downsizing, restructuring, and reengineering are, in fact, so pervasive that this story is really about America in the 1980s and 1990s. These methods for managing change have profoundly touched the lives of a high percentage of American workers. Tens of millions of workers have lived through them with their family and friends. One is left to wonder why we are creating a workforce that feels expendable and what the long-term effects will be upon productivity.

However, it is also important to acknowledge that these types of change in hospitals are many times necessary, as is the case for General Hospital. Hospitals must adjust to lower occupancy and they must lower their costs to compete in the managed care marketplace. There can be no doubt that this is an imperative for survival. However, this book makes it clear that the human side of the workplace can only be ignored at great risk when change is being contemplated. Organizations and hospitals are created by their employees when they come to work. They create them in their hearts and minds. It is, therefore, a necessity to plan and understand change in hospitals from a psychologically informed perspective.

This book examines the affects of downsizing, restructuring, and reengineering upon the employees of General Hospital from a psychoanalytically informed perspective. The story of General Hospital is filled with the psychological trauma of these three types of change, and it begs to be understood as a story of people doing their best to live through convulsive change in their work lives. The story that emerges from the interviews is a sad one that is filled with loss, guilt, fear, anger, and tears, but also some successes and hope.

THE WORK OF THE CASE CONSULTANTS

Consulting to the psychological side of organizational change, while not new, is also not well established as a practice and not understood or appreciated by many executives. It is certainly not the subject of many textbooks and, while often implicit in many organizational development texts, it is not usually explicitly explored.

This book explores the psychological side of a longitudinal case study of change by including the thoughts and insights of three psychoanalytically informed consultants, researchers, and university professors. Each was asked to read the case and independently develop his own independent understanding. Each interpreted and commented on the three sets of interviews in a serial fashion, as though he were entering General Hospital at three different times. Each was asked to summarize the story of each set of interviews, comment on its psychological side, and offer suggestions as to how downsizing, restructuring, and reengineering might have been facilitated by psychologically informed consultation. In this way, the reader is exposed to the ideas of three consultants working in isolation from each other.

This approach accomplishes two things. First, it enriches our understanding of the case and its story by assuring that the consultants developed their own unique understanding. Second, it also explores whether these consultants come to understand the story in much the same way because they share a common psychoanalytically informed perspective of organizational life. The voice of each consultant is intentionally not edited into a common style to retain the integrity of his independent work and to underscore the differences among them.

THE ORGANIZATION OF THE BOOK

The reader is provided three sets of twelve interviews that the consultants read. The remaining three sets of eleven interviews were not published due to space limitations. The consultants were polled to select those omitted (see Figure I.1). The deleted interviews are, however, available from the first author.

The book is organized into five sections. The first section provides an orientation to the literature on downsizing, restructuring, and reengineering and introduces the context of the longitudinal case study. The next three sections provide the case material generated by the three sets of interviews. It is hoped that they will be read in full to promote the development of empathy for the management team at General Hospital. It is important to appreciate the depth of experience and feeling and pathos of those interviewed at General Hospital, as it may just as well be taking place in your hospital or organization if it is going through similar change. This understanding permits the reader to draw his or her own conclusions about the nature of the change and its effects upon employees before reading those of the consultants.

It is also appreciated that all readers may not be interested in reading all twelve sets of interviews. The consultants were polled as to which interviews sets they felt were most important to read, and six were selected as most representative of the entire case. These interviews are the first six in each set and are, therefore, out of date order.

The interviews are followed by the three independent interpretations. Each consultant drew his own conclusions, which may differ from those of the other consultants and yours. It is in this difference that learning begins. Are they right? What did they seem to miss? How would you have approached the change process differently? The three interpretations are followed by an overview by the first author; the interviewer and story teller.

The book concludes with a fifth section that includes an update on the recent events at General Hospital and summaries written by each consultant after reading the entire manuscript (including each other's interpretations) and after a two-day research meeting to discuss the manuscript. The first author concludes the book with an overview of the final remarks of the case consultants.

In sum, the case materials, the three independent interpretations, the overviews, and the concluding section provide those who want to understand the psychological side of change a rich learning opportu-

Figure I.1
List of Interviews Published and Omitted

PUBLISHED

The following six interviews appear first and were selected as representative of the case in the event all the interviews are not read.

Jacob Dohrman
Brenda Early
Joseph Greene
Val Kasman
Ed Mills
Stan Pittman

The following are the remaining six interviews published.

Jeri Glover
Antonio Lozano
Peggy Lubin
Ted Olsen
Maria Meyers
Chris Regan

OMITTED INTERVIEWS

Copies of these interviews are available from the first author in the event the reader feels that it is important to read them.

Tom Frey
Judy Harris
Chris Forbes
Mary James
Doug Lofgren
Julie Nugent
Mike Payne
Bob Ryder
Rosetta Shelton
Matt Towner
Cynthia Winston

nity. The book also provides many ideas as to how to become a better change agent during a time when organizations must make demanding changes to become more cost effective so as to better compete in the marketplace. In particular, successfully participating in the new healthcare delivery landscape, which is filled with horizontally and vertically integrated networks, will demand the most from healthcare and physician executives. They must lead their hospitals in a process of constant change in order to insure the survival of their hospitals.

READING THE BOOK

When this work began, no one had any idea what would happen. What did ultimately happen to the management at General Hospital revealed such a depth of pain and suffering, danger, chaos, and personal and organizational disintegration that it staggered and humbled the three case consultants. They were each in their own way resistant to hearing the story. They did not want to believe that it actually happened. The three consultants happen to be Jewish, and General Hospital confronted them with some of the devastating aspects of the Holocaust. However, each had also either experienced or was experiencing the effects of downsizing, restructuring, and reengineering at his university. The experience revealed in the case was a familiar experience that was painful to relive.

This information is shared with the reader for one reason. The case is very likely going to be painfully familiar. This may make it difficult to hear the story or complete reading the story. The manuscript was shared with a few individuals for comment. What was surprising was that they all said, "Yes, this is almost exactly what happened where I worked." In sum, reading the case may lead to revisiting painful life experience that will, in turn, lead to resistance to reading and hearing the story.

A second aspect of this book is that the horrific story that unfolds at General Hospital will make executives who have led or participated in these types of change feel anxious, defensive, and resistant. The case will seem to be one of a kind, an anomaly, and certainly unlike anything the reader participated in. The interpretations may be rationalized as biased and unduly critical or negative. After all, change has to occur and how else can it be done? This book, however, unquestionably challenges the veracity of these types of change and, for those who have planned, led, or supported downsizing, restructuring, and reengineering, it is perhaps time to reconsider the use of these methods for managing change given the insights gained from this book.

In sum, this book confronts the reader with a journey into darkness. It deals with painful and distressing content that many may feel is better left alone. However, the reader is challenged to join with the consultants who, at first, tried to understand and find meaning in the case as it unfolded and who eventually became distressed and humbled by the experience described. In the end, they found themselves fitfully living with the case and its pain. They struggled with their own thoughts and feelings and the wish to be rid of the knowledge and to sooth those who were interviewed—to make themselves whole and restore their faith in human nature. The reader will no doubt share some of these experiences with the case consultants. This is an important journey to undertake with them because it is critical to find ways to make change in the workplace that do not recreate the experience you are about to read.

A WORD ON CONFIDENTIALITY

The case materials were developed in the context of a pledge of confidentiality to those interviewed to encourage open sharing of their opinions, feelings, and experience with the interviewer. As a result, names, titles, positions, the names of departments, and the name and nature of the hospital has been changed, as have elements of the overall context. Additionally, specific details, such as to the departments supervised and specific job duties, were omitted to further ensure confidentiality. An academic setting was selected because its familiarity to the authors; however, it might just as well have been a hospital that is part of a larger context, such as a corporation or network where there are managerial layers above the hospital. In this regard it also resembles national and international corporations, where what is going on at all levels in the organization is not readily knowable. Despite the many changes, care was taken to avoid altering the nature of the case materials so that they resemble the actual context and nature of the organization and the experience of those interviewed.

THE HUMAN COST OF A
MANAGEMENT FAILURE

Part I

The Literature Search and Research Methodology

Part I begins the book by providing a review of the literature on downsizing, restructuring, and reengineering. It becomes clear that these three approaches to managing change do not consistently produce favorable outcomes and, in fact, may more consistently produce negative outcomes which detract from operating efficiency and profit. Chapter 2 begins the case study by introducing the organizational context of the case. Once again, readers are reminded that all names are changed.

Chapter 1

Downsizing, Restructuring, and Reengineering: An Overview

Organizational change and, in particular, downsizing has become an all too common phenomenon during the past decade (Zdrodowski, 1993). Of the *Fortune* 1,000 companies, 85 percent report downsizing between 1987 and 1991 with 50 percent downsizing in 1990 (Mishra and Mishra, 1994). Of the companies that downsize once, 65 percent will often do it again the following year, and multiple downsizings are not uncommon. Fully 100 percent of *Fortune* 500 companies report plans to downsize in the next five years (Cameron, 1994; Vaill, 1989).

Downsizing (reducing the size of the workforce to achieve lower cost and better productivity), however, often does not achieve the intended outcome of creating a more cost effective, efficient, leaner, meaner, and more productive workforce. The titles to many articles on downsizing underscore its problematic nature as a competitive or perhaps even strategic response to competition and change (Filipowski, 1993). Some of the more interesting titles of articles are these:

- "The Pain of Downsizing" (Byrne, 1994—a *Business Week* cover story)
- "Downsizing with Dignity" (Zdrodowski, 1993)
- "The Dangerous Ploy of Downsizing" (Roth, 1993)
- "Downsizing: The Aftermath" (Preston, 1992)
- "Don't Rush Downsizing: Plan, Plan, Plan" (Greengard, 1993)
- "Building a Winning Team after Downsizing" (Pinola, 1994)
- "Of Butchers and Bakers: Is Downsizing Good for the Company" (Reich, 1993)
- "Downsizing Isn't Always Right Sizing" (Filipowski, 1993)

An article in a popular weekly magazine actually accused U.S. organizations of "dumbsizing" instead of downsizing, and it has been said that downsizing has consistently failed to create economic benefits (Cameron, 1994; Margulis, 1994). These observations are supported by the following survey results:

- Seventy-four percent of senior managers reported morale, trust, and productivity deteriorated after downsizing (Cameron, 1994; Filipowski, 1993).

- Fifty percent of 1,468 firms reported productivity deteriorated after downsizing (Cameron, 1994). Thirty-eight percent reported no change in productivity and 22 percent reported decreased productivity after downsizing (Filipowski, 1993).

- Only 46 percent of 1,005 firms surveyed actually reduced expenses. Only 32 percent reported increased profits. Only 22 percent reported increased productivity. Only 17 percent reported less bureaucracy (Cameron, 1994; Roth, 1993). And only 33 percent reported improved customer service (Reich, 1993).

- Many executives report that they do not consider their efforts to downsize to have been effective. Two explanations are that downsizing is not managed effectively and that downsizing creates resentment and resistance to such a degree that it actually hinders competitiveness (Cameron, 1994).

- Downsizing is a management-made disaster that leaves those who remain feeling fearful, angry, distrustful, uncertain, guilty, anxious, and as though their lives have been put on hold. They have, in the truest sense, become casualties of management-inflicted trauma who must be cared for but often are not (Armstrong-Stassen, 1993; Noer, 1993; Preston, 1992).

- After downsizing, 63 percent of employees are less loyal to their company and only 48 percent report that they "somewhat" trust their employer (Armstrong-Stassen, 1993; Heenan, 1991). Communication often becomes slick, controlled, packaged, and seemingly a substitute for legitimate caring for employees. The party line is offered and seldom are the fundamental questions that bother employees, such as, "What will happen to me?" answered. Truth is, in a very real sense, lost in jargon, announcement of plans, and phases of plans, and with its loss comes the loss of trust in management (Pinola, 1994). In the 1990s, less than one-third of workers describe management as trustworthy, and ultimately morale suffers seriously (Bryne, 1994; Heenan, 1991).

It is clear that downsizing, which is often accompanied by restructuring and business process reengineering (BPR), can, if not properly managed, lead to little improvement and unintended, but all too common, declines in organizational performance. Understanding the effects of these types of change is, therefore, critically important to make American organizations more effective. The purpose of this book is to add to the research and understanding of organizational change in the form of downsizing, restructuring, and reengineering by providing an in-depth look at the lives of an organization's members undergoing these types of management responses to change.

Downsizing, restructuring, and BPR have become popular responses to losses of competitiveness for three reasons (Klein, 1994). First, the global recession has shown that past business practices are increasingly inadequate. Second, there is growing disappointment with total quality management (TQM) and its ability to create the transformation needed by many organizations to survive. Third, restructuring and BPR are being effectively advocated as a solution to organizational malaise.

Restructuring and BPR are often discussed as part of downsizing, as is TQM, however, although they may all be employed concurrently or sequentially, they are each different from the others. Downsizing is an immediate response to declining profits by cutting labor costs, however, there is a growing recognition that a downsized organization also needs to reconsider its fundamental ways of doing business and thus enters the need for restructuring and reengineering. Organizational restructuring, which usually leads to organizational flattening and the implementation of concepts such as matrix organization and product line management, is a structural intervention. How the organization looks and functions is changed. BPR, in its purest form, is an intellectual exercise in organizational redesign, starting with a clean slate. The entire nature of the organization under study is reconsidered with the end user in mind—the customer (Goldwasser, 1994; Rigby, 1993). BPR is a systematic approach to redesign in which every aspect of the organization and its processes are reevaluated for their contribution to customer satisfaction. This broad definition subsumes restructuring. For our purposes here, restructuring is considered to be an intervention that can be undertaken without necessarily redesigning the entire organization and its work processes.

Much has been written about how to successfully conduct restructuring and BPR. Structural reorganization and BPR claim to promote horizontal communication and collaboration, the development of new information and measurement systems that provide better decision support, and a cultural change that emphasizes collaboration and the customer (Furey, 1993; Lowenthal, 1994; Rigby, 1993). This work is accomplished by carefully defining the scope of the intervention, planning the redesign process, and including the development of cross-functional project teams that have members who have sufficient breadth of knowledge and are known to be innovators and risk takers (Goldwasser, 1994). The goal of restructuring and reengineering is to better integrate people and work processes. Achieving this, however, requires careful evaluation of the impact of the change upon human resources, information systems, and related processes; and, if possible, the testing of the changes before full implementation (Farrell, 1994).

Successful organizational redesign also requires the strong support of top management (Hall, Rosenthal, and Wade, 1993).

Despite their promise to revolutionize organizations, restructuring and BPR can encounter many pitfalls. Their success can be compromised by unrealistic expectations for the change process, inadequate resources to accomplish the redesign and implement it, lack of sponsorship, the setting of unrealistically short time frames for the change process by senior management, lack of effective planning, the use of poor methods, defining the wrong scope for the work (often too narrow), and the use of BPR language without understanding it, which can promote a cult-like mysticism around the use of the language that alienates organization members (Klein, 1994). Also to be considered are resistance to change that encourages improving the design of a preexisting "cow path," excessive analysis without taking action (analysis paralysis), and fear that BPR will imply criticism and create dissent that threatens those in charge and by extension one's own career (Caldwell, 1994; Moad, 1993).

In sum, restructuring and BPR advocate rethinking the layers of management, how work is done, and to what end (the customer focus), whereas downsizing is aimed at cutting labor costs (hopefully without adversely affecting work). BPR can also lead to downsizing, but as a by-product of organizing work more efficiently. Organizations that downsize must consider reengineering in order to get work done with a smaller workforce. A process that may be started after downsizing and reengineering is TQM, which sets in motion the development of a new culture of continuously improving work processes and products with the customer in mind.

All of these elements are present within the case described in this book. Downsizing, restructuring, BPR, and TQM are all relied upon. The case points out the dilemma many managements face when it is clear that they have too many employees, but cannot necessarily wait to reengineer and adjust staffing levels to fit a revised organizational structure and redesigned work processes. Another question raised by the case is why top management allows a bad situation to develop in the first place, and why this same management is suddenly viewed as being able to lead more effectively when the need for highly effective leadership is at a premium in making changes of the magnitude of downsizing and reengineering. Last, this book painfully illustrates how these seemingly rational strategies for managing change can produce the many negative outcomes previously described.

Chapter 2

Case Study Context, Development, and Analysis

The healthcare industry is faced with changing technological, social, ethical, legislative, judicial, and marketplace agendas that demand the utmost from the management and employees of hospitals. How hospitals run is changing; as are how they relate to each other, physicians, employers, insurance companies, managed care organizations, and government programs (Medicare and Medicaid). Survival hinges on reducing the cost per unit of service while maintaining quality, access, and user friendliness. The need to change has created a wave (often consultant led) of downsizing, restructuring, and reengineering to become more cost effective as well as minimize the consumption of clinical resources by physicians.

The pace of change is quickening. In the 1990s, the leaders of hospitals are faced with the prospect of faster-paced marketplace consolidation, which is creating local and regional horizontally and vertically integrated healthcare delivery organizations. These huge networks endeavor to combine hospitals, nursing homes, multilevel long-term care facilities, freestanding surgical and diagnostic centers, ambulatory clinics, home healthcare delivery organizations, and physicians into an integrated and balanced whole. The resulting systems must then rationalize capacity by eliminating duplicated resources and services to lower cost. Governing boards and senior management of hospitals are faced with the prospect of engulfment by a large system where their identity and autonomy are lost. Those who have labored hard to build their hospital into a fine full-service institution may suddenly be obliged to close beds and cut hard-won programs in order to optimize the system. Inevitably, these huge, monolithic utility-like healthcare delivery organizations promise to transform the healthcare delivery landscape. The only limiting factor appears to be the judicial system, which may intervene to foster competition among the hospitals and physicians.

All of these influences create an extraordinarily dynamic healthcare delivery arena, which means that hospitals must constantly change to survive. The need to change is illustrated by the case of the General Hospital.

CASE BACKGROUND

General University is located in a metropolitan area. Its medical center campus is exclusively devoted to the health sciences. The medical center contains the schools of medicine, allied health, nursing, and dentistry, a large ambulatory care center, and General Hospital, a 650-bed financially successful teaching hospital.

The medical center is strategically located away from major competitors, which has sheltered it from competition. It, like all university medical centers, is a tertiary care and transplant center which, until recently, had not participated to any great extent in managed care contracting. The medical center's location and reputation permitted it to fill its beds and pay little attention to managed care contracting, operating costs, or improving its user friendliness.

A recent and sudden shift in the managed care market, however, resulted in a significant drop in bed occupancy (census). The census initially dropped 10 to 15 percent to 75 percent and, more recently, to the low 60 percent range. The sudden drop in the census was believed to be caused by managed care organizations deleting General Hospital from their lists of approved hospitals because of its cost. The situation was aggravated by the loss of clinical faculty (physicians) to major competitors, and reduction in the length of hospital visit or stay (LOS) that further reduced the number of beds occupied.

After observing the downward trend for six months, senior management of the medical center determined that the change required downsizing the hospital 10 to 15 percent to adjust to what was believed to be permanently reduced volume. Also to be addressed was the high cost base of the hospital. The hospital must be able to compete in the managed care marketplace in the future. Additionally, neither the hospital, school of medicine, or medical center had, at the start of the case, a strategic plan. This was viewed by senior management to be a problem.

The hospital's downsizing and cost-reduction process had three phases. Phase 1 involved cutting costs by downsizing. Phase 2 involved restructuring the organization to flatten its administrative hierarchy and reduce the number of departments. Phase 3 involved improving efficiency and cost effectiveness of operations (reengineering). Camford Associates, a consulting company, was employed to facilitate the first phase. The Strategic Planning Consultants Group (SPC) was employed to facilitate the development of a strategic plan for the medical center.

Camford began its work in May 1993. The initial review revealed that the hospital's budget had to be cut by approximately 10 percent ($40 to $50 million) to respond to the 10 to 15 percent decline in the census. Camford consultants utilized a time-consuming but participative consultation process that had the goal of gaining the support of all levels of management. The process also included benchmarking (comparing) hospital operations to those of other, cost-effective institutions to determine where cuts in staff should be made.

The downsizing process spanned five months (May through September 1993). During this five-month period, careful attention was given to the benchmarking process, the collection of considerable data about operations, and the development of targets for cuts. There was a major parallel effort developed to provide the staff of the hospital information about the changing marketplace and the need for General Hospital to make adjustments to its operations. The communication effort included open meetings with staff (where the Provost of the medical center, Dr. Maggiano, spoke) and the development of a monthly news publication, *Signals.*

The strategic planning process was kicked off in July 1993, when, at a mass meeting, the faculty and senior management of the medical center were presented with a comprehensive overview of the changing healthcare marketplace. Particular attention was focused on a phase in market evolution when managed care organizations move from including cost-ineffective healthcare providers that promote market penetration to deleting them after establishing themselves in the market. This change occurs suddenly (annual contracts are not renewed and referrals to nonparticipating providers are eliminated) and simultaneously includes most managed care organizations remaining in the market.

The Provost reported that he would lead the medical center in developing a strategic plan, and announced the formation of a strategic planning committee charged with creating a plan by October 1993. The planning committee subsequently appointed a number of subcommittees to deal with special planning areas such as ambulatory care and the development of user-friendly hospital services. Final reports were expected to be available early in 1994.

The schools of medicine, allied health, dentistry, and nursing were relatively unaffected by the reduced census and tighter financial times of the hospital. The school of medicine lost a few key physician faculty to competitors. It was also rumored that the school of medicine would participate in Phases 2 and 3—restructuring and reengineering.

Campus and Medical Center Organization

The medical center was moving toward financial and managerial autonomy from the university. The Provost commenced hiring a cadre of not always well-received senior level executives to lead the medical center. An important aspect of these appointments surrounded Dr. Arch Lewin's recent promotion to Assistant Provost of Health Services. Lewin, a close friend of the Provost, had been the director of the ambulatory facility for the past three years. His promotion, which placed him over both the hospital and ambulatory facility, was greeted with disbelief on the part of the faculty who, in general, had little respect for him because of his inability to deliver much-needed improvements in the ambulatory facility. The promotion, which was not discussed with the leaders of the campus, resulted in the immediate resignation of the Hospital Director, Mr. Frank Wirth.

The organization of the hospital and campus are provided in Figure 2.1. The Provost reports to the President of the university. It must also be noted that the university's administration was concerned that the reduced profitability of the hospital would undermine the university's finances in that surplus hospital revenues had been used to fund university operations. At the worst, the university had to build a financial "fire wall" between itself and the medical center should the medical center suffer a financial collapse.

In sum, the medical center, like many of its sister institutions, found itself engrossed in the need to change in order to survive. Organizational change may be understood from many perspectives. Perhaps the most compelling is that of understanding how the people of an organization create, operationalize, manage, and ultimately feel about change. This perspective leads to reliance upon psychoanalytically informed psychology to understand the human side of change.

THE PSYCHOANALYTIC PERSPECTIVE
OF PEOPLE AND CHANGE

This book is devoted to exploring the contributions that psychoanalytically informed organizational study can make to understanding the sweeping breadth and complexity of human responses to downsizing, restructuring, and reengineering. Organizations are most often thought of as having the primary task of producing something of value to survive. Accomplishing this task is associated with rationality in terms of organizational design and decision making. However, organizations may also be understood to have, at their core, a confluence of individual unconscious psychological defenses that form an interactive and synergistic socially defensive system. The system defends its mem-

Figure 2.1
Medical Center and General Hospital Organization Chart

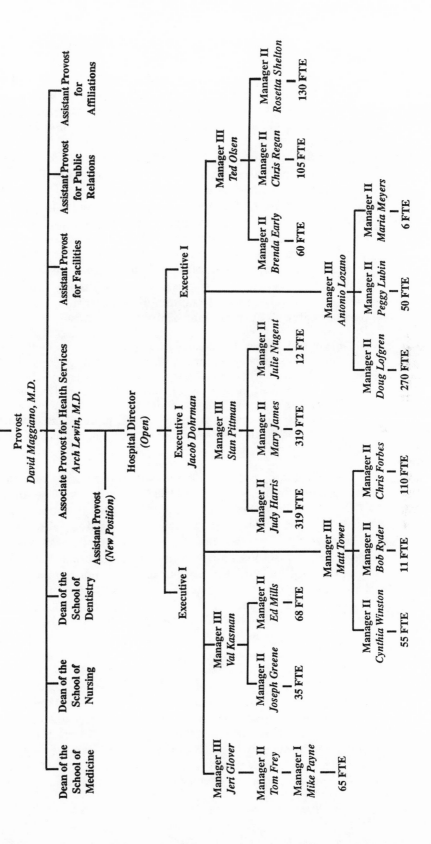

bers, groups, and leaders from anxiety that arises from changing patterns of organization life and threatening elements in the organization's
task environment and in society (Baum, 1987; De Board, 1978; Diamond,
1993; Jaques, 1955; Kets de Vries and Miller, 1984; Levinson, 1976;
Menzies, 1960; Schwartz, 1990).

These defenses are not all bad. Anxiety can block out thinking and
learning. Minimizing anxiety can, therefore, contribute to success.
There are, however, less adaptive and even destructive uses of these
individual and social defenses that are of special interest to psychoanalytically informed theorists, educators, consultants, and managers. In these cases, reality is distorted and responses to change are
dominated by less than thoughtful, reflective, or rational thinking. It
is these types of irrational, often overdetermined, responses to anxiety
that are best understood from a psychoanalytically informed point of
view. Michael Diamond offers the following notion that underpins the
psychoanalytic study of organizations. He states,

Organizational images, psychoanalytically speaking, are neither real nor fantasy: they are the product of imagination, and in this potential space between
reality and fantasy the riddles of organizational life reside. This is not meant
to deny the objective reality of organizations, but to emphasize the
psychodynamic position that the understanding of organizational dynamics
rests in the psychic reality of organizational participants. Interpreting their
individual stories, images, experiences, and perceptions of organizational
reality is what matters. (Diamond, 1993)

The significance of the unconscious in organizational life is further
underscored by Howell Baum (1987) who states, "The approach here
is psychoanalytic, investigating what people say about work and organizations and probing for unconscious meanings of bureaucracy and
accompanying feelings about it. Psychoanalysis assumes that people
have both conscious and unconscious intentions, that the latter frequently conflict with the former, and that conscious aims are often
frustrated by divergent unconscious goals." He continues by noting
that workers may say they are following rational problem-solving strategies, however, unconsciously they are frequently concerned about
avoiding anxiety, even if it leads them away from the espoused strategy of rational problem solving.

The notion that organizations have a parallel intrapsychic reality is
further elaborated by Howard Stein. "Projected outward and subsequently reincorporated, boundaries come to 'exist' in reality by the
strength of group consensus (literally, 'sensing together') on what a
group is and where it is located 'out there'—where it begins, where it
ends, how to recognize it" (Stein, 1993). He describes identity systems
as imaginary structures drawn from concrete aspects of reality that
link together important themes of the lives of people to create a global

sense of being, which leads to primary role identifications. If taken to an extreme, these identity systems become narrow, overly invested, and emotionally constricting. They exercise a straightjacketing effect where boundaries must be defended at all costs. In the workplace, these identities defend against the anxiety of change and, when they become rigid and ignore reality, can be understood to be antithetical to adaptive organizational change.

Diamond, Baum, and Stein are addressing the unconscious, unquantifiable, and hard-to-know-and-understand side of the workplace. Work life is filled with thoughts and feelings that motivate action. Thoughts and feelings are inextricably linked. It is, therefore, not possible to speak of a thought or cognition without acknowledging feeling and a lifetime of lost-from-awareness experience that contributes to the formulation of decisions and strategies. Organizational life is filled with these irrational influences which can become a dominant aspect of strategizing and decision making when the organization and its members are placed under the anxiety-provoking stress of change. Organizational members may feel victimized by the prospect of change and see themselves as helpless, powerless victims who must suppress their fear and anger. As a result, they may come to rely upon ritualistic defenses and routine to maintain some sense of control and familiarity, even if these are inconsistent with responding effectively to the problem of the moment (Diamond, 1993).

Workplace stress and the experience of anxiety are commonplace (Vaill, 1989). Workers and managers are continually made to feel anxious, and they frequently resort to the unconscious use of similar psychological defense mechanisms. These temporary individual and group psychological defenses may, under continued pressure, become rigid and enduring patterns of adjustment, which include losses of reality testing and self-integration and concomitant losses of organizational adaptiveness. These familiar rigidities constitute an important element of an organization's culture and, if abundant, become a socially defensive structure.

Gaining a better understanding of the psychologically defensive aspects of organizational culture is critical to helping organizations change. The path to this understanding leads to a door behind which are the private images that people hold of organizational life; their unconscious fantasies, expectations, attributes, assumptions, fears, and anxieties about themselves and others that become the psychic reality of organizational life that must be understood.

The key to the door of this psychic reality rests in the hands of the psychoanalytic perspective and its understanding of the phantom world of unconscious fantasies, dreams, and out-of-awareness thoughts and feelings of organization members. The door opens upon an understanding of organizational subjectivity and intersubjectivity, and the nature of the key lies in understanding psychologically defensive processes.

These processes are the avenue of exploration that leads beneath the surface of objective reality to the development of an understanding of the underlying out-of-awareness nature of organizational life and its hard to detect but often all too present influence upon presumed objectivity and rationality. It is to this exploration that this book is devoted.

The case at hand involves using psychoanalytically informed insight to understand how members of a hospital adjust to major change and how three psychoanalytically informed consultants interpret the change process. This book provides a one-year longitudinal case study of how a hospital's staff used downsizing, restructuring, and reengineering to accommodate a reduced inpatient census.

THE CASE METHOD

The first author requested permission in writing from Jacob Dohrman, Executive I of General Hospital, to conduct a longitudinal case study within his hospital that would involve interviewing approximately twenty hospital staff regarding their experience of the change the hospital was about to be put through. The request explained that the staff would be interviewed every four months over a twelve- to sixteen-month period, depending on how the research progressed. He was also provided the list of interview questions (see Figure 2.2).

A meeting was subsequently held to discuss the request. It was agreed during the meeting that interviewing senior and middle management was preferable (a fateful decision based upon the eventual restructuring that eliminated virtually all of their positions). This strategy would provide breadth versus depth based upon the twenty interview restriction arbitrarily set by the first author to acknowledge his time limitations. It was also agreed that the research process would not involve consultation to those interviewed. It was, however, agreed that the author would provide Mr. Dohrman a global overview of the trends that were found, without mention of the particulars or the providing of advice.

Upon ending the meeting, the author was given an organization chart from which twenty names were to be picked. This list was submitted to Mr. Dohrman who shared it with his senior staff. The author was subsequently invited to attend a meeting of the senior staff to explain the research project. No one expressed reservations and some expressed interest. It was agreed that each administrator would provide the author a revised set of names for his or her area of responsibility because the organization chart given to the author was out of date and incomplete. One administrator, Antonio Lozano, was asked to be the hospital's liaison to the author in the event of problems.

Within one week the author was provided a revised set of names from each administrator. A total of twenty-three senior and mid-level hospital administrators were ultimately selected for interviews. The

Figure 2.2
Directed Interview Questions

1. What is your title?
2. Briefly explain your job.
3. To whom do you report?
4. Who are your direct reports?
5. How many employees are under your direction?
6. What kinds of change do you contemplate will occur relative to your position?
7. How do you think it will affect those who report to you?
8. How will it affect those to whom you report?
9. What kinds of change have been recently implemented?
10. What has been the result?
11. How do you feel about the changes that will be made?
12. How do you feel about the changes that have been made?
13. How are you feeling about your work? Yourself?
14. How do you think those who report to you are feeling?
15. How do you think those to whom you report are feeling?
16. How many hours per week are you working?
17. Have you noticed any change in how you relate to others outside of work?
18. Have you had any recent illnesses? Health complaints?
19. How do you think others in the organization are responding to all the change?
20. Have you been feeling:
    Anxious
    Angry
    Left Out
    Unsupported
    Overworked
21. Has there been adequate communication regarding change?
22. Do you feel you understand why it has been necessary?
23. What would you have done differently?
24. Has the change been effective?
25. Have the impacts of making change been adequately foreseen?
26. Is there anything else you would like to tell me that has not been covered?

Word Associations
Job
Morale
Efficiency
Cost
Change

27. How did you experience the interviewer and interviewing process?

list included the Executive I, the senior staff, and many of their immediate subordinates.

The Interview Process

A list of twenty-six questions was used to direct the interview process. A twenty-seventh question was added for the last set of interviews. Five word associations were solicited at the end of each interview (see Figure 2.2). The interviews were conducted during a thirty-minute to one-hour time frame, either in the interviewee's office or the researcher's assigned office space. The interviewees were allowed to choose the site. The interview process involved an introduction to the first author, an explanation of the research, and an opportunity to ask questions. Interviewees were told that what they had to say was confidential and would not be communicated to anyone. They were also told that summary information would be shared with Mr. Dohrman and that the purpose of the longitudinal case study was to eventually publish a book. Everyone was told that their names and titles would be changed at the time of publication.

It was then explained to the interviewees that the author had a list of twenty-six questions, of which some were on the mundane side and others would require thought and reflection. The first question was asked at this point. The questions were read to the interviewee, and occasionally it was necessary to explain them. The researcher provided no direction to the interviewees. If major organizational events were omitted, the researcher inquired about them. When responses were vague or incomplete, further explanation was requested. Interviewees were allowed to say what was on their mind without being restricted to answering the questions. At the close of the interview, interviewees were reminded that another interview would be scheduled in four months. As an aside, several interviewees inquired as to whether their participation in a one-year longitudinal study was an indication that they would still be employed in a year.

The author took handwritten notes and attempted to write down the exact wording of key phrases and concepts expressed. The notes were usually typed up within twenty-four hours, and were edited into first-person responses. In this regard, the interviews are understood to inform the writing of the case materials and are not intended to be an exact replication of the interviews.

The second and third interviews were guided by the same list of questions; however, their wording was adjusted to compensate for the fact that the first interview was complete. For example, question one was rephrased to read, "Is your title still the same?" Question two was rephrased to read, "Has there been any significant change in your job?"

The Interpretation Process

Howell Baum, Michael Diamond, and Howard Stein, who are psychoanalytically informed organizational consultants and researchers, were recruited to provide independent case interpretations. Each was told that he would be provided a description of the hospital, its history, and three or four sets of typed interview notes at four-month intervals. Each was asked to briefly describe the basic themes of each set of interviews, discuss their significance, offer psychoanalytically informed insights as to what was happening in the case, and suggest what he might do to facilitate the change process were he to consult with the organization at this point. Each subsequent set of notes was to be addressed in the same way. Prior content would be blended into the interpretive process to create a longitudinal perspective. The consultants were asked to take the position of reading a longitudinal case an increment at a time. In this regard, they all started with the same data as do readers of the book.

The consultants were asked not to discuss the case with each other until the final set of notes had been interpreted. The first author, upon receiving the responses to each set of interviews, developed an overview of the interpretations. Upon completion of the final interpretation, the three consultants were provided a copy of the complete manuscript, invited to a two-day research meeting, and then asked to write a conclusion to the book that would permit them to expand upon what they had learned. The first author then contributed an overview to the conclusions. Ultimately, three sets of interviews were gathered (rather than four) due to the volume of material generated.

A NOTE ON INTELLECTUAL RIGOR

A comment is in order on the intellectual rigor of this approach. The use of a directed interview methodology and the restriction to three interviews did, no doubt, limit what might have been volunteered in an open ended, undirected, more strictly psychoanalytic interview process. However, this format did permit those interviewed to "add" additional undirected comments at the close of the interview, and no effort was made to limit anyone's response, even if discussion strayed considerably from the questions asked. When asked if there was anything else to report at the end of the interviews, many interviewees said that they thought they had covered just about everything and that the interview had been very thorough. The use of the word associations was provided in an effort to solicit additional unconscious undirected associated content. A related issue involves the first author's lack of probing follow-up questions. This limitation was set to avoid introducing interviewer bias, in that the content selected for elaboration may be selected for reasons unique to the interviewer.

A second aspect of developing any case is the selection of the content to be reported. Implicit in the selection process are unconsciously motivated editing processes of the researcher. The method used here permitted the first author to focus his attention on collecting data, without the impending need to use them for consultation or for eventual interpretation in a manuscript. As a result, the first author could focus his attention on data collection and thereby avoid biases surrounding their eventual use. A related aspect of the data collection was the use of handwritten notes as opposed to tape-recording or videotaping the interviews. These methods, while clearly providing more complete and accurate data, also create so much data that is not readily conveyed in a manuscript of limited proportions. Ultimately, the author must choose the data presented, which introduces unconscious process into the selection. However, the purpose of this book is not to provide a definitive case that is beyond reproach. Rather, the purpose of the case is to provide the reader a level playing field with those who interpreted the case material. Everyone has access to the same data from which to learn, draw conclusions, and compare those conclusions with those of the three experts. It is, therefore, the written case that is the data and not ultimately the organization and its members from whom the data are drawn.

A final consideration is the question of what claims may be made based upon this research. The case is not developed as proof for any hypothesis. The case and interpretations are also not provided to prove the validity of the psychoanalytically informed approach to understanding organizational life. Rather, the case and the interpretations are provided to illustrate the nature of change and how it may be understood to contain psychodynamic elements. The reader is left to conclude the validity (or lack thereof) of each of the three sets of interpretations and the psychoanalytically informed approach to interpretation. In sum, this case and its interpretations make no claims of conclusive scientific validity. This work is, however, provided to illuminate the complexity of a story of organizational life that unfolds from the interviews and the depth of feeling that is involved in organizational change.

A NOTE ON SECTION INTRODUCTIONS

Each of the three sets of interviews has an introduction to keep the reader informed of the evolution of the overarching operating environment of General Hospital. Part V begins the conclusion to the book with an epilogue to bring the reader up to date on recent events following the last of the interviews.

Part II

The Downsizing

The General Hospital contracted with a consulting company to reduce the number of its employees to respond to what was thought to be a permanent 10 to 15 percent drop in hospital occupancy. Phase 1 of the consultation process (downsizing) was reasonably participative and took five months (May through September 1993). The reductions occurred October 1, 1993. The date of each interview is noted in the case. A hiring freeze during this period led to attrition. During this same period, the longstanding President of the University retired, and the Provost of the medical center began to hire a new layer of senior level executives (assistant provosts) to operate the medical center. Most of the interviews were conducted prior to the date that employees were terminated.

The reader is again reminded that the first six interviews (which are out of date order) have been selected as representative of the case in the event there is insufficient time to read all of the interviews. It is also again noted that all names and titles have been changed and that responses to questions were edited into a narrative.

Chapter 3

The First Set of Interviews

VAL KASMAN, OCTOBER 5, 1993

I've been a Manager III for four years and here for nine. I manage the operations of ten departments. My duties include budgeting, human resources, operations improvement, patient and physician relations, program development, and marketing. I report to Jacob Dohrman and I have twelve direct reports and about 515 employees, down from 529.

I do not believe that my role will change much over the next year or two. The hospital will have to recruit a new director who will have to get oriented. I believe Dr. Lewin has ideas about how ambulatory and the hospital should work together; for example, radiology currently handles outpatient services. In the future, outpatient services may be split off and run by ambulatory. This would reduce the scope of my responsibilities. I also anticipate some mergers or breakoffs of my departments. I am less certain about the long term. There might be one administrator for ambulatory and hospital services.

My staff are likely to be affected by the downsizing. In one case, a Manager II may be cut; this was the employee's idea. Some departments may merge while others may have their outpatient responsibilities removed. There is also the possibility that some of my departments might pick up new responsibilities during restructuring.

Jacob has no one to report to; he will be a candidate for the Director's role. He also has to deal with medical center consolidation and the development of one patient registration system, one medical record system, and one department of nursing. It is hard to say how he will fit in.

Some of the recent changes are the reductions, Dr. Lewin's appointment, Frank Wirth's departure, and attrition due to the hiring freeze, which has created maldistribution. There is a need to redirect the department heads' attention to the low census; they are used to managing with a full hospital. Now their jobs may not be needed anymore.

The result is that there is increased awareness of the national healthcare marketplace. There is more sensitivity to waste, productivity, and material resource consumption. It has also been necessary to take a harder line with the physicians and their demands. Frontline administrators now feel empowered to say *no*. The physicians seem to be accepting the situation. On the negative side, there is increased anxiety which, at times, borders on paranoia. Everyone is feeling vulnerable. There is the feeling that we will never let this [the layoffs] happen again, like the Holocaust. Right now, staff are not in the right places. Some areas are below the recommended levels. There are also multiple levels of review all the way up to Dr. Maggiano, who approves all hiring.

I feel good about the expected changes. I can step back from what is going on. I'm not concerned about myself or my role. The changes will make the center more competitive. The questions, "Who are we?" "Where are we going?" will have to be answered. We must learn to move patients through the system faster, while avoiding such things as collecting redundant information about them.

I am strongly behind the reductions. I feel that Phases 2 and 3 will be fun, although they will be hard work and create more anxiety, but I cannot wait to get started. I am eight months pregnant, but I want to come in for meetings immediately after my delivery. I feel that reengineering is something that we should be doing every day.

I am a little nervous about how the center is responding to changes in the external environment. Other centers are on the move and we are not. It is a little scary. So far the change feels good. We did what we needed to do and we did it in a positive way; we did a good job. There was a minimum of adverse anxiety.

I am feeling very good, in the sense that I believe in what I am doing. The reductions did not present me with conflicts with my personal standards or style. My workload is incredible. I picked up extra departments after Jack Heath [a Manager III] left without replacement. Planning and implementing change is also a lot of additional work. The opportunity to assume more responsibility is challenging to me. I do not want to miss anything.

My staff are feeling relieved. It was hard. There were some tears. Men even wept. They came to me to ventilate. There is now a sense of increased self-esteem, arising from the fact that we survived the reductions and we handled them effectively: "I did it, and I did it well." There remains a tremendous amount of uncertainty. No one knows about what will happen to all of the vacant positions. Phase 2 will be hard, especially on those who have been here for twenty-five years.

Jacob is relieved but anxious about his position. He is worried about who will replace the Director. He has not had time to develop a bond with Dr. Lewin. I feel sorry for him. He is an expert at operations. The whole process that has just been played out came out of his head. He located the consulting company. No one else may give him credit. This needed to be done. I'm not sure whether anyone realizes what he has accomplished. He does not know about his possible promotion. He will deal with it.

I've been working fifty-five to sixty hours a week, including taking several hours of work home most days. Even so, I have just been my usual delightful charming self at home. Two weeks ago, I was probably a bitch to live with. It was stressful. I tried to not take things home. I have had less time to spend with my family and, in particular, my daughter. My health has been good.

Across the organization some will never get it and will continue to complain. They complain about not getting overtime and keeping their jobs. I have observed insensitivity on the part of the schools relative to what the hospital is going through. The reductions have been referred to as Black Friday and D-Day. It is no joke. We are trying to become lean and mean. Other sections of the center should be expected to do the same.

I have been feeling anxious but not angry, left out, or unsupported. I am feeling overworked. There is a lot to do, but it is my responsibility. Communication has been adequate and I understand the need for change. In general, there has been a goodly amount of effort, but there is never enough.

If it were done again, I think we should have planned better for the initial communication of the cuts. Dr. Maggiano announced them on July 2. We ended up spending a lot of time on the back end. Everyone needed support from the front end. There was perhaps more anxiety after the initial announcement than at the end. The administrators should have been around more to lend support and demonstrate a caring attitude.

The change has been effective. We met the goal, but it is too early to tell if it worked. Attrition has been unbalanced. I think that there have been some unforseen consequences. Where imbalance in attrition has occurred, it must be dealt with.

Word Associations

Job	Personal satisfaction
Morale	Good
Efficiency	Essential
Cost	Not there yet, needs to be lower
Change	Positive

STAN PITTMAN, SEPTEMBER 28, 1993

I have been a Manager III for eighteen years. I am responsible for operating my department. I report to Jacob Dohrman and I have a total of eight direct reports. I recently issued 1,673 checks. Staffing varies between 1,600 and 1,900.

I do not see much change relative to my position. There are more meetings. I always shared information freely with my staff. I do not know what will happen when the new Assistant Provost role over my area is filled. This is my greatest concern. I feel comfortable with the current reductions.

My staff are frightened and concerned. One of my directors will be cut. They are acting with less maturity and rationality. They are being forced to consider changes in their methods. They are rallying around which has impressed me. There is also fear, open hostility, and anger.

Jacob is nervous. His primary concern is, "Who will replace Wirth?" He wonders if he is a candidate. This is an awkward time for management credibility. Strangers are coming in to make change. Jacob has been supportive of my department. He is much friendlier and more relaxed at meetings than in the past. The new Assistant Provost may not change how operations work. I also know that the planned unification of my department with others in the center has not been successful elsewhere.

Recently, recruiting has been frozen. We are looking at using less skilled personnel which means the traditional roles must be reexamined. Pay practices have changed. Overtime has been cut. We are sending staff home without pay when there is no work. They may take vacation at these times but some do not like to. There are more resignations and leave-of-absence requests. Many are leaving to take more-certain jobs elsewhere.

The result so far is that quality is fine. There are a lot less patients. I have been receiving more compliments from physicians on the quality of my department. My department could become more powerful with everyone pulling together. My staff have a higher level of education than in other departments where there is less understanding for the need to change. There is also less friction at the staff level and fewer patient complaints. The staff seem interested in what is going on and are coming up with cost-saving ideas.

Change was inevitable. Some things have detracted from the process. The loss of Frank Wirth, Dr. Lewin's appointment, the change in the university's president, and recruiting for a new Assistant Provost have created a lot of change that has been thrown at everyone at one time. It would have been better if some of it could have been held off. Managers can only reassure others so much if they are uncertain themselves. I understand Dr. Lewin's appointment and, in fact, foresaw it, based on his personal relationship with Dr. Maggiano.

I have been surprised at how smoothly it has gone. We have avoided pitfalls that occurred elsewhere. Everyone knew we had to do it. I have been fortunate to have good staff. The open communication in the past set the stage. We have also invited in Maggiano, Lewin, and the new department chairs to speak to us and permit us to better coordinate our planning with the center.

I would like for it to be over. I have always been busy. There is always something going on. We just simply have to do it with less people. I have been in my profession for a long time and can remember times when staffing was low; they got it done then. My staff are frightened, unsure, and wary. Some feel a great sense of satisfaction in what they have accomplished to respond to the call for change. There is also hostility. It is scary.

Jacob is more relaxed. He feels that we can meet the targeted cuts. He seemed sincere when he thanked the staff for the hard work. He is also probably surprised it has gone so smoothly. He is more comfortable than expected; he's usually a hyper guy.

I am working forty to sixty hours. I do not work sixty hours often. Outside of work I am short tempered, rude, and intolerant. I am better at work, where I have to be supportive. I have also been traveling home frequently to take care of my sick mother. In general, I have been well, although I had a bad cold.

I feel that the more educated people are responding better; they understand what is going on in healthcare. There is some negativism, which seems to be inconsistent with what is going on in health care. This is occurring primarily in the ancillary departments. They just do not seem to be on board and often want to fill open positions. There is more grumbling in these areas.

I have not been anxious, although I am about filling the new Assistant Provost position. I have not felt angry, left out, unsupported, or overworked.

Communication has been adequate and I understand why change is needed. The average staff members seem out of touch. They seem mostly focused on their fear of being cut. In some other areas there may not have been adequate communication.

If I was asked to do it again, I would not do it any different. In general, it seems that the hospital is the only unit being affected and this is unfair. The open forums were well received. It is hard to tell at this point if the changes will be effective. I do think the impacts of the changes were foreseen. We did not just jump in on a reactionary basis. We took the time to do it right.

Word Associations

Job	Work
Morale	High
Efficiency	Getting the job done
Cost	Splurge, in the past too much money was spent
Change	Occurring

JOSEPH GREENE, SEPTEMBER 29, 1993

I have been a Manager II for twenty-four years. I direct my department's services for the hospital and some outpatient services. Occasionally we provide service by the type of service [cancer]. I also run some small programs. I report to Val Kasman. I have two Manager Is and a secretary who report to me and I also supervise some staff. I have 35 FTEs [full-time equivalents], but will lose 4.5.

I do not expect change relative to my position immediately; there is already more work for me. We have to be creative to cover all of our responsibilities. I have not cut services yet. I will be losing one clerical person. I have shifted to voice mail, dispersed some clerical work to others, and "farmed some work out" to the clinics. The staff also have to do clerical work now. Some professional services may have to be dropped. The staff have volunteered more effort. It took seven changes to compensate for the loss of one employee. I believe that we will lose some of the creative time that made us great, such as making videos and writing journal articles.

My staff are more anxious; everyone is asking, "Am I the one?" A lot of time is being wasted talking about rumors. They are discovering that they can exist with fewer staff, but things are slower and some things are not getting done. The changes will affect them by increasing their responsibilities; they will have to stretch themselves. I have not heard a lot of complaints. It is quiet now. They are very aware of who I am talking to.

The recent change of not filling open positions has led to reallocating work. I have also reduced my operating budget a bit in the areas of travel and continuing medical education. I will have no flexibility to exceed budget. Everyone must be more cost conscious. I am developing uses for outside donations. Other than what has already been done, I am not sure yet if I can get the job done after the shoe falls. There is an atmosphere of pettiness. Staff are making dumb mistakes; there are more complaints; people are edgy. No one has done layoffs before. I had my own float pool which is now virtually eliminated. How things are depends on the volumes of the day.

I am aware that acute care hospitals are losing admissions and that change is necessary. I know that ambulatory has created their own department; this is not in the spirit of being seamless. Someone has changed my title.

Everything has needed to happen. I am proud of my staff; they are good people and they have been flexible. I have let them participate. I feel good about the people above me. Frank Wirth's departure had little impact. It is disconcerting that the hospital has to do it alone. The top of the organization is continuing to add people and hire expensive consultants. Who am I to say? Maybe it is appropriate.

My work is not as much fun recently. I am more emotionally torn, fearful, and disillusioned. I am not that far from retirement—three years; I could make it if I was laid off. The younger people feel more anxious. I feel good about myself. I feel I have been meeting the challenge because I have good staff.

My staff are anxious, apprehensive, and insecure about the future. They do not appear to be angry. They are experiencing what many other organizations have been through. It is our turn. There is acceptance, but also hope that they will not to be a victim.

Val is incredible. She supervises eight departments, which is an enormous load; she is nine months pregnant; she also oversees several demanding services. She has less time to communicate. There is simply no time left. She has good people to work with. She has been sensitive to us, level headed, and very managerial. She does not appear to be anxious. She has a job and must do it and she is working lots of hours to do it.

I am working forty-five hours a week. I have a small department and the workload is not too great. I think my family thinks I am crabby and preoccupied. I have been healthy; some allergies. Others are preoccupied with the change. They obsess over every rumor. Some are talking about what they might do if they have to leave. The focus is on self.

I have been feeling anxious about the future. I have not been feeling angry or left out. I get about as much information as can be given. I have not felt unsupported or overworked. Communication has been adequate. I understand why the change is needed.

I am not sure how I would have done things differently. There is not enough hindsight yet. The impact so far has been manageable. In general, I would like to see things progress more slowly to maintain good will and sensitivity and respect for employees. Val is sincere about the loss. Things have been handled pretty well. I feel frustrated because last year the hospital had record profits. We have to watch our step because we're mirroring the outer world. I would not have done too much differently in the department. The data supported change. So far the changes have been effective. We are holding our own. I am worried about meeting spikes in volume when they occur.

Word Associations

Job	Okay
Morale	Good for what is happening
Efficiency	Better at it
Cost	Effective
Change	Difficult

BRENDA EARLY, OCTOBER 12, 1993

I am a new Manager II. I provide administrative support for medical directors and guidance for supervisory personnel. I handle the budget, human resource management, facilities, planning, and quality assurance. The whole area needs to be reworked. I report to Ted Olsen. I have nine people I directly supervise and 55.5 FTEs after the cuts; 60 before.

I am currently involved in proposing an expansion of the area. More facilities are needed to provide services for ambulatory patients. In the short term, I am looking at the current space for better utilization, which is creating turf battles. I also need to replace a retiring supervisor.

My staff are feeling positive. Everyone will benefit. I am redefining work rules and creating more responsibility. Ted has got a difficult job. Recruiting is frozen, but several of my areas need to grow. It will be tough to support growth versus the current philosophy of "don't do anything." He faces resistance in getting support. I have a lot of respect for Ted.

Cost restructuring is the recent change. I am reevaluating how staff are scheduled. We used to work overtime to cover absences; no overtime is permitted now. We have to flex between the Monday–Friday staff and the weekend group. We cut back on starting at 7:00 A.M. There was nothing to do then; cases started at 9:00 A.M. We are also sending some people home when there is no work. There has been attrition, but we have not felt the attrition to be a major loss. One lab had more people than other labs, but they were lower in pay. We have absorbed losses because we were over staffed by 10 FTEs. The loss of a secretary is difficult. We are talking about a lot of ideas.

So far the changes are still permitting the work to get done. The schedule has been fairly consistent. I am feeling positive about change, if it is done on timely basis. We are not quick, and this concerns me. The environment requires quicker responses; the system needs to change.

The department needs to be made over from scratch. It had no manager for almost a year. It should have changed long ago, if only to improve patient care. Institutionally, the change had to be made. The problem hit fast. The fact that they did not have any plans in place, such as affiliations or managed care contracts, concerns me. There is a lack of vision; we are late in getting started. The changes in leadership at the top [Dr. Lewin] have left me concerned. I can't tell if they are good. There are unknowns and anxiety. I can't get a readout. It is the physicians versus hospital administration. The relationship is not good for taking care of patients.

There does not seem to be a good work group. Everything is done by committee. There are no decisions. There are too many people involved. We are sitting back and waiting. There is no leadership in my department. The employees get it from the faculty when they are upset. Some faculty may leave out of fear of a new faculty leader in their department.

I like what I do. I'm good at it; it's rewarding. I like to be considered to be a resource person. I am spending time with my staff. They are good people, although one does not like the change and is having difficulty switching gears. The systems here are a little archaic; there is a lack of information. The physicians are a little distant. They are paranoid about the hospital side. I enjoy working with Ted. He is fair, easy going, and does not like hesitant leadership. I'm feeling good about myself. I'm a happy person. I'm goal directed and I like work. I have a good image of myself. I'm self-confident and happy outside of work. I got married six years ago. My job is no longer the only thing my life. I come from the outside, and I feel less connected.

I met with my staff to reassure them after the cuts. This was helpful. I am an honest person. I involved my staff in planning the cuts. People were very anxious until the cuts were made. I'm relieved it is over. I'm still anxious that it is not a one-time occurrence. The shakeup in my department over the loss of our Physician Director is bothering us.

Ted and Jacob are tired and drained. They have to deal with difficult decisions. Referring doctors are boycotting us. I feel a little need to talk to someone—to Dr. Lewin. What is on the program? Why was my Director removed? Jacob will not talk to Dr. Lewin. It would be professional suicide. I'm frustrated and fed up with the leadership. There is a lack of communication between faculty and their leaders.

I'm working forty-five hours. In the past I have worked long hours that were not appreciated. I have not noticed any change in how I relate to others; the cuts are part of normal conversation. This has not affected my relationship. I am not alone either. My last job bugged me. There was lots of pressure. I am not close to the situation here. My health is good. I injured two discs in my back a year ago, and they were treated in the spring.

Many others are not prepared. It is difficult to anticipate how they will react. It is almost like we are in a glass bubble; people do not know what is going on outside. The hospital used good techniques and consultants to prepare people. It has taken its toll. There are lots of family members working here.

I have not been feeling anxious, but I might get out of healthcare. I'm not feeling angry, but I do feel left out. The department heads are not treated as professionally here as where I worked before. There is no big-picture information. I have not felt unsupported. It is cyclical. We deal with the same issues over and over. There are mixed messages. "What do you want?" Things are slow.

Communication has not been adequate, although I understand the need for change. The biggest problem was that everyone was supposed to be told on Friday, but then it was moved to Thursday for some departments, and no one told those departments that were not changed. The rest of the information has been okay.

The centralized exiting process was not dignified. Everyone was herded like cattle to slaughter into the auditorium. It was too public and embarrassing. The human resource department is doing the job of the managers, who were probably not prepared to handle the layoffs.

So far I think the change has been effective and most problems foreseen. Some departments got to deal with problem people that they wanted to deal with all along. There will be long-term benefits. Duplication has been reduced. I'm frustrated with the lack of decision making and the fact that change has been limited to the hospital. The whole organization needs to be linked together.

Word Associations

Job	Security
Morale	Positive. It is mixed now.
Efficiency	Quality, effectiveness
Cost	Control
Change	Constant

ED MILLS, SEPTEMBER 17, 1993

I have been a Manager II for twenty-four years. I manage inpatient and outpatient operations. I oversee all services, including hiring and planning, and I report to Val Kasman. I have two Manager Is who report to me and I have a total of 68 FTEs. After the cuts I will have 63.

I am serving on committees working on organizational change. I am interacting more with some disciplines than in the past to achieve efficient resource use. There is more participation. I believe my department will do the same things and more. It will become more visible as a focal point to achieve cost containment.

The change is not easy for my staff, and it will be ongoing. It was a different experience at the start, but it was also exciting. They feel that they are part of the solution. Val will be working more closely with me to define direction and goals. She has to work closer with all of her departments and get involved with interdepartmental connections.

I have 8 or 9 frozen-open FTEs which will cover the reduction process. These open positions have given us a taste of what it will be like after the cutbacks. They have already felt the pressure of not having adequate staff. Quality may become a problem. More errors are occurring and of a more serious nature. There is little time to double check. The staff are stressed. The change has not been well received. It is not clear how quickly some of the open positions can be filled, which is a point of anxiety.

The changes have been necessary; they are long overdue. Resources have been overutilized and cutting back will not compromise patient care. Overutilization has been the result of a lack of cooperation and no one perceiving a need to do better. It will take a couple of years to accomplish the change.

I agree with the downsizing conceptually, but I also feel anxious about it. It is not clear how it will impact operations. Those left will have to do more. It bothered me how aggressive the change effort has been. It has focused only on cutting positions, without regard to their impact on operations and patient care. Those orchestrating the cutting are not sensitive to patient care. The cuts proposed by the consultants appear to be arbitrary and driven only by the decline in the census. Little appreciation is shown for what it takes to do the work. Some areas of the hospital are still functioning at the maximum and they are disproportionately heavy users of my service. The consultants did not respond to these considerations when asked. All support departments [ancillary services] will be asked to do more as work is gradually shifted to them. No consideration is being given to this. Current and future cuts will also make recruiting difficult.

Work is more stressful and demanding. There are more meetings and less time to work with my staff. I feel that I am under pressure and being challenged to meet new expectations. I have never had to make decisions about layoffs before. I'm lucky attrition will accomplish the task. It is a difficult notion to cope with. I feel that I have little control over the process.

My staff are anxious about the process and uncertain about their jobs. They have been reassured that they will not lose their jobs. I am trying to build up credibility with them as a source of information. They appear to appreciate my being straightforward. During talks with them, they always remember the number to be cut [437] and the date [October 1]. They also wonder how this could be happening so quickly.

I do not think that our employees understand the current situation in healthcare. Val is also under a lot of pressure. She is accountable for the change process, and she is concerned about her job too.

I am taking work home. There are more deadlines. The workload reminds me of when the hospital first opened. I am working fifty hours per week. I am more impatient at home and see a little less humor in life. I have less time with my family, and I am preoccupied and less thoughtful. My health is generally good. I aggravated my hernia on a home project.

I would like to think that everyone else is going through the same thing. I think everyone is anxious. I believe there is more stress in some departments where people actually have to be laid off.

I have been feeling anxious and a little angry. I am having to change my work style. I have not felt left out or unsupported, although I feel overworked some days.

Overall, communication has been good and I understand why the change is necessary. If I had a voice in designing the overall process, I would have planned it differently relative to the ancillary departments. In my department, I am not sure. I didn't have to deal with cuts.

The change has been moderately effective. It has set the stage for a change agenda. There have been a few casualties and there will be more. There is a new awareness level. They all understand that they have to pull together to increase productivity. Departments are only dealing with change at their level. I am not sure what will happen interdepartmentally. I feel that the ancillary departments should have been left to last so that the effects of all the other planned change could be assessed relative to its impact on the them. Some may have to absorb more work. Val understands this. My voice and hers are not being heard.

The culture of the organization for twenty-five years has been top-down. People were used to receiving dictates and having to cover their butts. The hospital has traditionally relied on consultants. Senior level managers have not looked in on their departments and are out of touch with how things work. Val is somewhat in touch, but those above her are out of touch.

I do not think the impacts of the changes have been adequately foreseen. They are not anticipating major interlinkages. I feel that there is a strong likelihood of a roll-down of work onto my department.

Word Associations

Job	Mine
Morale	Could be better
Efficiency	Much improvement needed
Cost	Waste
Change	Stressful, dynamic

JACOB DOHRMAN, OCTOBER 4, 1993

I am an Executive. I am responsible for the daily operation of the hospital, development of all budgets, human resources, and the nursing service. I used to report to Frank Wirth and now, at least temporarily, I report to Dr. Lewin. I have ten direct reports and there are approximately 3,300 hospital employees left after the reductions [down from 3,800].

What happens to my role will depend upon the future organizational design of the hospital's administration. In the long run, those I report to will provide clearer long-term operating objectives, as compared with the past. The strategic planning process needs to be rolled out. The result will be more precise and measurable goals and accountability. The changes will provide the board and my superiors greater ability to understand, measure, and assess what is happening in the hospital.

The recent change is that the reduction in force has been implemented. There has been an evaluation of current services to locate additional savings. This review highlighted a significant number of areas to be reengineered to provide adequate levels of cost-effective service. The reduction in force went well. Managers were educated in how to deal with it. It is too early to tell the effects. There have not been any negative effects from attrition; there are no apparent imbalances. There has been a hiring freeze on since the spring.

I am feeling positive about the changes. This is a time to reflect on where the organization is and what it needs to do to remain financially viable in the future. The hospital needs to fit its goals to those of the center. This is a springboard to reengineering and TQM. The goal is to maintain high quality and become more user friendly, while remaining cost effective. I feel positive about the changes; the organization can absorb them. Adjustment is possible.

I'm feeling very good about myself. What has been done so far will position the hospital well for what needs to be done in the future to respond to the marketplace. Middle management and the clinical staff will support administration. Up to a few days ago, my staff were working under a lot of pressure and stress. Today [after the layoffs] there is some immediate relief. However, the pressure will still continue; future goals will have to be met. Phase 2 represents a positive undertaking. The staff may be more comfortable with the idea of Phase 2 and targeted outcomes. Those above me are feeling tentative and concerned about the future of the hospital and medical center. They feel positive about the past four-month process.

I work fifty or more hours a week. I have not noticed any changes in my life outside of work. I'm just as affable as ever, and I have been well. Overall, some people are anxious, but feel that the organization has moved to a proactive posture to deal with the needs of the center in order to remain strong in the marketplace.

I have been anxious at times. I have not been feeling angry, left out, unsupported, or overworked. Communication from above me is adequate and I understand the need for change. I need less information because I understand the situation and the organization and I am involved in the Steering Committee for Strategic Planning. Below me, the notion of strategic planning becomes more abstract. I feel that we did a good job communicating about the need to cutback and restructure. If I had it to do over, there is not much that I would change. It was a good process for the time allocated. The release of the employees worked well. They have also adjusted the use of consumable supplies to reduce costs. The attrition process also went well. At this point, it is too early to predict the impacts.

Word Associations

Job	Good
Morale	Good
Efficiency	Striving
Cost	Working on
Change	Exciting

ANTONIO LOZANO, SEPTEMBER 14, 1993

I have been a Manager III for three years. I manage seven departments with about 300 employees. I also work on projects and participate in committees. I report to Jacob Dohrman. Jacob's superior, Frank Wirth, just resigned because he did not want to report to Dr. Lewin. This will provide Jacob an opportunity to assume Frank's role. If this happens, his job might not be refilled.

Now that Jack Heath [a Manager III] is gone, I expect to pick up some of his departments. I also believe my role may expand and become hospital-wide. If this happens, those who report to me will have less of my time. They will need to be more efficient in meetings, delegate more, and work smarter and not necessarily longer hours.

Changes continue to be made. Open positions are not being filled and staff are having to accommodate the cutback. So far, everyone has been cooperative. We used a bottom-up approach and my staff are coming to me with ideas on how to manage the cutbacks. I am, however, somewhat concerned about how top management is managing the process. I am not sure if another round of cuts will be made before entering Phase 2. I am worried that they will get too greedy in Phase 1.

Nonetheless, I feel positive about the changes. The hospital needed to downsize. Many other hospitals have had to do it. It is about time, but no one likes layoffs even if they are sensitively handled. Now that

Dr. Lewin is in charge it may be better that Frank Wirth left before all of this happened.

Lately there is more work but also a little better morale. People are less intense and there are fewer meetings. People are exhausted from the effort, stressed-out, and anxious to get the cuts behind them.

Those who report to me are feeling stressed and pressured. They feel it tenfold, as it is they who have to face the people who have to do more. The employees are less anxious about Phase 2 [restructuring] than senior management, because it is the manager jobs that will be on the line because departments will be merged. I think Jacob is taking it a day at a time. I do not believe that he is sure how he is feeling about the process.

I am working fifty hours a week. There is more stress, but my work has always been stressful. Everything is okay. I go to a health club to work the stress off. I have been healthy except for a cold two weeks ago.

Most employees are pleased that they were given an opportunity to talk at public meetings where the cutback was discussed. They are stressed out. They are becoming accustomed to it, but they are also taking it home. It has become part of our personalities.

I have been feeling anxious. I cannot get some projects done now. I haven't been feeling angry, although my opinions may not be being listened to. I haven't felt left out, although at times it would have been nice. The senior staff have pulled together to support each other. The consultants have also been a big help. I have felt overworked during the last three months. There is lots to do. I would like to get back to a normal routine and shift from crisis management to the usual burnout. I'm not getting other things done, such as growth projects.

Communication has been adequate and I understand why change is needed. Given the same problem and how well it has gone, I would approach it the same way again. The change has been effective in terms of cost reduction, but it is too early to tell about the effects of the cutbacks. If the census goes down more there will have to be more cuts.

I do not think our current situation was adequately foreseen. We should have started two years ago. The departments are getting their work done. There has been enough dialogue. I have not put my departments at risk with the cuts to date. I am waiting until Phase 2 to cut more.

Word Associations

Job	Security
Morale	Needs improvement
Efficiency	Getting there, there is a way to go
Cost	Reduction
Change	Inevitable

PEGGY LUBIN, SEPTEMBER 15, 1993

I am a Manager II and responsible for a department that runs twenty-four hours per day, seven days a week. I report to Antonio Lozano. I have three supervisors and a secretary who report to me and fifty-plus employees including the float pool.

When it comes to change, I know of institutions that have eliminated my position, but some have expanded it. The changes are making my staff anxious and fearful. Other institutions have cut all the assistant managers. I expect work to increase as the hospital becomes more involved with managed care. So far, all cuts in my department have been handled by attrition.

Antonio is supportive. I discuss changes that I want to make with him. Everyone is uncomfortable and wants to get the cuts out of the way. Attrition has led to changes in scheduling. Scheduling is a problem with a 24-hour, 7-day-per-week operation. We are starting earlier in the morning which requires some staff to start work at 4:00 A.M.

The results of the changes so far are more work. I am using a TQM committee to look for cost-cutting opportunities. Lots of ideas are being generated. This has been a great experience for me and everyone. They are functioning as a team, which is positive.

The change was necessary. Healthcare has changed. The new ideas generated by my staff opened my eyes. I was used to the status quo, and I did not see the possibilities for improvement. Thus far the changes have not been that negative, but I do not know about the future.

In the past, I made proposals but they were not implemented or were changed. I am heavily involved in my professional organization and I know the national trends. I feel I was not listened to by upper management. Dr. Maggiano stopped a recommendation and then reduced it by half. The consultants are now recommending the same thing I did. I feel that I saw the future and was ignored.

I am keeping very busy and I like it like that. I like to work on lots of projects. I'm not married and my children have left home. There are days that I feel concerned about my position. Four of my colleagues lost their jobs. My position could go either way. The uncertainty is a killer.

My staff are anxious and uncertain. There are occasional tears. They ask if I can tell them what will happen. They all have family responsibilities. Because I involved my employees in the change process, they are pulling together as a group to accomplish work and create change. Antonio is feeling uncertain. He would like to get the cuts out of the way. I cannot tell my employees that all the cuts have been made by attrition.

The ambulatory facility continues to recruit new employees and hired many of mine who were looking for a way to bail out. The good news is that this created the attrition needed to avoid cuts. The bad news is, if Dr. Lewin is over both ambulatory and the hospital, it might be asked of him, "Why is ambulatory expanding when the hospital has to cut?" It is not fair.

I cannot tell my employees that none will be laid off. This has been difficult. When I recently called a meeting, everyone arrived believing I was going to announce the cuts. I understand why I cannot tell them and I'm not angry.

I am working fifty hours per week. I may cut back on participation in my professional organization. I have had no change in my social activities, but when I do something social, such as gambling, it feels more like I am just filling up time. The problems at work never go away. I did not buy a new car or build a deck on my home to save money just in case I get laid off. Recently, I have been pretty healthy, although I had a virus that was passed around in the office.

Everyone is feeling the same: "Let's get the change over with." The big changes were the appointment of Dr. Lewin and Frank Wirth leaving. This has created a lot of uncertainty.

I have been feeling angry and left out sometimes. I feel supported and I'm not overworked. Communication has been satisfactory and I understand why change is needed. I do think that the cuts should have been made much more quickly. Six weeks would have been good. The change process has been well handled. The workshops that were held by the consultants were effective. I would not change much regarding how I worked with my staff. Dr. Lewin's appointment was the disturbing surprise. I was hired by Frank Wirth and reported to him for many years.

I think the changes have been effective, however, something more is going on. Physicians are unhappy. Some have left. It is more than just the change to managed care. There is a disturbance in the medical center. I hear angry comments from physicians about Dr. Lewin. The doctors report that they cannot talk to their leaders, and when they do, it is negative. Slow decision making and implementation is a problem. I do think that the impacts of the changes have been foreseen so far.

I do not know Dr. Lewin. I feel that the hospital is being blamed for all the problems. It is being punished, although I know that change is needed. I feel that the hospital has been targeted, as compared with ambulatory, which is expanding. All our hard work and past success does not seem to count. Dr. Maggiano is hiring a layer of assistant provosts who will run the hospital, which makes it seem like we did not know what we were doing. It was this layer of people that blocked many of the recommendations for change in the hospital. I am angry and frustrated about this process.

Word Associations

Job	Good
Morale	Down
Efficiency	Up
Cost	Down
Change	No choice

MARIA MEYERS, SEPTEMBER 16, 1993

I have been a Manager II for nine months and an employee for six years. I manage a staff of clinicians, a support staff, the budget, day-to-day operations, marketing, and the coordination of the graduate practicum. I report to Antonio Lozano. My department has 6 FTEs and three part-time staff.

I fear my department will be merged into another department. The possibility of merger of the department is rotten. I do not want it to happen. The merger will not be well accepted. Our department was established by splitting it off from another department after three years of politics. We all felt good about the change and were looking forward to a bright future. It if happens, Antonio will have fewer people reporting to him.

Everyone is increasingly aware of productivity. The part-time staff and 1 FTE will be lost. Another 0.5 FTE is in limbo. There was a lot of hush-hush talk among the staff. However, they have learned more about the decline in referrals and wonder how the hospital could have been so unprepared. Now it seems like everybody is in the same boat.

My staff are accepting the fact that they can still do quality work with reduced staffing. I have reshuffled their responsibilities to accomplish this. We are not short of staff at this point. I do not feel positive, merely acceptant. I am trying to defend my current staffing level. There is a constant demand for meetings and statistics.

I feel that I have risen to the occasion and am getting more done because I have to. I am constantly busy. There are lots of meetings. My staff are frustrated, scared, and wondering if they should be looking for a job. They are also rising to the occasion to meet work demands. They are trying to work hard to ensure that they have a job. They are scattered geographically and there is not much togetherness.

Antonio is stressed and frustrated to a degree. He has been struggling with the split off since he started working here. He seems overworked, but he has remained sensitive to the issues and has shown empathy for our having to make the cuts. I see him as a person rather than as an administrator.

I am working forty hours per week. I have not noticed any change at home. Initially, I worked at home nights and weekends. It was tougher then. I have not had any health complaints. In the hospital there is a time bomb waiting to explode regarding announcing the layoffs. Anxiety levels are high and different from the past. I have been feeling anxious but not angry, unsupported, left out, and overworked.

There has been adequate communication and I understand why downsizing is needed. I would like to have been able to have informed my staff sooner. I could have told them definitely that none will be laid off, but that we lost the 1 FTE, that the 0.5 FTE is on hold, and that the pool slots are being converted to a half-time slot.

I think the changes have been effective, after an initial adjustment. The prospect of being merged into a larger department after all the work to split us off is regrettable. The dreams of a new department and great success have been lost. The change has been too fast. The possibility of losing departmental status is bad. I may also lose my job as director. It is a shame to lose the progress after years of effort.

One aspect of the change that has made people feel bad is that the hospital is the target and ambulatory is not affected. Staff have left to go to ambulatory, which is hiring. The feeling is that ambulatory is not bearing their portion of the burden.

Word Associations

Job	Work
Morale	Spirit
Efficiency	Always
Cost	Watch
Change	Hard

TED OLSEN, SEPTEMBER 24, 1993

I am a Manager III. I have a mix of line and staff work. I have fifteen departments reporting to me with about 650 employees, and responsibility for $160 million in revenue. I report to Jacob Dohrman.

It is hard to foresee how things will change for me. My position has changed constantly, which has been exciting. I feel that I might become more involved in operations.

Those who report to me will continue to answer more questions from me. They will have to be more accountable for operating effectiveness and making changes quickly. I do not believe Jacob will move up. The scope of his role may contract. His role has not expanded much because of Frank Wirth's departure.

The recent change is that open positions are not being filled. There is also a lot more information available. This is the result of the change forcing hospital finance to change. The information was not available before, or perhaps not known to exist. The result so far is that the departments have learned that they can do well with less. Department managers have done a great job selling the need for the downsizing. The changes had to be made; there is no question. I feel that there is some vulnerability remaining, in that the current cuts are responding only to decreased volume and are not systematic in nature, which will be covered in Phase 2.

I feel positive about the changes. The consulting company has been a big help. They have been sensitive to the nature of our work. The company and their process has been a big piece of the comfort level. I reluctantly signed up for reductions when this started. [He was asked to sign next to a cut figure on a blackboard as part of a group process.] I felt that there was a gun being held to my head. If the process had been done poorly, I would have left. I do not understand the need for another layer of decision makers. I also question the need to hire a Hospital Director. I am comfortable with Dr. Lewin's style.

I truly hate my job now. I am working unbelievably long hours, which has unbalanced my personal life. I do not like to have to deal with the issue of terminations and I miss the support I used to get from Frank Wirth. Jacob does not provide it. When it comes to those who report to me, changes are occurring in how they feel from week to week. First they were afraid of losing their jobs. Then they were anxious about what they had to do. Then they were supportive, cooperative, and satisfied. Now they are sitting on pins and needles waiting to do what they have to do. The process has taken too long, but it had to take time to do it right. I wish that it were over. Most have bought into the change. A few have not.

I am not sure how Jacob is feeling. I am not a mind reader. Jacob is probably nervous, perhaps just as much about Wirth leaving as the cuts. He probably feels comforted that we have met our targets, which has been revealed by new information in the last few days.

I work seventy to eighty hours per week now. I do not see my family much anymore. I am more short tempered, especially with my wife. We argue more. Our social life has not changed much. We did not have much of one anyway. I have been well. I had a cold in the middle of it all and took one sick day. How everyone else is feeling varies a lot. Some do not understand what is needed and are resentful. The hold-outs are resentful and bitter. I heard a joke in the lunch line which I think I was intended to overhear. The staff were joking about receiving pink slips in their paychecks that day. Everyone is anxious and feeling vulnerable. There are perhaps ten times as many people who are anxious as need be concerned. I think this is the result of them being part of a whole that is being cut.

I have not been feeling particularly anxious. Sometimes I feel angry, unsupported, and overworked. I have not felt left out though. There is never enough communication. I worked hard at communication. I was a member of the communications committee. I understand why the change is needed. I also do not think I would have done anything differently if I had it to do all over again.

It is hard to say if the downsizing will be effective. I will not know until October 1, or later. I am convinced that it will be effective. We have considered the impacts of making the change. I feel that they have taken fairly quick action on some things that happened fast, such as the drop in the census.

Word Associations

Job	Boss
Morale	Important
Efficiency	Numbers
Cost	Effective
Change	Cost

CHRISTINE REGAN, SEPTEMBER 28, 1993

I have been a Manager II for four years. My job is a combination of clinical director and manager of budget and policy. Day-to-day operations are run by an assistant. I report to Ted Olsen, and I have six direct reports and 105 employees until recently. I have twelve open positions that will not be filled.

There is a need for someone in my role. I am not convinced that I need an assistant. My departments are fragmented and I deal with a number of administrators. I do not foresee much change on a daily basis. My department may be reorganized, and my position changed then.

I do not believe there will be a significant impact on those who report to me. Personalities may be a bigger influence. Everyone is used to working independently. My immediate staff have been supportive and cooperative. They see the big picture. At the employee level there is open hostility. There needs to be a correlation between the cuts and activity. I think that the changes have favorably impacted those above me. They have reduced costs and they can still deliver good quality service. I will be delighted if there is no change. On the negative side, patients may have to wait longer.

I have redesigned, cut roles, and reallocated staff. I modified the scheduling process to deal with peaks and valleys. I am also using underutilized space creatively during nonpeak hours. So far volume is up over last year. We are accomplishing as much this year as last, with less staff. The big change is that we have been able to decompress the department.

The change has been a long time in coming. When I came here I was amazed at how cost ineffective things were. I feel more positive than negative. Some patient care practices have to change before I'll feel more positive.

Sometimes I feel frustrated about my work; it takes so much time. There are so many layers to get change through. I feel very good about myself; I'm coping well. I am not building a career because I'll retire next year. I'm feeling flexible.

My staff understand and embrace the change. They have been supportive. The employees are grouchy and holding their supervisors responsible. Ted feels pretty good about it. We are accomplishing what we need to do. He is concerned about long waits, the quality of service, and keeping the numbers up. He is always supportive. I want to do a good job for him.

I am working about forty-five hours per week. I have not noticed any change as to how I relate to others outside of work. I love people outside of work. I was stressed a little bit at the start, but I have not been sick. I really do not know how others are feeling. I think my department is fairly isolated from what is going on in the hospital. I feel that there is a difference between those who are relatively new and the long-time employees. Those who are new are not surprised about the cuts. The long-time employees wonder why it is all happening.

I was initially anxious. I had never had to cut. I haven't felt angry, left out, or overworked. I have felt supported, but there is no support at the grassroots.

There has been adequate communication and I understand why change is necessary. I do think it may have taken too long, although it is well planned. There is this approach versus the fell-swoop approach that does not include much planning but gets it over quickly. I think it has been effective so far and that the impacts have been foreseen. In one or two cases they had to regroup before implementing the change.

Word Associations

Job	Work
Morale	Good
Efficiency	Adequacy
Cost	Expensive
Change	Needed

JERI GLOVER, SEPTEMBER 29, 1993

I have been a Manager III for three years. My job involves centralizing my department's functions. I report to Dr. Lewin. I have five direct reports and 225 employees under my direction.

I will assume more responsibilities by picking up some of Jack Heath's departments. My staff will be affected in two ways. First, they will need to deal with more personnel issues. Second, they have to be able to think about their work differently; they must focus on reengineering and be able to step back and look at alternatives. Regarding my superior, I used to report to Frank Wirth. I do not know Dr. Lewin. I expect that he sees the fall in the census as an opportunity to change how the hospital makes decisions. He will move the hospital toward self-directed work teams that involve the staff in problem solving. I don't know if he has gone through staff reductions before.

A number of changes are being made. There are twenty-five frozen positions in my area. The hiring freeze has caused Tom Frey to reorganize and cross-train employees. The change is necessary; there is a need to do even more but I feel positive. The center is way behind other organizations which have been dealing with a lower census for ten years. There are lots of opportunities to reduce costs and learn from others.

The holding of positions open has been difficult. It is good that we don't have to lay off employees, but it is hard on the departments. There are delays in getting approval to fill positions. The request must clear multiple layers of management and none have been approved yet. Everyone is having to continually adjust. There does not seem to be adequate planning; in particular, the attrition is unplanned. People are coping and the work is getting done. There is a trade-off between firing staff and accomplishing the reduction through unplanned attrition. We are not always getting the right positions vacated. However, the attrition has gotten middle management used to having to work with less.

I have added to my current responsibilities. I need to reinforce the change with my immediate staff. I have to begin looking for strategies for working with less. I have also put a lot of time in on the reductions and the development of the workforce-reduction policy, and I have spent a lot of time working with the coordinating council of the hospital and the consultants. I have been through this twice before. I feel that everyone is vulnerable and I do not feel safe.

My staff know that they will not be released and are feeling secure in Phase 1. They have been involved in the reductions and I have worked with them. Everyone is worried about Phase 2, which is not talked about. They are also anxious; most have not gone through reductions before. I do not know Dr. Lewin, and I will have to speculate how he is feeling. I respect him and his self-directed work teams. I feel comfortable not knowing.

I am working fifty-five hours per week. The difference is that I feel sad about the whole process; I'm taking it home. I am more quiet and withdrawn, but I have never been a very expressive person. I have been healthy, although I recently broke my leg on vacation. In general, people are very anxious; they are talking among themselves and listen to every rumor. I have been feeling anxious but not angry, left out, unsupported, or overworked.

Communication has been adequate at my level and I feel that I know why downsizing is needed. It is different for my department heads. I'm not sure that they know that tomorrow is the day that the cuts will be announced. Information has been intentionally withheld because the department heads cannot be trusted to not pass the information along. If they did, it would be chaos.

If I had it to do over again, I feel that I need to find a way to follow up with the department heads more often. I appreciate that, from their point of view, things have been done piecemeal. I do not agree; they were not communicated with all along. They do not know what the senior staff is working on. This has created a double bind. If we tell others, the information will spread like wildfire.

I think the downsizing has sometimes been effective. This is a 24-hour operation. Staffing imbalances are being worked through. I think the impacts were foreseen, except for one group. Physicians wanted to be involved more than they were. The initial thought was that they would be included in Phase 2.

The consultant's approach, which involved department managers, was excellent. Everyone had a say in what they gave up, which created ownership of the changes by managers and staff. The changes being made at the top of the organization are not being talked about. This is unfortunate. There is no certainty as to how many internal candidates there are. They are not being proactive when it comes to redesigning the organizational structure. Jacob's style is not particularly proactive, it's more reactive.

Word Associations

Job	Insecure
Morale	Low
Efficiency	Needed
Cost	Information
Change	Needed

Chapter 4

Case Interpretations
and Overview

The interviews presented in Chapter 3 are filled with a rich and some-what distressing story about change. This chapter is devoted to under-standing the nature of the story from a psychologically informed perspective. The three case consultants offer their insights into what is happening to the employees of General Hospital. The first author concludes the chapter with an overview of the work of the three con-sultants and the case developed thus far.

INTERPRETATION BY HOWELL BAUM

Themes

No special psychoanalytic sensibility is needed to understand what has happened in this hospital. In response to concerns about the hospital's profitability, senior management called in consultants, who recommended a change process that started with cutbacks and firings. (*Downsizing* is both a bad euphemism and bad English.) People who did not know whether they would be fired and who were not privy to decision making became anxious, angry, suspicious, and stressed. There is no puzzle here.

Significance and Hypotheses

Anyone who has ever been a patient might also be struck by the virtual absence of any discussion of patient care in staff interviews. Perhaps staff are too anxious about their own well-being to think about others, including the hospital's clients. Perhaps these middle and senior managers do not normally think about patient care. Perhaps it is the culture of this hospital to be concerned first about finances.

Strikingly, though the description of the consultants' work is sketchy, there is no sign that senior managers asked the consultants to consider patient care a primary concern in their recommendations. After all, the three phases of the change process form an odd sequence, where redesign of the structure (presumably to better serve missions that include patient care) follows, rather than precedes, cutting departmental staffs.

At the least, it is clear from the first that this hospital is concerned about making money. That this is so, either in general or in the current situation, is neither surprising nor inappropriate, but one must wonder whether this emphasis has displaced concerns for patients and, if so, what that means for those who work in this hospital. One hint of disquietude is several staff members' complaints that the doctors were not sufficiently consulted on changes that should be made. At least symbolically, doctors represent curing and caring.

Reading just these interviews, one can get only a sketchy picture of events in the hospital. It would be helpful to know more about the deliberations among senior managers that led them to decide to hire consultants, how they and the consultants talked, and what the consultants have done. It would help to know more about Arch Lewin's background with ambulatory care, David Maggiano's selection of him, and whatever about him led Frank Wirth to resign posthaste. (These pseudonyms themselves are wonderful: "Arch Lewin" is easy to think of as the Arch Enemy who caused the hospital to lose a Frank man of Worth, thus leaving Jacob as the Doorman between the Arch Enemy and the rest of the staff.) Further, it would be useful to hear from workers who care for patients, not to mention patients themselves.

The pain caused by organizational changes leaps out on every page. Some managers rationalize their own or others' suffering with tacit allusions to the reality that doctors, to heal, must often inflict pain. Yet it is hard not to ask how the managers of especially a healthcare institution could initiate steps that cause so much suffering. Some of the pain was certainly avoidable. And one must wonder whether, after so much suffering, the hospital will be able to function effectively. On the basis of available information, it is difficult to say much about avoidable pain; it is unclear both how the hospital was operating and what top managers want to do with it. However, one can say a great deal about the extent and depth of staff suffering, and one can speculate about the meanings and consequences of such suffering in a healthcare institution.

Budgetary and surgical language converge here in a focus on "cutting." Over and over again, staff members speak of people being cut. And yet these cuts are not the first injuries suffered by staff; they are only the first that top management have inflicted on their subordinates. In fact, the story begins with the retirement of the university president, the departure of physicians to work for competitors, and the protest resignation of the hospital director. The hospital staff are, indeed, in mourning for an unstanched stream of losses.

They have lost positions, and they have lost people. The people first left one at a time, more or less voluntarily; then, in a rush, many were fired at once. Tom Frey reports he has "lost some highly skilled technical people." Julie Nugent says the hospital is "losing major physician leaders." Others say, more simply, their colleagues and friends are gone. The change process causes more losses. Frey is "losing [his] global focus." Maria Meyers feels not only that she may lose her job as Manager II, but that her unit will lose its "progress after years of effort." Her "dreams of . . . great success have been lost." Mary James is concerned staff have lost their "loyalty to the center."

One after another, staff use violent metaphors to express how they experience the change process. Peggy Lubin says the "uncertainty is a killer." Meyers speaks of "a time bomb waiting to explode" regarding layoff announcements. Ted Olsen feels there was "a gun being held to [his] head" to cut his units. And the question is, Bob Ryder says, "How long can a gun be held to someone's head before they say 'shoot'?" When the layoffs were finally announced, Brenda Early observes, "everyone was herded like cattle to slaughter into the auditorium." Val Kasman says the layoffs were "like the Holocaust."

It should be unnecessary, but it is important to say that, while these metaphors are not literally true, they describe how hard people feel the cuts and being part of a cutting process, even when they retain their jobs. Moreover, although individuals, even talented and beloved ones, can usually be replaced, it is much harder to repair the losses of focus, dreams, and loyalty.

Many of the staff seem like zombies—living dead. Some are simply victims of the violence of change—the gun at their temple went off. But others have killed or maimed themselves so that they no longer feel the pain from outside. Some have quit. Others request leaves of absence; some take vacation. Less formally, others engage in absenteeism by calling in sick. Still others turn up at the hospital but withdraw from the work.

Some staff members retreat along complicated psychological routes. Stan Pittman observes that people who report to him "are acting with less maturity and rationality." Joseph Greene gives other examples of immaturity: "There is an atmosphere of pettiness. Staff are making dumb mistakes." In psychoanalytic language, they have regressed: They have mentally retreated from a painful situation in which they are adults and have responsibilities by acting as if they were children who could not possibly be employed in this hospital or responsible for anything there.

For some, this regression is part of another reaction to the violence and losses of the change process; Cynthia Winston uses the psychoanalytic label when she notes that people "are depressed." Jeri Glover, Judy Harris, and Mary James speak of being sad. Glover says she is "more quiet and withdrawn." Indeed, people seem withdrawn not only from work (even if they spend many hours on the job), but also from others outside work. Greene, simply, is "preoccupied." Matt Towner is "not as willing to be social." Peggy Lubin says, "When I do something social, such as gambling, it feels more like I am just filling up time."

Many people withdraw from their spouses. Lofgren, Mills, and Kasman report spending less time at home with their families. Although real work demands may keep them at the office, others, who also put in long hours at the hospital, say they are not as interested in their spouses as before. Olsen and Ryder argue with their wives. James is "more removed from my husband . . . more quiet than usual." One would speculate these people are less sexually interested in their spouses as well. That, too, would be a sign of regression, from mature relations with other persons to self-preoccupation, or, more precisely, to imaginary mental relations, the social life typical of infants.

Meyers, who seems to feel an exceptional obligation to speak truthfully, metaphorically describes people who doubt their potency and work both manically to reassure themselves and magically to keep their bosses from firing them: "My staff are frustrated, scared, and wondering if they should be looking for a job. They are also *rising to the occasion* to meet work demands. They are trying to work *hard* to insure that they have a job" (emphasis added). She herself feels such pressures: "I feel that I have risen to the occasion, and I am getting more done because I have to. I am constantly busy."

Depression is a complex phenomenon, but a central thought associated with the leaden experience is that one is not worth very much. If only we were better, we may imagine, this would not have happened to us. Thus people may blame themselves for what also makes them ashamed. Even rage against the world seems fruitless, for the aggression seems impotent, and we feel worse yet. Arguing blindly with one's husband or wife may be one of the few ways one can momentarily feel efficacious, even though one may know one's spouse has nothing to do with it, and one feels ashamed of trying to make him or her feel as tormented and worthless as one feels.

Extensive cutbacks are inherently traumatic. There are no easy ways to fire anyone, and personality differences make little difference in how people react. Nevertheless, two recurrent themes point to conditions that increase the pain (if that is possible). Repeatedly, people speak of uncertainty. Any planning process without foreordained conclusions will, for better or worse, be uncertain. Yet Glover and Lubin say more when they speak for many in noting they don't know Dr. Lewin. If they knew the top man, they might better anticipate the eventual good or bad news.

Instead, rampant rumors substitute for solid information. Frey says, "Rumors are running amok." Glover reports, "In general, people are very anxious; they are talking among themselves and listen to every rumor." Joseph Greene observes that working the rumor mill displaces working on the job: "My staff are more anxious; everyone is asking, 'Am I the one?' A lot of time is being wasted talking about rumors." Most end up assuming the worst while twisting rumors every which way to find a glimmer of hope in them. Greene suggests that "they obsess over every rumor. A lot of time is being wasted talking about rumors. Some are talking about what they might do if they have to leave."

Even under normal conditions, in any large organization subordinates want to see their bosses and know what they think. When people cannot get realistic information about what their bosses expect and how they will evaluate subordinates, people may resort to speculation built on fantasy. For example, they may unconsciously equate their boss with earlier authority figures, such as a parent they remember from infancy: large, omnipotent, omniscient, omnicompetent, and wielding the power of life and death. When people think of their boss in these ways, they may feel ashamed at their own seeming smallness and inadequacy, and they may resent that their boss apparently treats them in such a demeaning way. Nevertheless, this definite image, as bad as it is, reassures workers by seeming to make the boss predictable (see Baum, 1987).

The less subordinates know about their bosses, the more likely they are to imagine them as people who would put a gun to their head or kill them. Sometimes, when people are traumatized, they try to invent activities in which they can control events that symbolically represent the injuries they were forced to experience passively. Lubin's gambling looks like an example that shows one way she copes and reveals still another frightening fantasy about unknown bosses: By playing with cards, she tries to master the kind of seemingly random events top managers inflict on the people who work for them.

Worse yet, as Mike Payne observes, "The rumor mill destroyed faith and hope. . . . Everyone feels betrayed; they have worked here for many years." Part of the explanation is that people came to believe the worst of top managers, and, getting no reassurance from them, withdrew their loyalty. Another part of the explanation is that some of the dire rumors were, in fact, true, as Harris explains: "The informal information process has included lots of rumors that have been denied by management, but subsequently have proven to be right. I don't like the implied dishonesty."

Despite almost ritualized affirmations that communication has been adequate, staff members complain both that they have not been told what they want to know and that what has been said, as Harris points out, has been duplicitous. Top managers do not trust middle managers to get as much work as possible out of their subordinates before firing them. Glover explains that "Information has been intentionally withheld because the department heads cannot be trusted to not pass the information along. If they did, it would be chaos."

This predicament leads to the kind of deception found in Stan Pittman's department. Pittman says, "One of my directors will be cut." Nugent, who is in the same department, comments on this prospect and layoffs generally: "There will be one executive in charge. . . . We never had to lay off people before. We have been getting training, a script for laying people off. We need to prepare. It bothers me that I know when dealing with a person who will be laid off. It is two faced." Knowing who will be cut, Pittman complains (as noted earlier), "They are acting with less maturity and rationality." Lying to them, perhaps feeling forced to mislead them, he says he is surprised they do not go along with him.

Work is hard enough when a situation is inherently uncertain and when some people will inevitably be fired. What makes the change process in the hospital insidiously worse is the added invisibility and anonymity of the top managers and the objective untrustworthiness of managerial communication. Subordinates might assume the worst and withdraw emotionally from a toxic situation.

The firings and the way this phase of the change process went will affect the next phase, as well as later life in the medical center. Jacob Dohrman reports, "The reduction in force went well." He is "positive about the changes; the organization can absorb them." Here is where management is different from surgery: A cut body recovers far more easily than a cut organization. The troops are shell-shocked. People who worked for the hospital for many years were fired. Those who were not fired might reasonably imagine that these were not the last cuts they face. Even keeping a job is not the same as surviving: many have lost focus, dreams, and loyalty.

Moreover, survival is not a simple matter. Kasman says (as noted earlier), "Never . . . again, like the Holocaust." If some staff experienced the cuts like the Holocaust, they may also react to them as people did to the Holocaust. Some Holocaust survivors came to feel profound guilt that they had survived at others' expense. They felt others deserved to live more than they did. Such diabolical calculations in no way reflect the reality of the Nazi Holocaust or firings at the medical center, but they point to debilitating feelings workers may struggle with. If keeping their jobs unconsciously means they forced others to lose theirs, they may, for example, punish themselves for their seemingly unwarranted—and thus hollow—victory by acting in ways that defeat both themselves and the hospital.

Symbolically and practically, it remains to be seen how these "walking wounded," if they feel unwell and betrayed by the medical center, are able as a collectivity to cure and care for patients. What will be crucial in the next few months is whether the top managers who inflicted this pain on the staff can respond to the trauma and help to heal the center. Otherwise, some individuals will do better than others, but the organization will suffer. After all, improving productivity is more than a matter of cutting staff.

Suggestions

It would be presumptuous for the reader of an interviewer's notes on conversations with second- and third-level managers to offer advice to Maggiano and Lewin about improving the situation. The available information does not tell much about who the hospital leaders are, how they think about the hospital, what they want to accomplish, or what instructions they have given the consultants they hired. Moreover, quite simply, they have consultants and are obviously not looking for additional advice. The intervention has created serious personnel problems, even if it may address short-term financial problems; some believe the intervention has also created problems in caring for patients. There is no evidence here that Maggiano or Lewin sees these problems or wants advice on them.

It would be a contorted act of the imagination to say what Maggiano and Lewin should have done, because they do not seem to be the kind of managers who are concerned about problems central to the hospital's long-term health: staff working conditions and morale, and the quality of patient care. If they had, by chance, hired a consultant who had such concerns, he could have pushed them to frame a diagnosis of the hospital's condition not only in terms of its finances, but also in these other matters.

That approach would have defined issues, opportunities, and constraints differently. In addition, it would have led to a different intervention process, in which representatives of staff of all ranks, as well as patients and community members, would have participated continuously in analyzing situations and identifying possibilities for action. Such a planning process would have avoided many of the painful consequences of the actual intervention, where those at the top concealed their thinking and intentions from everyone else. At least as important, it would have constituted a significant reform in the hospital's structure. Finally, of course, it would have led to different interventions and probably broader support for them. And yet Maggiano and Lewin did not choose such a course.

If consultants concerned about the institution's long-term vitality approached the hospital in search of a client and an assignment, they might turn first to staff members like those interviewed here. These consultants might persuade staff of the possibility of preparing their own, alternative, restructuring plans to show top managers directions that could simultaneously serve the ledger books, staff, and patients. However, the work would require someone to pay the consultants, and might demand more dreams, focus, and loyalty, not to mention self-esteem and courage, than staff have left.

INTERPRETATION BY MICHAEL DIAMOND

Themes

Healthcare delivery systems are undergoing profound changes. In order to survive, General Hospital is downsizing and cutting costs. Directed by a national consulting firm, the employees of the hospital and medical center were faced with a three-phase approach to change: First, cut costs by downsizing; second, flatten the administrative hierarchy of General Hospital and reduce the number of departments; and third, locate avenues to improve operational efficiency and cost effectiveness.

The consulting firm helped complete Phase 1. Their recommendation was for a 10-percent cutback to respond to the 10- to 15-percent decline in census. Based on interviews of twenty-three hospital staff, I will suggest how General Hospital employees are coping with the changes. In so doing, I will try to identify thematic patterns that emerge from the interviews. Then, I will suggest what these themes signify about the feelings of workers and the implications for systemic change and development at the medical center. In trying to more deeply understand the meaning of these interviews in the context of the organization, I begin with an overview of critical incidents that comprised the change effort at this time and that triggered emotional responses among staff.

Critical Incidents

What are the critical incidents that required adaptive responses from leaders and that produced stress for hospital management and staff at General Hospital? First, the hospital has moved toward financial and managerial autonomy from the university. In an era of healthcare reform (managed care and managed competition), the medical center requires sufficient independence to formulate policies, change institutional structures, and implement strategies consistent with an overall business plan. Although relative autonomy may seem like a rational organizational strategy for the medical center, it produces a substantial increase in the power and authority of two center executives, Maggiano and Lewin, which may not be conducive to the welfare of the hospital and its employees.

Another critical aspect of the case is Maggiano's leadership of the center. His values, personality, and leadership style inevitably shape the hospital employees' organizational identity (Diamond, 1993), and thus, the pattern of superordinate–subordinate relationships throughout the hospital. Moreover, the move for hospital autonomy from the university occurred during Maggiano's administration and appears to have been influenced by him.

Next, his more recent (apparently unilateral) appointment of Lewin, a close friend and head of the ambulatory center, to the position of Assistant Provost for Health Services (a position that now incorporates ambulatory and the hospital), is quite important to hospital workers. In fact, Lewin's appointment was denounced with expressed feelings of condemnation by many of the interviewees. Most indicated a lack of respect and confidence in his administrative abilities. In reference to the new appointment of Lewin, many workers commented on the resignation of Frank Wirth, the Hospital Director—a position now vacant. It is unclear at this time whether the position will be filled or assumed by Lewin. Most of the staff implied that Wirth resigned in reaction to Lewin's appointment as Assistant Provost. Some indicated that if Wirth had not resigned he would have resisted the downsizing initiative. Finally, the hiring of a consulting firm by Maggiano to cut costs and downsize is another critical incident affecting the morale and performance of hospital management and staff. The consultants produced two meetings that, I believe, require our attention and were significant to the perceptions of management and staff at General Hospital. First, a meeting took place at which senior managers were asked to sign a document that confirmed their commitment to their stake in the cuts. Apparently, each manager was asked to step forward and sign their name beside the level of cuts for their section. Second, many interviewees said that hospital staff were processed for termination at a large meeting in an auditorium. Both meetings have a rather ritualistic character that I will discuss. I believe they help in understanding the emotional state of the institution and its members.

Ironically, Provost Maggiano has established a new layer of vice presidents who report to him. It appears that little is known of these positions, such as the rationale for their institution and their concomitant functional responsibility and authority. It is frequently the case that executives do not feel obliged to share decision-making rationale with management and staff. However, many hospital managers and staff are puzzled and, in some cases, resentful over the added layer of hierarchy, and some indirectly criticize Maggiano for creating a new managerial level while simultaneously looking to merge and eliminate positions.

Significance and Hypotheses

Prominent among hospital managers and staff of General Hospital is the presence of anxiety over uncertainty and loss of control. They are undergoing a serious effort at downsizing and cutbacks, which the majority agree with in theory. Their anxiety is fueled by the fact that they seem to have little to no input into where the cuts are targeted and whether the level of cuts is effective. In fact, from the interview data and those provided by the description of the three-phase approach, it appears that the consultants, in alliance with Maggiano and Lewin, are operating unilaterally. However, many interviewees claim the process of change is participative. Nevertheless, the data in the interviews and the case description signify a contrary process of decision making at the top and directives to implement at the middle and technical core of the hospital. The senior managers or unit heads decide whom to fire, but the percentage of cuts is decided by the executives and their consultants with apparently little input from hospital workers.

Moreover, the two meetings set up by the consultants (first, to gain commitment from senior managers and second, to process cuts) signify deep mistrust of hospital management and staff, and defensive behavior on behalf of the consultants. The consultants may be overly identified with Maggiano and Lewin in the minds of many hospital employees. The meetings seem designed to humiliate staff and depersonalize superior-subordinate relations. Are the consultants aware of their own aggressive feelings and the consequences for the hospital workers? Are they aware of the dynamics of "projective identification" between clients (Maggiano and Lewin) and consultants? I don't believe so.

Both meetings were public spectacles intended to coerce compliance and suppress dissent among hospital managers and staff. The consultants seem to be carrying out the intent and untested assumptions of Maggiano and Lewin. There is no evidence of any serious challenge from the consultants to the additional layer of hierarchy (the newly appointed vice provosts), and there is no evidence to suggest that the consultants are advocating for greater participation among hospital managers and staff. In other words, it appears the consultants and Maggiano and Lewin have merged unconsciously, and the merger has taken the form of a "twinship or alterego transference" (Kohut, 1977). The emotional foundation of their relationship is based upon a need for what Kohut called "essential alikeness" or "twinship" between them. In the consultation, this is problematic for the consultant–client relationship in that it interferes with the consultant's requisite independence and impartiality and does not allow for sufficient scrutiny of the roles of the two executives.

For example, at the senior managers' meeting, management was required to sign—on a blackboard—their names next to their respective unit and the assigned level of cuts. There was no opportunity to discuss the merits of the downsizing in certain areas, or to entertain ideas on various strategies for adaptation in a changing healthcare environment. From the interviews, it did not appear that workers had an opportunity to question the cuts in one area or the lack of cuts in another.

In particular, it was noted by numerous interviewees that ambulatory is growing at the same time the hospital is retrenching. For example, the managers of two departments independently commented to the interviewer that they viewed ambulatory as "not taking its fair share of cuts." It is expanding, they said, and "it's unjustified." There is a rationale for this distinctive treatment of ambulatory services. However, there was no opportunity (or no perceived opportunity), to debate the merits of the rationale, and because Lewin was the head of ambulatory prior to assuming his new position, it is highly suspect in the minds of many hospital employees. Consequently, Lewin and the consultants are the targets of hospital employees' aggression and negative feelings, which ironically mirror the executives' and consultants' negative projections aimed at the hospital employees. If these decisions and actions are valid and rational, why is it that the executives and consultants did not present their case and encourage staff to challenge and advocate their own views?

Many unit heads and staff feel that they were asked to take on more than their fair share of cuts, despite the fact that attrition was delivering a large portion of the downsizing. In fact, if the consultants, executives, and staff do not examine the nature of these negative feelings and projections, the linkage between ambulatory and the hospital (inpatient services) could be jeopardized. Feelings of envy and rage among hospital workers are typical reactions to cutbacks that negatively affect divisional and organizational relations. The consultants and executives of General Hospital appear oblivious to the psychologically regressive consequences of downsizing.

Most everyone seems to agree that the downsizing and cost cutting are necessary for the hospital to survive in an era of decreasing census. However, they do not support the decision-making authority of Maggiano and Lewin. In other words, many employees disagree with the process and implementation of change. They feel the change was announced, and then implemented too late. They generally disrespect

Lewin and mention with suspicion the apparent good friendship between Maggiano and Lewin. Seeing the obvious contradiction between
Maggiano's words and actions, the hospital management and staff cyni-
cally and skeptically view the introduction by Maggiano of a new layer
of vice provosts into the hospital system. Finally, some workers claim
that the downsizing (much of it through attrition) accomplished at
this point in time has reduced costs. However, few believe that the
quality of hospital service will improve. Some say it will suffer.

Assessment, Preliminary Conclusions, and Suggestions

By minimizing participation, Maggiano, Lewin, and their consultants have committed a serious error that will diminish the quality of
performance of hospital personnel. The planning and directing of the
change effort is too centrally located among the consultants and the
executives. There is insufficient vertical and horizontal collaboration
in problem solving and decision making. The methods of downsizing
employed at General Hospital appear to contradict the philosophy of
contemporary managerial approaches to change and service-delivery
improvement, such as TQM and the like. When the methods of change
contradict the philosophy behind the effort, people in organizations
acknowledge the contradiction and become angry and resentful.

Maggiano and Lewin need a consultant who will encourage them to
look at their own roles and actions. The lack of support for their leadership is serious and ought to be addressed by them. Resistance to
more deeply examining their roles and the perceptions of their staff is
inevitable, but can be worked through and overcome. The nature of
their relationship and interactions with the staff must be openly examined and considered in the context of the critical incidents of recent organizational history previously discussed. Individual feelings
and their implications regarding the departure of Frank Wirth, the previous Hospital Director, must be openly discussed. The rationale for a
new layer of vice provosts must be shared and debated between executives and staff. And the role of the consultants must be seriously examined. Is the process consistent with the intended outcome? Why
are the consultants not encouraging more participation? Employees'
feelings of inequitable and unfair treatment, opinions about the tardiness of the change effort, and experiences of stress due to change must
be addressed.

Feeling uncertain and out of control, the employees of General Hospital are anxious. This collective anxiety produces regressive behavior
and tendencies among groups and divisions to operate on the basis of
unconscious fantasies and untested assumptions rather than valid information. The degree to which workers are left out of decision-mak-

ing opportunities for change has the effect of increasing these feelings of helplessness and powerlessness.

To avoid deterioration of performance and morale, I, as their consultant, would encourage an exchange of feelings and ideas between the hospital staff and Maggiano and Lewin; organizational boundaries between executives and staff are inhibiting effective communications and emotionally loading their mutual roles. At this point in time, however, I would want to share the feedback from the interviews (maintaining staff confidentiality) with Maggiano and Lewin prior to structuring any face-to-face meetings. The purpose of these face-to-face meetings would be to surface problems and commit to addressing them.

As a psychoanalytic organizational consultant, I would move to clarify intentions and expectations between and among executives, consultants, and hospital personnel. I would work to minimize defensiveness by countering projections of aggression with valid information and facilitating the sharing of knowledge across role and divisional boundaries. I would assist in publicly clarifying divisional and individual tasks and roles, issues of authority, and responsibility. I would assist staff in publicly and directly addressing undiscussable and threatening issues. I would support them in sharing negative feelings and acknowledging the place for emotions in problem solving and change. In other words, I would help to lift suppressed feelings and ideas that comprise the unconscious life of General Hospital. Finally, I would help the executives to more deeply examine their roles and the impact of how they work as a team on the hospital management and staff.

In sum, I would suggest restructuring the change effort in a fashion that would empower hospital management and staff to participate in charting their own destiny. I would ask them to identify areas of waste and mismanagement and involve them in working teams as a component of a strategic plan for the hospital that is grounded in the realities of changes in the healthcare industry.

INTERPRETATION BY HOWARD STEIN

Introduction: Self and Subject

I wish first to explain how I work; to situate myself in relation to the task. For what we see is where we see from. A principal source of data about the organization in this book is how I emotionally respond to what I am reading in Dr. Allcorn's interviews. I serve as a kind of resonating instrument. It is the basis of what I know about the organization, and what I do. How the data "make" me feel, think, and want to act (technically, the "countertransference" they induce in me) are part of the organizational data themselves.

Let me illustrate this approach by describing my reaction to reading the interviews and to the task of writing the interpretation. When I first read the interview transcripts, I could not read them all in a single sitting, or even two or three. The feelings and imagined scenarios, only recently dealt with by those interviewed, were overwhelming. So I fed myself or titred myself in smaller doses so that I could better absorb the accounts of life at General Hospital—a luxury those interviewed did not have. I knew I was resisting the material; trying somehow to control both my feelings of reeling with the change and my response of wishing I could do or say something decisive and feeling helpless. I keenly felt that I was everywhere in the presence of violence, mutilation, and death.

Even later, as I wrote this first set of interpretations (although I had written much in the first couple of months after receiving the interviews), I stalled and put off writing something final. Part of this reluctance was my unconscious transference toward Dr. Allcorn, the senior author—but even this I take not only to be my fantasy of Dr. Allcorn's individual judgment of my contribution, and my feeling of some sibling rivalry among us three interpreters, but also, and primarily, to be part of the General Hospital data themselves, since uncertainty and fear in upward chain-of-command, and uncertainty of identity, pervade the interviews too.

But that is not all. Part of my inability to complete the assignment as early as I had wished was my own feeling of being overwhelmed and rendered helpless—paralyzed—by the institutional history I was reading. How does one (i.e., an executive, a consultant) possibly hold on to such a momentous series of events as were occurring at General Hospital? Somehow I had to be able to hold on to these feelings in order to feel, via identification, what it must be like to be the interviewees, and more broadly, what it must feel like to work at (or to have worked at) General Hospital. There were times I forced myself to sit at the typewriter or computer and just write: "Get on with it; don't feel; work." I used all these "crazy" feelings as cues not only to myself, but to General Hospital via my visceral reaction to reading the interviews.

When I read the interview transcripts, as when I consult in person, I listen to each individual both as a distinct person and as if the person were somehow also speaking at some level for the entire group. That is, I read and listen as if people are playing important roles in one another's imaginations. I listen to an individual as if he or she embodied the organization as well as being a distinct, separate person. Stated differently, I work with and listen to organizations much as if I were reading a novel or short story, or attending a play or opera. Shakespeare's tragic heroes—Othello or Macbeth or Hamlet—require the entire cast of characters to sustain them to be "themselves." Everyone participates in the drama. My task as organizational analyst is to identify the surface drama and the often unvoiced but hinted-at underlying drama.

Third, there can be no absolute distinction between a description of the "facts" of the organization (e.g., General Hospital, the interviews) and my "interpretation" in the form of hypotheses about the significance of the facts and the meanings I give to them. We all harbor the wish for objectivity—for undistorted, unedited, and unselected facts. (We talk of "letting the facts speak for themselves.") Yet we know that we also select "facts" to fit with what we think is happening. Having three organizational consultants offer independent assessments, interpretations, and recommendations is one way to keep ourselves honest about the extent to which we organize—often for unconscious purposes of avoiding anxiety and conflict—the very data we then purport to interpret.

Themes

I emphasize at the outset that this enumeration of themes, while heuristically useful, is also artificial. Each theme interpenetrates with the others into a configuration. Each theme is part of the same picture or experience.

Main and Subsidiary Themes   In many great novels, movies, symphonies, and operas, there is not only the obvious, conspicuous "big theme" introduced at the outset, but one or more subsidiary themes that could be missed, yet make the first theme even more powerful and poignant, often by contrast. In this first set of interviews, there is the obvious theme of the hospital's large-scale, traumatic downsizing, and the unexpectedness of the event to many of the interviewees. An equally important theme, though, and one woven in by many interviewees, is the appointment of Lewin and the resignation of Wirth. Leadership succession, and the associated sense of loss, anxiety, uncertainty, grief, and resentment, thus become a part of the story of General Hospital's downsizing. There is not only the scale of the loss at layoffs and the uncertainty of the future in Phase 2, but the loss of an apparently reliable, even admired, leader and his replacement by the surprise appointment of Lewin and the loss of an apparently reliable line of reporting as well. My fantasy is that perhaps interviewees would have felt less abandoned and overwhelmed by the change had Wirth remained, or had someone other than Lewin—and with their advice—been put in.

Metaphors   Organizational metaphors (and similes) serve as a path to understand how members of a work group imagine themselves and their situation and what it is like to be there. They also serve as one among several "royal roads" to an organizational unconscious; that is, to fantasies and effects that underlie and organize recurrent images. As I read the transcript of the interviews, I wrote down the following metaphors and similes. (I have tried to keep as much of the spirit, if not the letter, of the quotations as possible. The reader can keep me honest by reading the text to see what I missed or what I might have overinterpreted.)

There is this story about leaving a garden, walking through a park, and then ending up in a wilderness. I believe the employees are feeling that they have left the garden and are now lost in the wilderness but, in reality, they are really in the park.

Change monster.

All bets are off.

The summer from hell.

Change will leave us stronger by tearing the organization down and rebuilding it. The survivors need to hear this. They have to feel good about what is left. I want to avoid the feeling that what is left is a battlefield full of destruction.

Survival [organizational].

Let's get the change over with.

Targeted cuts.

They were not listening.

Disturbance in the medical center.

The hospital is being blamed and punished [as if the personified hospital were bad].

Hospital versus ambulatory care center.

Fluff [superfluous].

Hospital unprepared.

Merger is rotten.

Merger of departments versus split-off departments.

Rumors are running amok.

I'm afraid that when problems arise, my department will be scapegoated.

"Am I the one [targeted to be fired]?"

Hospital as the target.

Black Friday.

D-Day [invasion].

How long can a gun be held to someone's head before they say "shoot"? [reductions].

It was important to hear that the ship is not going down and a message like, "This too shall pass."

Flatten the organization [administrative layers].

Everyone was herded like cattle to slaughter into the auditorium [to process those laid off].

It is almost like we are in a glass bubble. People do not know what is going on in the outside [boundary issues].

Everyone is feeling vulnerable. There is the feeling that we will never let this (the layoffs) happen again, like the Holocaust.

Reengineering is challenging.

The reader might say that, in so enumerating and isolating the core metaphors, I am taking them out of their conversational or narrative context. I agree. I do not discount the more obvious, sequential narrative context. On the other hand, if I may be further metaphoric, the official context can be seen as a kind of "smokescreen" to divert attention from the "fire." And the fire is itself clearest when we consider only the metaphors, by themselves, as closest to the underlying, unconscious context. It is emotionally draining to read the above list because it feels so overwhelming. There is nowhere to hide. There is no protection from total vulnerability. Perhaps that is what it feels like to work at General Hospital.

Control versus Out of Control   Western civilization, not only post-Enlightenment Europe and America but all the way back to the Old Testament, is built upon the attempt to control the external world and the expectation that we should be able to exert such control. Submission to nature (fatalism) is downright un-American. In modern America, biomedical institutions, their personnel, and high technology represent the apex of the quest for control over nature, disease, death, and loss.

If half a century ago hospitals still represented to most Americans the place to go for one's final illness and death, today they represent to the public, to patients, and to healthcare workers of all professions the place where near-miraculous cures are ordinary when maximum control over the environment can be achieved. Think of the terms we offhandedly use: *The Mecca, The Medical Center,* and after Samuel Shem's classic novel, *The House of God.* A world-famous, high patient volume, high quality, "big bucks" profitability organ-transplant center such as General Hospital represents the symbolic apex of this death-defying fantasy made reality. Within this framework, "downsizing" is an affront to those interviewed. "How is this possible?" they ask, partly in shame, partly in guilt, partly in rage.

The interviewees' recurrent agony presupposes that this sort of thing should not happen in places like this: "We who are in control are suddenly totally out of control," many protest. To be "out of control" in American biomedicine and in the wider technological society is intolerable. Worse perhaps than the layoffs themselves, was the interviewees' sense of lack of control, lack of preparation for, and lack of the ability to anticipate and somehow absorb and master the event. It was as if the event, for which they were partly responsible, also overtook them.

Further compounding the sense of "out of control" is the fact that senior administrators, who are expected and who expect of themselves to come up with organizational "saves," now have to engage in at least symbolic killing (elimination by firing) of those whom they wished to save. There is the sense that "We should have known" or "We should have been told," as if the past could perhaps retrospectively be changed and the trauma averted. It remains harrowingly unclear whether any-one, at any level, really "knew" or was as much "in charge" as many interviewees had wished or presumed. Still, there is the assumption, especially in tall, impersonal, hierarchical bureaucracies, that "some-body knows" or "somebody is in charge."

Further, we Americans claim to thrive on change—the Western or cowboy insistence on being able to keep "movin' on" and never want-ing to be "stuck" or "fenced in" by civilization and domesticity. Yet we also yearn for settledness, even as we gripe about how it fences us in. We prefer to be masters rather than victims of change. When change feels as if it is happening too us, rather than being caused by us, we become unsettled, even alarmed. General Hospital is no exception. Accusations of leadership's lack of vision, disorganization at the top, rumors amok, and poor communication of facts are all attempts to ex-plain the suddenness of the change, the sense of victimization by it, and to regain at least some symbolic control.

The Expected Story Line versus the Unexpected Story Line   Hospital organizations, like ethnic groups, nations, families, and individual persons, have often implicit notions about how a story ought to go: how it should start, what should happen to make it a good story, and how it should end. General Hospital personnel, together with those interviewed, are struck by how discrepant the real turns in the story are from what they expected, needed, wanted, and, in many cases, had labored so hard and long to accomplish (e.g., "The need to cut back first appeared in the campus newspaper," or "It took me three years to build the department up from what was a disastrous earlier situation. I feel I just made it about a year ago. I now feel that I will have to dismantle my efforts, which is upsetting.")

It is as if their story now betrays them, that it is no longer their story, even though they are responsible for its new outcome. Last year's record profits must somehow be emotionally as well as cognitively recon-ciled with this year's low patient census. Those interviewed must some-how give up the old story, enforce the new story, and justify to themselves doing both (e.g., giving up old ways, making changes). They must, in short, craft new selves, let go of old selves, and explain to themselves and to others why they are doing so—and try to feel good and just about it. That is to say, they must somehow deal with the anxiety, aggression, guilt, shame, and other undesirable emotions that are evoked by the new situation.

"Us" versus "Them": Hospital versus Outpatient/Ambulatory Care As the interviewees describe the uncertainty and the layoffs, they often distinguish between inpatient and outpatient (hospital versus ambulatory) units, and speak of this relationship in terms of conflict, if not bipolar opposition. It is as if the good in life is a limited "pie," a zero-sum game, and that whatever ambulatory gets is at the expense of the hospital. If somebody gets, somebody gets something taken away; in this scenario, someone has to be deprived. I have a feeling that some interviewees (and some of their subordinates) have a sense of injustice, if not betrayal, as if the fantasy were, "If we are to suffer, then we all should suffer equally. If hospital gets cut, then ambulatory should also."

Communication This word keeps cropping up throughout the interviews: the need for better communication, the wish there had been better communication, or communication as solution. Communication is an issue both with those to whom the interviewees report, and those who report to them. Lurking behind communication lie vulnerability, helplessness, and perhaps the wish to have averted the past. Also, there is the question of how to live with being the bearer of so much (unexpected) bad news when administrators and managers wish to be "good" people. Perhaps this wish to view oneself as "good" (that is, kind, generous, loving, not hurtful) helps to explain the wish to get on with things and not dwell on the downsizing itself.

Boundary Uncertainty Throughout the interviews, I am overwhelmed with feeling that there is not a single area in work life at General Hospital where boundaries are not uncertain, not up for grabs: from individual role responsibilities to whether the medical campus will be administratively separate or merged with the rest of the university. Even boundaries high at the top have been blurred, or are at least confusing (e.g., the appointment of Dr. Arch Lewin, a close friend of Provost David Maggiano, to Assistant Provost [with authority over both the hospital and ambulatory facility].) Not only is whether one will have a job (and more, what it will entail) undefined, but virtually all identities at General Hospital feel uncertain.

One recurrent boundary theme is that all workers are expected to expand their personal role boundaries and work group boundaries.

One major anticipated type of change is the redefinition of work group identity, from department to hospitalwide. What people do is an intrinsic part of who they think and feel they are. One recurrent demand is for personal and group boundaries to become more inclusive and to crosscut traditional divisional and departmental units.

Functioning (Doing) versus Feeling   Many managers in the 1990s try to avert feelings of anxiety, shame, guilt, and sorrow by focusing entirely on the mechanics of layoffs and reallocation or restructuring of work. The interviewees gave some room for feeling, though I felt that the overall mood was one of what many in the American West call "circling the wagons" when under attack: the wish to get the cuts (even the anticipated ones in Phase 2) out of the way so that routine business-as-usual can be restored, or at least restructured. "Doing" or "action" can be a way of avoiding "feeling" responsible for hurting others. Metaphors are one way to avoid feeling and focus attention on doing. For instance, the term "cutback product" in the initial interview makes everything sound mechanical and involves no hurt. There are no people, only products and productivity.

The Experience of Change   The experience of change, and in particular, of time, takes us to the heart of the downsizing. A recurrent theme is the belief that it could have been foretold, maybe even prevented. The suddenness of the announcement and of the actual layoffs made emotional preparation impossible on the part of workers and on the part of the supervisors (the interviewees) who are (and who feel) responsible for their workers. There is a sense of being a passive victim of circumstance, rather than an active architect of it—an intolerable feeling of being out of control (see previous theme). The feeling that "We should have known long ago this was coming," and that "They [upper management] knew this, but didn't tell us," is in part an attempt to control what the supervisors themselves could not control. It is also an attempt to go back before the trauma and retrospectively imagine ways of gaining control of what was in fact lost. (In football, this is called "Monday morning quarterback.")
    A further aspect of the experience of change is increased responsibility, the expectation of oneself and of others of getting more done for less (i.e., money, people). These changes involve several conflicts in values and goals: among them are service versus income generation (profit); getting more for less, yet implementing TQM; creating more lateral responsibility and self-directed work teams versus more vertically top-down, hierarchical, authoritarian decision making; having better communication vertically and laterally with people, while shoring up the hierarchical command structure responsible for eliminat-

ing so many positions; eliminating positions versus expanding positions; and being humane while being ruthlessly efficient. All along, there has been the wish among interviewees to do good and to see themselves, and General Hospital, as doing good. Still, questions lurk as to whether all this reduction was done for nothing, that more reductions are yet to come, and that perhaps even this may not save the hospital. A chronic undercurrent of vulnerability and the fear of further scapegoating vie with many interviewees' wish to keep a positive attitude and a task-intensive attitude that is even more resolute than business as usual.

A final, yet major, change in General Hospital is a dramatic shift in self image: Those used to managing in a full-census hospital, where only recently there had been record profits, must now manage everything on a smaller, much more watchful, less grand scale. Ambition and sense of identity are invariably involved: There is surely a parallel downsizing of the inner landscape, where each person must deal with the disparity between who he or she wanted to be, once was, and who one now chooses, or feels compelled, to become. Here, we are at the core of people's sense of worth, its connection to interpersonal relationships in the workplace, and the role narcissism often plays in filling the void when ideals, roles, and identities can no longer be achieved in reality.

Significance

As I try to understand "What does this all mean?" to those interviewed and to their hospital, I must keep in mind that the question of significance is simultaneously local (from individual to department to General Hospital as an institution) and national. I read the interviews and see much the same unfolding story as at my own medical campus, the University of Oklahoma Health Sciences Center in Oklahoma City. We are all in the midst of something profoundly—and profoundly disturbingly—American: the modern phenomenon of "downsizing." It has become a buzzword as much as the war in Bosnia–Herzegovina, homelessness, street people, Somali warlords, and drug lords. How we understand it, and the significance we ascribe to it, influences how we hypothesize about its psychodynamics and how we propose to be of help.

As Americans, how do we go about culturally assessing what downsizing (or "RIFs" [reductions in force], or "rightsizing") is really for? That is, what is its goal? It is, for instance, only or primarily an instrumental, pragmatic, reality-oriented, tough-minded economic task or set of activities? Or might it also be (as I am inclined to believe) largely if not primarily an expressive activity; one filled with symbolic, conscious, and unconscious meanings and motivations fueled by unarticulated feelings and ritualized acts? Put differently, are we to view downsizing as an economic necessity with no further explanation needed (or an explanation is needed only of the emotional response by executives and employees to mass layoffs themselves) or as a shared cultural compulsion? Certainly, the frequent business and national media characterization of "downsizing mania" and "downsizing frenzy" suggests an expressive element. That is, this is the current way or modus operandi to solve virtually all organizational problems.

The fact that the administration of such widespread pain to so many people (by putting them out of often long-standing jobs) is spoken of in the language of euphemism (e.g., downsizing, RIF, rightsizing, reengineering, restructuring), suggests that we are avoiding the inner meaning and motivation behind what we are doing nationally. The metaphor of downsizing is further buttressed by the even deeper, unself-questioned metaphor of economic "bottom lines" (in the accounting sense of ledger lines and profitability). We treat bottom lines as if they are virtually God-given, palpable realities like granite. Yet they condense deep cultural values, meanings, and feelings we tacitly agree not to talk about. Two and three decades ago, and during the 1980s Reaganomics of excess, bottom-line thinking was culturally unthinkable. This argument, if even partially correct, situates "economics" inside culture and history, rather than as their engine.

The entire process of mass firings is emotionally sanitized and rationalized in the idiom of economic necessity for the survival of corporations as if these were organic bodies. The language of sacrifice is often used (e.g., to cut one part off in order to save the whole; that is, life is renewed through sacrificial death).

I am struck by how, in many organizations, the language of layoffs is that of a military campaign to preserve the imagined organismic integrity of the business, hospital, university, department, corporation, or other unit. Workplaces are not only anthropomorphized, but animated with lives of their own for which large numbers of people must be sacrificed so that the integrity of the body be preserved. Why, though, do we have such emotional investments in, and fantasies about, workplaces? They are not organisms, yet we experience them—and our attachments to them—as if they were living beings.

To put it simply, how much downsizing is necessity, and how much of it is atrocity? How rational is the creation of an entire underclass of expendable scapegoats? Do we as executives and managers (and students and consultants) of modern American bureaucracies have the moral capacity to distinguish between these anymore? Should we be psychodynamically examining only the consequences of downsizing on decision makers and employees alike, or should we also explore the nationwide psychodynamics of downsizing as itself a kind of mass ritual sacrifice? What should be our unit of study?

I worry that downsizing is itself a nationwide euphemism (metaphor) for well-rationalized atrocities; a making of many people into vulnerable, helpless, disposable scapegoats so that the rest of us can feel more assured, safe, and good, even if we also have to work harder. Likewise, the "bottom line" as metaphor and euphemism often serves as a final authority; a conversation stopper. It is as if, by our cultural logic, there is no further recourse or reply. Do people become more like dead, disposable commodities and the decision making about them more emotionally deadened if we think entirely in terms of economic bottom lines? Does that absolve us (because we allow it to do so through group identification with language) from feeling guilt, shame, anxiety, responsibility—and even human kinship—toward those whom we fire? That is, can an entire way of economic thinking and decision making itself be an ideological system that, like much religion and politics, masks a great deal while it directs attention to a single acceptable type of explanation?

To pursue this logic, I wonder how upper and middle management at General Hospital play into and use, in their own personal motivations, this national drama of RIFs and bottom lines. Does group loyalty demand that downsizing itself be unquestioningly implemented; taken simply as a necessary, if also sad, fact? As we further explore the meaning of the interviews and of downsizing at General Hospital, I simply ask the reader to honestly take nothing at face value, even something as seemingly concrete and now ubiquitous as downsizing. If we review labor history worldwide, we discover that corporate problem solving by mass firing is a very American-type solution (in contrast, for example, with the often idealized Japanese solution of moving workers around an organization rather than expelling them). That is, it is very cultural and not merely very economic. As we discuss the General Hospital interviews, we need also to see them against the backdrop and depth of an American way of problem solving.

Hypotheses

I offer the following psychoanalytically informed hypotheses as attempts to account for and explain (at least in part) the themes previously identified, and to explain the significance and choice of these particular themes for the people interviewed.

General Hospital, the medical center, General University, and individual departments serve simultaneously as work groups and "symbolic objects" of intense personal identification. In the latter capacity, they are at once extensions of the self into the outer world and internal presences of outer realities (i.e., introjections, identifications, ego ideals). They represent and condense many different types of values. If, as both conscious and unconscious representations, they literally contain a vital part of the self, what does it feel like when that vessel, that container, is threatened, broken, or can no longer be counted on to hold the self together?

Clearly, the agony of many of the interviewees derives from the fact that, for them, their job (and General Hospital) is not "just a job" or "paycheck," but a world. It is part of an identity that is under siege. Boundaries under attack heighten the sense of vulnerability, and, under the pull of regression to earlier modes of experiencing oneself and the world, muster narcissistic defenses against vulnerability; specifically, the threat to the fantasy of merger with and invulnerability in "the organization" (symbolic heir to symbiosis with the mother and the early protective family).

Separation anxiety and abandonment anxiety are intensely felt by the interviewees. My fantasy is that it is increasingly difficult for them to be good-enough, parent-like leaders when they now feel like overly responsible, overworked, and recently abandoned children themselves. The regressive pull of these circumstances, and the reorganization of personality and institution around primitive defenses that protect managers and workers against feelings of annihilation, rage, persecutory anxiety, and abandonment (to name but some of the most obvious reawakened inner monsters), cannot be underestimated.

Downsizing is one expression of the problem of human aggression. On the one hand, interviewed administrators often expressed regret and empathy toward those who were fired. However, I would want to explore the possibility of unconscious satisfaction at socially acceptable discharge of otherwise unconscionable aggression. It is as if to say, "I didn't want to hurt all these people, but I had to for the institution's survival or for the sake of my boss." It is a way of displacing, projecting, and rationalizing one's own aggressive impulses— making them someone else's and making them necessary, thereby disowning them or at least alleviating oneself of anxiety, guilt, shame, and remorse. Here, downsizing becomes a socially acceptable, projective pretext for aggression. That is, one can ascribe his or her motives to the need or will of the organization or senior executives, rather than having to take personal responsibility for morally unconscionable deeds. It is as if to say, "It is really 'not me,' but my role to do this."

The inability to control events, anticipate them, and prepare for them is experienced as an assault on interviewees' narcissism (and perhaps that of many others at General Hospital). Traumatic events are those which people cannot absorb within the borders of their mastery; they feel punctured, invaded, and violated, as if their very substance were about to leak (if not drain) out. Every psychosexual phase and issue (Oedipal, separation–individuation, body integrity, and so on) is condensed into the experience of this event. The failure of shared (cultural, organizational) defenses leads to the need for, and the attempt to develop, new defenses against catastrophic feelings. The interviews suggest that one way many adapt to this feeling of being so out of control is through working at tasks even harder toward mastery; depersonalization or mechanization serve as a way of diminishing the emotional magnitude both of what is happening and what one is participating in.

The magnitude and relentlessness of change deepens the suffering (for comparisons interviewees made with war and death camps, see the metaphors discussed earlier). The interviewees try to comprehend emotionally what they are doing; to make sense of it in part by utilizing defenses against violations of their personal conscience and temptations to act out intolerable wishes (e.g., splitting, emotional isolation, numbing, rationalization, and acting out through a rush into "work activity" to avoid thinking and feeling).

Leadership succession (Lewin's appointment and Wirth's resignation) is officially presented as a fait accompli; business as usual. In addition to individual styles of dealing with change and loss, especially around leadership, there is a group style (including a group-coerced style of emotional adaptation) which is built upon, among other things, identification with the aggressor and mutual identification among managers. Several interviewees spoke of the need for empathy, but there is relatively little recognition of the magnitude of unexpressed grief and the various guises it takes. Task- and policy-oriented preoccupation is one form of emotional "isolation" or "numbing" to adapt to the new chain of command.

Another form adaptation to leadership change might take is a splitting into the idealized lost leader (Wirth) and the disparaged new leader (Lewin). The past may grow rosier, and the present (and future) more dismal, as a result of this emotional bipolarity.

Social change at General Hospital is rife with what Alexander and Margarete Mitscherlisch (1975) called "the inability to mourn." Not only is there loss of the previous leader, Wirth, but the very need for downsizing attests to the changed status of General Hospital. Emotionally, the organizational experience is similar to that of a world power suddenly becoming a second-rate power, or worse. The economic injury is experienced as a narcissistic injury. While "task" is always important to accomplish, many interviewees, despite their wish to have empathy, flee into task (from discrete-local to overall restructuring) from feeling loss and grief over the change.

Organizational metaphors express and reflect shared intrapsychic social reality. "This is what it feels like to work here," is what the upper administrators interviewed are saying through their metaphors. "Downsizing," "RIFs," "rightsizing," and the like are themselves widely used metaphors; often Orwellian "newspeak" euphemisms for caus-ing, or participating in, great suffering. Through socially shared and justified euphemisms, we can borrow our conscience from others and cede personal responsibility to "The Organization," thereby diminish-ing the feeling that we are causing harm and diminishing our own sense of responsibility, anxiety, guilt, and shame.

Let me introduce a grim parallel that differs certainly in degree and in behavior from the situation at General Hospital, but not in the un-derlying mental function or purpose of metaphor in it. During World War II, Nazis (and especially the SS) commonly referred to the exter-mination program—the systematic attempt to eliminate Jews from the face of the earth—as the "Final Solution to the Jewish Problem." Adolf Eichmann was in charge of what was euphemistically called the "Of-fice of Jewish Emigration," which is to say, the coordinated collecting and shipping by railroad of Jews from all over Europe to slave-labor centers and death camps. While certainly less extreme and less repug-nant than these, current American euphemisms of downsizing and the like allow administrators to hide from what they are in fact colluding with and implementing.

The use of these metaphors makes the activity sound more routine and mechanical and less emotional and wish-ridden. They provide a sense of control over what feels beyond personal power. And they make it more acceptable for policymakers and administrators to do. When one is implementing highly euphemistically symbolized policies, it be-comes easier to "follow orders" and act as if "it is really not I who am doing this." One creates a split between private and public morality.

The further the split is rationalized (and made easier), the greater the social "mass," so to speak, of the language and of the belief. Downsizing, after all, is on the tip of the tongue of most Americans; it pervades the print, television, and radio media. We are suddenly far beyond the institutional boundary of General Hospital, and in "every-where America." Through a cycle of projection and identification, downsizing becomes easier for more and more people to participate uncritically in it, since "It is our culture;" "It is our way." We can take downsizing for granted, and not question its appropriateness as a prob-lem-solving strategy or look for alternatives. It is easier to be anony-mous and impersonal when one identifies uncritically with the cultural stream. It becomes more dangerous when policy, such as downsizing, is used to implement unconscious wishes, fantasies, and rages.

Suggestions

What would I do if I were the consultant? This will be my shortest section. Its essence is that I would want to hear more, to listen more, and to obtain over time what editorialist Paul Harvey calls "the rest of the story." I would want to know more of the interviewees' evolving feelings, hopes, expectations, identities, and emotional (interpersonal) and task roles in the organization—all of which I would try to learn by gaining their trust through availability over time. The primary role I would seek would be that of an applied fieldworker. At the same time, I would constantly be checking with the interviewees about their expectations of me. As part of my applied fieldwork role, I would seek permission from those interviewed (and from their supervisors and direct reports) to go outside the "glass bubble" of the interview proper, and walk through General Hospital; to talk with others in order to gain differing perspectives on the new and old history. In addition to talking and listening, I would want to be allowed to observe such things as interpersonal interaction and the use of space and time as part of my effort to explore the relation between what the interviewees were saying and what they and others were actually doing during this downsizing process.

I would start with my own emotional reaction as a key to the interviewees' world. As I read the interviews, I felt overwhelmed; I felt like running, like hiding, like there was nowhere to hide, and like retreating into a frenzy of work and intellectualizing. There was already too much hurt (and the anticipation of even more hurt) to bear. I would guess, out loud, that this might be part of what they were also feeling: flight from feeling as part of problem solving. I would stress that I could offer no quick fix, only an abiding, persevering presence; to be with them, to be their sounding board, and to tell them what I think and feel I am hearing—which is also a crucial part of what they offer to those who report to them.

With all the ambiguity of upper-level decision making and powerful feelings about "communication" of the layoffs, I would pose such questions as: "What is real anymore?" "How do I know?" "What is rumor?" "What is honest?" "What is lie and deception?" "How can I continue to live with such uncertainty and responsibility?" How can I feel when there is so much I'd rather not feel about?"

I would listen for "slips of the tongue," metaphors, and other "windows of opportunity" to learn about feelings, fantasies, and wishes at General Hospital. I would ask the interviewees to say more about these phrases and images, in the spirit of free association: Together we would come up with their meanings, underlying effects (unconscious feelings), and the like.

I would try to create a safe enough interpersonal environment (what Winnicott [1965] called a "holding environment") in which interviewees could continue telling—piecing together—their stories; to create an atmosphere in which new and unimagined story lines might emerge. To put it metaphorically, the more playful the intersubjective space between consultant and client, the more playful the prospective intersubjective space between client and organization.

My preferred role is more medium and listener than interventionist. In the spirit of clinicians such as Donald Winnicott, Michael Balint, Harold Searles, Vamik Volkan, L. Bryce Boyer, James Grotstein, and Thomas Ogden, among others, I seek to create a "good-enough," safe-enough interpersonal mental space in which novel solutions might have the chance to emerge and rigidity could be reduced.

I would also try to serve as an ego support, an ally (as in a consultant–client "therapeutic alliance") for interviewees as they try on problem-solving ideas with me (e.g., how to achieve broader work groups in the hospital), and at the same time to listen for and interpret the use of problem-solving modes and tasks as a means of avoiding powerful feelings and wishes (unconscious resistance). I would stay with the client in his or her phenomenological experience of the here and now, but I would also be attuned to possible influences of past formative experiences—about which I would inquire via my own feelings or more direct questions. If on occasion I wished to delve into the past—a frequent accusation made against analysts, as if they were only interested in the past—it would be for the sake of the present; for clarifying the client's role at General Hospital.

I would acknowledge the lure and purpose of the flight from feelings into action, doing, restructuring, nonfeeling, depersonalization, and euphemism, but I would try not to collude. I would try to remain as an "observing ego" throughout the consultation. I would pay careful attention to the emotional tidal pulls between myself as consultant (countertransference) and the client or interviewee (transference). When I felt tempted or pulled to collude in emotional numbing, for instance, I would acknowledge this also, and wonder aloud what it meant not only for me, but for the consultation. In short, I would strive to persevere with them on their own "turf," just as they are trying to persevere in their overwhelming, unexpected role at General Hospital.

OVERVIEW OF PART II

The purpose of this section is twofold. A synthesis of the case and the findings of the three consultants is presented, and some of the insights of the first author are provided.

Synthesis of Case and Consultants' Findings

The interviews reveal a great deal about work life at General Hospital. The mandate for change came from the top and the instrument of change wielded by Maggiano and Lewin is a consulting company explicitly hired to locate a level of reduced staffing consistent with the lower census, and to orchestrate layoffs as needed. Much effort went into avoiding laying people off. The management of General Hospital was willing to absorb unbalanced attrition, both by the type of work being performed and by shift. This process of attrition seemed to be less painful to the executives involved than actually having to face the prospect of terminating employees.

Another major theme in these interviews is that the reduction in force was overlaid with other changes, such as the appointment of Lewin as Assistant Provost for Health Services, the resignation of the Director of the Hospital Frank Wirth, and the development of a layer of new vice provosts that no one understands the purpose of. Change is also occurring in a vacuum of strategic direction. No strategic plan exists to point the way to the future or indeed help these executive avoid problems. In fact, the imposition of the new layer of vice provosts and the use of the consulting company was experienced by the members of management of the hospital as though they were doing something wrong.

The story of General Hospital as seen through the eyes of the three case consultants is a sad story that includes many losses. Good feelings of working at General Hospital and dreams about the future have been lost. The hospital's sense of innocence and its caretaking culture were in part lost in the face of an unyielding, rational, bottom-line view of fiscal reality. In particular, caring among the staff for each other has been lost. A sense of fair play, trust, and loyalty have been lost. The old ways of doing business and familiar relationships have been lost. Certainty about one's role and one's future has been lost. A sense of control over one's work and life has been lost. And also lost has been the sense of individual invulnerability and self-worth.

In the place of these losses there have been some additions to the experience of working at General Hospital. A sense of helplessness and despair has been added. Anxieties about the future has been added. A sense of loss of control and great personal vulnerability has been added. A sense of being coerced into actions of an organizationally violent nature has been added. A sense of guilt, suffering, and depression has been added. A soulless, unfeeling, uncaring experience of self that kills the pain associated with one's actions has been added. The experience of disempowerment and worthlessness has been added.

These incredible changes and experiences happened all at one time, which has led organization members to defend themselves against the change as best they can. There is evidence of withdrawal, denial, rationalization, intellectualization, and dissociation of feelings from thinking and experience. There also exists the experience of having become a passive victim. There is a search for a sign (however magical) that "I" will survive and there will be a tomorrow, next week, next month, and next year. However, the magic of survival is accompanied by feelings of survivor's guilt.

These trends identified by the three consultants speak of a human experience of significant scope and power, and they speak to the strength of the human spirit to somehow find a way to survive in the worst of times. The consultants have together found a story in the narrative of the interviews that provides every reader pause for reflection when contemplating downsizing.

But one must ask, "Change to what end at General Hospital?" One might ask why the threat of layoffs was put on the table as the focus of all of the activity when attrition was taking care of the problem of overstaffing. At the same time, if finding the right levels of employees is so rational a process, why rely upon attrition at all, as it clearly resulted in imbalances and losses of some employees who would have been better kept. This is a fascinating paradox. Clearly the sense of pain and guilt that accompanies layoffs is so great that attrition is by far the easier way out. The staffing imbalances that developed at General Hospital are apparently more easily suffered through than the pain and guilt associated with layoffs.

The case study's consultants also identified important splits in the organization. Middle management has become split off from the out-of-touch upper management. A split developed between the hospital and ambulatory and between the hospital and the rest of the medical center, the campus, and the university. There is a split between Frank Wirth, who appears to represent good, and Dr. Lewin, who appears to represent bad, in the hearts and minds of those interviewed. The case consultants also noted the following: Downsizing, as a response to hard times, has become part of an accepted cultural tradition. If you do not need it, get rid of it. Labor is disposable. There is also the possibility that the sequencing of the change process was wrong. Perhaps it would have been wiser to reengineer and then downsize.

The case consultants raised the issue of top management dropping the leadership ball. Why was the hospital not engineered correctly in the first place? Why did there seem to be a vacuum in leadership to better market the hospital to avoid the downturn in the census? There is also the issue that top management may by unwittingly displacing their deficiencies and anger onto the staff of the hospital. This creates the experience of the bad hospital and bad hospital employees that empowers them to act to make change.

Last, it is also clear that the change represented by the downsizing led to the experience of loss of control and uncertainty about the future on the part of those interviewed, which is perhaps more of a factor than the anxieties about laying off staff. It is also worth noting that mourning all the above losses and additions as well as the losses of fellow workers, working relationships, and friends must be part of the change process. It is one that does not appear to be present in the case thus far.

In sum, the case consultants, while each developing his own unique understanding of the case, have also identified common themes that describe a process of change that is filled with loss and, in particular, the loss of certainty. The case can also be further understood by inspecting the thoughts of the first author.

Additional Comments

The case consultants have done an excellent job of ferreting out most of the content that the author identified during the interviews. However, a few additional items may be added.

- The need for change was reasonably well communicated and generally understood by everyone. The communication was reinforced by the obvious evidence of empty beds and less volume and knowledge held by many that these changes have occurred at many other hospitals.

- The consultants noted that there is a lot of change going on at one time. The loss of Frank Wirth and the appointment of Dr. Lewin, the addition of more assistant provosts, and the hiring of the consulting company are all overlaid on the need to change General Hospital by reducing staffing. One might wonder if Maggiano and Lewin perceive all the change as part of a plan that is not overly complex to understand and does not seem to be too stressful from their point of view. An analogy may be aptly drawn to generals in the Pentagon planning a battle that is to be waged by troops halfway around the world. This intellectual side of planning change may be contrasted to the feelings developed by those going through it.

- The lack of any overarching strategic plan for the hospital or medical center provides no clear direction to those suffering through the change. Where is the end point and what will it be like? Also worth noting is that the hospital does not have a marketing plan, which appears to have aggravated the problem of the lower hospital-bed occupancy.

- The top of the hospital's organization is felt to be slow at making decisions and poor at listening. The addition of another layer of executives, it is felt, will further slow down the decision-making process and impair hearing what the hospital's managers have to say.

- A paradox exists between the wish to carefully plan a staff reduction of this nature and the wish to get it over with quickly. By the time the cuts were finally made, most of those interviewed were stressed-out and ready to have it finished.

- It is noteworthy that responses to the change varied by age, tenure, length of time in a particular role, and the length of time a department had departmental status. Clearly, the personal attributes of those experiencing the change have a major influence on how they are experienced and coped with.

- Throughout the process, the relationships between the Manager IIIs and the Manager IIs who work for them remained positive.

- Many felt good about the changes and it is clear that there are many new ideas being generated as to how to better operate the hospital.

In the case, top management, as represented by Maggiano and Lewin, may experience themselves as bad (as inflicting change) and the staff as good (suffering through the change). The compliment is that the staff feel top management is bad and contributed to the problem as a result of a lack of foresight and that they have done a good job and are being caused to needlessly suffer.

The opposite scenario may also simultaneously exist. Top management may feel that the staff are bad (change is needed because they failed to do a good job of managing themselves) and that they are good and leading the hospital to salvation. At the same time, the staff may feel that they must be bad, or why else would they be being humiliated, and even punished, by top management. At the same time, they may also feel that top management is their only hope and must, therefore (or perhaps hopefully), be good, wise, and leading them to a better future.

The simultaneous existence of both of these scenarios is likely. Top management experience themselves as bad to the employees and respond by becoming more distant and remote, while also feeling that they are making all the tough decisions and taking charge even if others do not like it. The staff of the hospital may simultaneously feel that they are good because they have been successful up to now. They, while acknowledging the need for change, are also feeling victimized and disempowered by how they are being treated by top management. At the same time, they may feel that they must be bad or else why would the change be needed, and a new layer of management and consultants added to help them run the hospital.

The psychological side of this paradox finds each side trying to dispose of their bad feelings onto the other. Both top management and the staff of the hospital want to have good self-feelings. Each is willing, therefore, to unconsciously locate the origins of bad feelings in the other side. Top management wants to experience themselves as good people who have shouldered an onerous burden of having to change the bad hospital to make it into a good hospital. They may also want to feel that they are infallible. Therefore, it is important for them to rid themselves of their bad qualities and limitations by locating them within the staff of the hospital. This permits them to feel good and experience themselves as infallible while encouraging the staff of the hospital to feel that they are bad, limited, and, therefore, must seek help from top management.

The hospital's staff, in contrast, also want to feel good about themselves and tend to locate the cause of many of the problems in top management. They then feel that they are the innocent victims of bad top management.

In sum, when work life becomes stressful, psychological defensiveness increases and results in many distortions and oversimplifications of reality that detract from meaningful decision making and work. This becomes much clearer during the second set of interviews.

Part III

The Eye of the Storm

It is now four months after the initial interviews and downsizing, which was accomplished without major incident. During this time, little additional work has been accomplished toward planning and implementing Phase 2—reengineering which is expected to flatten the hospital's hierarchy, combine or eliminate administrative roles, and reduce the number of registered nurses by replacing them with lower-paid personnel.

During the past four months a number of important changes have occurred. First, an informal hiring freeze has been implemented after the reduction in force. This amounts to a continuation of the freeze that was in place before the reductions. The hiring freeze created attrition that minimized the number of employees who had to be laid off. A committee has been developed to review requests to fill open positions. Requests approved by the committee are subsequently approved by Jacob Dohrman, Dr. Lewin, and Dr. Maggiano. The result is a slow and meticulously documented process that must consider every aspect of operations in order to demonstrate need. This process has as its aim avoiding filling positions which, if filled, it is thought may have to be eliminated in Phase 2.

A second change has been the selection of a new consulting company to lead the work of Phase 2. The selection process was handled at the highest levels of the organization (Dr. Maggiano, Dr. Lewin, and Jacob Dohrman) without much sharing of information with, or participation by, senior and middle management. The company ultimately selected was SPC, which assisted the strategic planning process. SPC has a national reputation for cutting the staffing of hospitals, including replacing nursing staff with lower-paid personnel. This aspect of the company was underscored by a recent article in a major national business newspaper that highlighted the fact that nurses do not like SPC's method of using more nursing aides. This article has been broadly circulated in the hospital.

A third aspect of the past few months has involved the lack of progress in locating and appointing a new Hospital Director and Assistant Provost. Dr. Lewin has provided no information about the process to anyone. A fourth change has been a lower-than-expected hospital census (60% range). This change has helped, in some instances, to ameliorate the ongoing hiring freeze. In addition, the number of public forums diminished after the reductions and none have been held for the past few months.

At the same time as the hospital is being cut back, the ambulatory facility continues to have many job postings, and some of the schools have a few.

Signals *continues to explain the need for change. Recent issues have mentioned the following points:*

- *Resizing has been accomplished.*
- *LOS has been reduced, which has lowered the census.*
- *Customer needs must be put first.*
- *Relationship building is occurring with primary care physicians.*
- *The hospital is becoming more cost effective.*
- *The hospital is entering into risk-based contracting for healthcare delivery.*
- *Quality indicators are being developed.*
- *A Healthcare Strategy Council has been created to develop a strategic plan by late Fall 1993 (something that was not accomplished and may not be accomplished until Spring 1994).*

- *An environmental assessment has been completed.*
- *The hospital is developing a formal network of relationships with other hospitals.*
- *The hospital continues to have a strong financial performance.*
- *There is a developing effort to create an integrated health delivery network.*
- *The hospital is expected to become separately incorporated from the university. The new corporation will, however, still be under the university's direction.*

The new University President has announced a major fiscal retrenchment of the university, which has led to some reductions in staff and will eventually lead to more. The newly developed deficits are considerable, and are a by-product of reduced contributions of hospital surplus revenues to the university. An early retirement program has been announced for employees who have ten years of employment and are sixty-two years of age.

The interviews for this chapter were conducted at points on either side of the date of the announcement of the new consulting company and a general orientation to its methods. Rumors about the choice of the company were accurate and it was, therefore, no surprise. The reader is reminded that the first six interviews have been selected as representative of the case in the event all twelve are not read.

Chapter 5

The Second Set of Interviews

VAL KASMAN, FEBRUARY 9, 1994

My title, job, and direct reports are the same. I still report to Jacob. I have a lower number of employees. We RIF'd 80 FTEs, and there has been significant attrition since.

I've heard that SPC is looking at our positions and I suspect one or more of us will be asked to leave. They might also change my role or I could have the same role but different departments and responsibilities. Above me, the new Director will change things. Jacob could move up or perhaps out. Below me, staff could go or there could be a change in their responsibilities. We aren't keyed into the process. I don't know what will happen.

Many of my staff may not be reporting to me or they may be asked to leave. There is a tremendous level of anxiety among the department managers. Jacob might be promoted or asked to leave by the new Director. He might leave voluntarily. His job might be reorganized into a new role. He's probably stressed about all of this.

The biggest issue is attrition; there is an intense review process before the positions are even brought forward for approval. In the departments, we are looking at reorganizing and flattening. We are also reassigning workloads to cover for vacancies I haven't filled. We are evaluating product and drugs costs, TQM, and operations improvement.

We've done a very good job on the labor budget; it's cut to a minimum. We are looking at restructuring. That's positive; everyone is really really looking. They understand they won't get anything unless they need it. We have improved cost containment. On the negative side, there is lots of stress; people are taking on more work. The department managers see the stress in their staffs and they are taking on their own extra work. There is a lot of tension and anxiety. There is a lot of resentment toward administrators and Dr. Maggiano and Dr. Lewin.

When we went through the RIF, it reached the FTE target and productivity data were up. It was our understanding that we could fill vacant positions. Now they are not being filled, regardless of how good the data look. They really hate us for it. I'm between a rock and a hard place. We shouldn't just fill because something comes open, but we are chronically short of staff in some areas and we should respond.

I have mixed feelings about the future. I'm totally supportive of reorganization and flattening. I've heard an effort may be made to umbrella some functions under one administrator that are currently distributed, such as oversight of housekeeping. Everyone is nervous; this is a big nut to crack. No one tells me what will happen.

I think in looking back at the RIF I feel positive. It was needed and we achieved results. I'm disappointed in the selection of SPC. We worked well with the first consultants. SPC's name springs fear to people's minds. Everyone is nervous about their approach.

I feel good about myself. I've only been back a full week. I'm more refreshed than others. I'm enjoying my work. I hope I'll still be here to enjoy it. I'm not enjoying the bureaucracy that has developed. Dr. Maggiano wants to approve everything. Requests to fill vacancies have to go through a committee, then to Jacob, and then to Dr. Lewin before they go to Dr. Maggiano. Meanwhile, they are talking about empowerment, grassroots approaches, and self-directed teams. People ask why we can't fill open positions. I don't know if Dr. Maggiano and Dr. Lewin see that what they are saying and doing is inconsistent. It is seen as very hypocritical by the department managers. I hope that it isn't long term.

My staff are frustrated with the hypocrisy. They are exhausted, stressed-out, and they have stopped talking to each other. They feel threatened. Everyone has always been willing to volunteer. Now there are no volunteers. They do their work and go home. Jacob is feeling stressed-out and exhausted. I never see Dr. Maggiano. Dr. Lewin has been around, but I don't know how he feels. They have got to be anxious about the work. Jacob is anxious about promotion; if not him, who? He is frustrated with being unable to push decision making down; he doesn't feel empowered.

I'm working the same hours as before. I haven't noticed any changes in how I relate to others outside of work, and I haven't been ill.

People are stressed and tense. I've heard that fuses are short with others in the organization; that there is no more friendliness and camaraderie. They're discouraged. This used to be a happy organization, but it's not so happy now; not because of the RIF but because of the hypocrisy. We didn't jump right into reorganization and we lost momentum. We were feeling good and it turned out to be a sham.

I've been feeling a little anxious. They will be looking at my job. I'm somewhat angry over the loss of empowerment. I feel left out and unsupported; it's the whole empowerment thing. Jacob has been supportive. I feel overworked, but it's expected. I don't think that there has been adequate communication regarding the changes, but I still believe many of them are necessary.

If we started over, I would have begun reengineering right after the RIF to continue the momentum. I would have also communicated more. The open forums and *Signals* are positive, but what is communicated is really administrative lip service.

The changes have been quantitatively successful. The budget looks pretty good. Employee relations haven't been good. Everyone cooperated on the RIF. They promised the resources and haven't kept their word. People are working double shifts in some areas, which is going to eventually jeopardize quality. We foresaw many of the impacts of making the changes but we haven't addressed them through reengineering; it's a shame.

I don't think there is much else to add. One thing is what is going to happen with ambulatory and the schools? The hospital is taking all of the responsibility for reform. The feeling is that Dr. Lewin is from ambulatory, where they viewed the hospital as the golden goose and getting everything and fat. Now it's time to make the hospital just like ambulatory, which he believes is run much better; he'll whip the hospital into shape. It's unfortunate we can't all be doing it at the same time. Ambulatory has forty-five positions posted, and each school has a few.

Word Associations

Job	Challenging
Morale	Low
Efficiency	Better
Cost	Reduced
Change	Positive

STAN PITTMAN, FEBRUARY 4, 1994

My title hasn't changed, but there has been some change in my role. I still report to Jacob. My direct reports haven't changed, and I'm not sure how many staff are left—possibly 1,500.

I have no idea what is going to happen. Either I'll get the Assistant Provost position or it will depend on who gets the position. SPC will produce a dramatic decrease in resources. It's very frightening; there are horror stories. Some organizations got rid of them, others got cut off at the ankles.

There is a lot of conflict. There are justified complaints now. The level we are at is generating concern about quality. Many people have been here for a long time. They are frightened, insecure, and depressed and it affects how they work and what they have to say. I don't know how it will affect those above me. Dr. Lewin inferred our department will be separate from the hospital. It is up in the air. He isn't saying.

The recent change is the reduction. Position review was going on before; everyone was empowered and cross-trained. We are looking at using nonlicensed personnel. We have to prepare our professional staff to work with them. Some task groups are working on efficiency. The result is I think we have a very angry and depressed staff. There are a lot of complaints from the physicians. It is a step back; there is no empowerment. Uncertainty is worse than the shortage of staff. When you spot an operating problem, you don't know what the name of the game is; where to go.

Recently, Dr. Lewin is out visiting with the staff, which is okay. He asks staff about the performance of administrators, which is divisive. It's like ratting on them. I heard that a manager in ambulatory can't appoint someone to a committee without Dr. Lewin approving. He doesn't share back the information he gathers; it would be a courtesy to me. We were open before. In the public forums, Dr. Maggiano and Dr. Lewin said that the staff would be supported, but now I don't have the resources and it makes me look bad.

I think I'm upset now for their not following their change plan. We need to be able to flex-up for increases in the census. Position review is a joke. Dr. Lewin doesn't approve anything and he isn't talking to Jacob. It is a waste of time and energy.

I'm trying to be objective and give it all I've got, but it's very difficult. I don't know what I'm supposed to be doing. I need to give direction without knowing the direction. I should be getting a medal for my positive portrayal to the staff; for casting the organization in a positive light. I have to either put up with it or get out. I'm very nervous, depressed, and upset; I've never felt like this during my professional life—so disempowered.

How are the staff feeling? Number one, very insecure. That covers everything. Frustrated; they are supposed to be leading but they are getting no direction. They understand it is not me. The changes have led me to be more open with Jacob and I'm extremely comfortable about it, which is a credit to him. He and I are in a similar position. We don't know where we stand. We need the courtesy of information on the process. Are the Director and Assistant Provost positions filled today; in six years; has the decision already been made? Where do we stand?

I'm working about the same hours, but I'm getting here earlier. I'm not sleeping as much lately. I'm getting up earlier—around 3:00 A.M.—and going to bed earlier. I'm physically and emotionally exhausted; worn out. It's like classical depression.

I have noticed a change in how I relate to others outside of work; it's difficult. I'm not as interested. I can't separate my mother's death from this. The holidays are also a factor. I've also had a lot of sore throats, diarrhea, and abdominal pain.

Everyone is feeling angry and frustrated. People are verbalizing their feelings more. I've been feeling anxious, angry, left out, and overworked, but I feel supported by Jacob and my staff.

I definitely don't think there has been enough communication. I don't know if I understand why change was needed. Some we should have done, others have no explanation; the change in consultants is unexplained. The rest be damned.

We prepared for it, but no one was listening. I don't see doing anything differently. The reduced resources are inconsistent with keeping the quality up.

I don't think the change is effective. I don't know the direction. There are too many different goals and they are getting mixed up. I don't think the consequences were adequately foreseen.

There is not much more you can say. Lots of other organizations have gone through it. It's different here because we have been a caring organization. Dr. Lewin recently said in a meeting that there are no birthrights; people who have been here fifteen years may have to go.

Word Associations

Job	Work
Morale	Feeling
Efficiency	Good
Cost	High
Change	Going on

JOSEPH GREENE, FEBRUARY 4, 1994

My title and job are unchanged. I still have the same reporting and I have one less person reporting to me. I have about 31 FTEs. I lost 4.5 in the cuts.

My position could be eliminated or expanded. I don't know. It could move up, continue as is, or move down to a lower grade. I heard just about anything can happen with SPC. If we move to product line there might only be a small central core left.

My staff will be emotionally impacted. This was a strong, creative, hardworking department. The loss of 4.5 FTEs affected them. Now there is more work and less time to work on things people liked.

I don't know about my staff. I'm not sure if they will remain. I might report to another discipline. I might also report to a different level of management; possibly to the new director.

Our reductions had already been met before the cuts. We are adjusting to a two-person office, rather than three. We are starting to prioritize work. We are dropping our volunteer efforts to support programs. There are no registry personnel to fill in for special projects or absences. We've lost two more staff and there is no sure way of replacing them. We are hard pressed to do some things. Our quality is down. There is no overtime. Morale is starting to be affected. They don't enjoy going on vacation because those who are left have to pick up the load. It used to be that someone invited to be a speaker was praised, now it's not good. Our workload isn't really down that much. When you stop to think that in the last six months we are down 500 admissions, that's only about three per day. The staff have hardly noticed the dip. If they close an entire unit, then I'd have an extra worker to reassign. We don't control referrals either. There is no drop in our workload.

People are working hard, long, and with less enthusiasm. The frills are gone (what people liked to do). I think that there is enormous apprehension, but change is also always exciting and a challenge. Change is expected today, but it is not always for the good. We'll drift back after SPC leaves. People are stretched to the limit incorporating the change.

The changes had to be made. I can't ignore the fact that the healthcare system is changing; more ambulatory, home care, extended care, and less acute care in hospitals. But that doesn't necessarily mean that there weren't a lot of things done well before.

I'm working harder than ever; you just do it. I feel good about myself; there are no problems with me. People are being challenged about what impact this will have on them. They don't see it affecting their work. They have risen to the occasion; extending, adapting, volunteering to help others. I haven't seen them bitter or angry. No one knows what is coming. They have a job to do and they do it. The two people who left probably left because of the uncertainty here. One also got more pay and a higher title. We'll have to rebuild too, just be like the hospital where my employee went. Those above me have the same feelings. I think this kind of change affects everyone; everyone is worried.

I've been adding on an hour a day. I keep coming in earlier, before 8:00 A.M., and staying later. I guess I'm putting in forty-five to fifty hours per week. I used to be sympathetic to those going through tough times. Now we are no longer different than other institutions. There is a lot more talk about early retirement; is my future here? People are reevaluating their lives, careers, and where they want to work.

I haven't been ill recently, but there has been a lot of illness in my department. Within my age group everyone is questioning taking early retirement. Everybody is anxious. Some seem to be inspired and challenged by change. I have been feeling a little anxious but not angry, left out, unsupported, or overworked.

Communication has been adequate in terms of what can be said now. We are just entering into a process. I understand the need for change. I thought we were current with the times. We provide good service.

Before, I said I worked for the medical center. Now it seems more like it is split apart into hospital, ambulatory, and the schools. Now I say I work for the hospital. It is hard to get things done across lines.

It is hard to get the top people here to talk to each other; they're now very separate. People are territorial where there used to be flexibility. It's self-preservation and control. I'm discouraged about the development of a second department, even though ambulatory is paying for it and wants to control it.

Something happened; things are askew. I hope it will be brought back together. The cutbacks equalled fewer services. There may be more risk-management issues. We are feeling that we can't help patients as we would like to. I'm not sure these effects were foreseen.

Word Associations

Job	Very difficult now and challenging
Morale	Precarious
Efficiency	Highly
Cost	Held, reducing
Change	Good, hurt

BRENDA EARLY, FEBRUARY 8, 1994

My title and job haven't changed. I lost a key supervisor who retired and it has taken a long time to get permission to refill her position. I still report to Ted. I have the same direct reports except for the one open position. The number of employees under my direction keeps changing. The ballpark number is fifty-eight. I lost three to attrition and the equivalent of two more because of cuts in overtime.

My gut reaction to the future is that there will be more and more responsibility and accountability for lower-level managers. We won't be going through all the layers. It is happening some now. We will be asked to be creative in doing more with less. I will probably lose some people to reengineering, but I can't afford to lose my direct reports, who are supervisors. I hope the newly upgraded position which I can fill will take some of the load off of me. I'm working on cross-training the technicians. We need more flexibility on evenings and weekends. We are shifting services to meet demand. I'm preparing staff to be more of a team, to pitch in and break down the specialization so we can get coverage when we need it. I'm reallocating effort. I'll probably reduce staff in some areas. I can't cut now because I need time to train people to assume more responsibilities.

There's lots of anxiety in the department; feelings of strain because of not filling open positions. Illnesses have been hard to cover. Everyone is a little angry. If they aren't busy, they are expected to work elsewhere. We are trying to deal with flexible staffing, but it's difficult because people have to take their vacation or leave early without pay. The more they help, the more jobs can be saved. They were in the habit of not taking lunch, but with the lower volume I'm insisting that they do take lunch so that we have better overlap at shift changes. I'm asking people to change a lot of habits and I'm the new supervisor. I'm trying to do things in small doses to avoid overwhelming them. I'm trying to spot opportunities and work through change with my staff. The situation differs area by area; some are more flexible than others.

Anything that improves efficiency and reduces cost is positive for my boss. He's pulled in a lot of different directions. He's supportive of my trying new things.

There is lots of change. Flexible staffing is sending people home if there is nothing to do. I've cut overtime 50 percent by regulating start times. I've started to encourage work groups to be more available to fill in for absences. We are monitoring patient waiting and procedure time. We are beginning cross-training. We need to work with the doctors to control volume. We don't have a good system in place. We are spending more time shopping for supplies and developing product evaluations. We are moving to a primary vendor. We are developing an inventory system. We need to work on a cost per case with the doctors, but there are not much data. We are trying to use cheaper drugs.

The results have been positive. We are starting to see that we can change. In some instances we're better than projected—overtime is below projections. The reduction in staff has been a little harder for some people than others. We haven't been able to fill open positions quickly, plus illnesses and pregnancies create open positions we can't fill. The workload has been manageable through all of this. We're not as busy, which has been good and helped us work through having fewer people. Peaks have been difficult. Morale is not as good as it was. It cycles up and down; up after the cuts and over the holidays, but down now. People are disillusioned about not being able to fill positions and concerned about the volume of work. They are trying their best, but they aren't being recognized for their effort with raises. There has been an increase in sick time and tardiness, some of which may be do to the weather. People are more edgy and there are more personality clashes. The doctors are showing a lot of anxiety, which feeds over to the staff.

Change was inevitable. My concern is that the workforce has changed in the last twenty years and there are two types of workers. There are older workers who are loyal, dedicated, like their job, and are willing to come through. Younger employees came in when it was plush and their image of how much they can do is lower. Reengineering may not take this into account. One group requires more training; they are not taking into account individual differences. I would pick the workhorses to stay, but I can't always do that. They are focusing too much on the numbers. We must factor in variation in services; they don't take acuity into account. They are lost in the averages and their information hasn't been validated.

Sometimes the facility itself is not conducive to patient-centered care. There is some frustration since June, when I started. I inherited the staff. I've been working on developing my staff and I have higher expectations. You can get them to do anything for you if you treat them as important and needed. There isn't enough effort to develop employees. They are ignored, as compared to the students, residents, and nurses. They are not encouraged to participate in training. I've had to start over training my supervisors. They used to take direction from the doctors and are stifled. They always feel that they have to talk to Dr. So-and-So about changes. They are a frustrated group of people who want to help but really don't know how.

People accepted the reduction targets. We came through in Phase 1 better than most, but I'm concerned about the next phase. They aren't ready. Our ability to manage our resources has been taken away. It was kind of a lie that we are not able to fill. We are being treated globally; there is no concern for the local level. The committee has no decision power and just ties up things. Jacob then sits on the requests; he's insecure about Dr. Lewin. I'm concerned about these decisions being made at the top. There needs to be more trust and support in our peer group. We wouldn't ask for the positions to be filled if we didn't need them. It is very counterproductive. There is probably a better way to do it, according to preestablished criteria.

The criteria are always changing. There's a lot of anger with it. The consultants were good. I'm not sure why we had to pick a second group. We should have thought it through to use one consultant. There doesn't appear to be any concern about the requests the consultants make. It's counterproductive to hire two.

I feel that there is a big pool of water, and we are getting in deeper and deeper and it is hard to stay afloat. Work is almost overwhelming. I set limits. I'm resolved to do what I can do; no more. What gets done, gets done. You can't squeeze a turnip. I feel okay. I have good self-esteem. I know my limits. I wish I had more help in the department so I could accomplish more. I wish I could give more to my supervisors to develop them. I have to pick and choose.

My staff see how busy I am and the amount of work we have to turn in. They are feeling pressure and also becoming more aware of their own limitations. Some of my supervisors need to be upgraded, but I can't get the change. It has become a constant effort to keep things going and to fight fires. It is very stressful.

Those above me feel the same. They are tuned-in and sensitive people. They are being pushed to the limit. They are having difficulty getting things accomplished. Ted admits he is frustrated. He is calming because he puts things into perspective. We share some of the same opinions. He's real supportive. There is lots of pressure on the senior staff because of the current leadership. They are anxious and stressed.

I control how much I work; I guess I'm working forty-five hours per week. Occasionally I take work home, but I usually avoid it. I'm not going to kill myself. I'm rather good about recognizing when I have to leave work. I don't think I've noticed any change in how I relate to others outside of work. My friends are in healthcare and we are all affected. I haven't had any illness, either.

Everyone is responding in the same way. Some have only worked here and it's harder for them to adjust; they can't put it into perspective. Everyone is concerned about the workload and accomplishing some of the grandiose ideas [reengineering and patient-centered practice]. They are frustrated about resources and replacing people.

I have been feeling anxious. I'm working on a lot of projects. I was angry a couple of weeks ago when I was trying to fill vacancies. I have felt left out. The department managers receive superficial information. People need to feel that they are a part of the organization. They don't hear about the positive. There is no big picture, or it's not being shared. We need to hear about new techniques, research, and facility changes in order to develop an institutional focus. I haven't felt unsupported, but I have felt overworked like everyone else.

They have done a decent job on communicating some things. I learn more from the university's paper. I understand why the changes are needed.

If we did it over, I don't think that it is necessary for Dr. Maggiano and Dr. Lewin to sign off on personnel requisitions. I wouldn't have hired the second consulting company. I'd have stayed with the first or picked one to start that could do the whole job. I'd have gotten the doctors more involved with their administrative counterparts. We need a good team to do the work. They did a fairly good job on educating everyone about what we had to go through. We were successful at making a quick reduction; everybody participated. I'm not aware of whether ambulatory or the schools are cutting back. There can't be special groups.

The changes have been effective. We accomplished our goals and it is too early to tell about the rest. In my area, the impacts of making the changes were for the most part foreseen. We probably didn't think through how to cover illnesses or the other losses which were not anticipated.

We've covered the gamut today. The time frame of this interview affects my responses.

Word Associations

Job	Stressful
Morale	Low
Efficiency	Effectiveness
Cost	High
Change	Constant

ED MILLS, JANUARY 24, 1994

My title and job haven't changed. The intensity of the problems I face is greater. I still report to Val. My direct reports are the same. I have 64.5 FTEs, but I can only fill 56. I have attrition below the original targeted cuts and the organization is unwilling to fill them. There is no trust in the organization at every level of management; some is subtle and some is obvious. I'm puzzled. We're a few months into the change, but there is only rhetoric.

We had the opportunity to refocus with the agreed-upon resources to reach out to our customer base. In particular, my department is being assaulted. There are proportionally more open positions. I'm down 5 percent on volume and 10 percent on staff. My staff would like to buy into the program; they keep asking how much more they will be pushed to do. They initially bought in; they responded. We were making headway and they were generating lots of ideas and volunteering extra time. Now, morale is undermined. They can't see any end. They wonder, "How much longer?" They don't mind bending in the short run. There is too much focus on the business side now and not enough on the people side.

The rationale for not filling the positions is not being shared from the top down; from Maggiano. Something is not in synchrony. There is an absolute breakdown between the top and the rest of the organization; dictates versus explanation. If we are supposed to be a team, the top isn't participating. There are no change details out there. I have no clue what kinds of affiliations are being developed, and how the departments will change to support them.

The initial effort to sell the change was good, but Phase 2 is an unknown arena. There are few specifics or directions. They are taking a reactive position to redeploying the remaining resources to operate the hospital. The needs must be defined. They are keeping several thousand employees in anxiety about the possibility of more layoffs.

My turnover has not been associated with the changes. Now they want to use a different indicator to relate staffing to volume. Nowhere are there sophisticated information tools. The benchmarking exercise was good and gave us a better idea of what to do. There is more to it than meets the eye. It is frustrating to the department heads. The changes ignore risk exposure to errors. There is no question that they are up. A few critical incidents have been reported. Some may not be being documented.

There is no certainty about the future. The question is how many levels of management will be decided on. My position might be eliminated. Some areas might be added to my responsibility. Another university tried to cut my position, and it did not go well. Someone has to coordinate my department.

If my position is cut, my staff will have some trouble. They would have to assume responsibility for directing their areas and coordination among their areas. They will not be able to see the big picture. Those above me don't have the clinical expertise to provide direction. They wouldn't know how to coordinate the other dimensions of my department, which has lots of connections to work areas. If departments were added to my responsibility, there would be a reduction in managers for these areas. I'm not sure how it would affect the people above me. It would depend on who the merged departments used to report to. Decision making is very cumbersome here.

Few changes have been implemented. I'm totally paralyzed. We are being asked to do more. I don't have the people to support areas requesting help. Nursing is now looking to us to do things they did before. The ancillary areas need to do more, not less, to help the caregivers, but the ancillaries are being strangled. There is no vision for the department as to how to support the organization. What is our role?

We have to avoid change for its own sake. Maybe more direction will emerge in Phase 2. I have heard the statement made that, "We are right where we should be." I'm skeptical. If we are where we should be, why are our census and revenues down? I hope our expenses are.

We can't just budget for the census. Cutting for cutting sake is not the answer. We are way behind in developing affiliations. We have made some progress on cost containment, but there needs to be a lot more. The doctors must contribute by changing their ordering patterns. They are cooperating. The awareness level is much better. There is the sense that we all have to participate.

So far, the change within the department has been very negative. Opportunities to support other areas has been strangled and there are missed opportunities for us to do more. We are not being asked to do more, perhaps because others are frustrated and not looking for opportunities. It's the status quo. No one is moving off square one. We aren't really doing anything new, other than cutting.

I'm looking forward to a better vision of what the changes will be. I don't know if I'm part of the solution or part of the problem and they will cut my position. If I knew what the game plan was, I could try to support it. There is no game plan, and I'm getting nervous. There are no initiatives. Our referral base has eroded. Many of the referring doctors are from our institution. This is probably the result of poor diplomacy and the taking of referred patients as our own patients.

I feel negative about the changes so far. We are spinning our wheels. Cost containment for the sake of cost containment isn't good. We aren't initiating in the marketplace. We need to get on with it.

I like my work, but I'm frustrated about not being able to move ahead. Everyday is a human resource and scheduling day. Everyone is trying to get the work done. I personally feel frustrated. I can't see any progress being made. I have a broader vision and we are not moving in its direction. Managed cared is not the problem. We have alienated our referring doctors who have patients that are not part of managed care.

My staff aren't as frustrated as I am. They are looking at their jobs in a different context and are focused on volume statistics. They are not thinking about how to increase the census. They are more involved in day-to-day survival. They don't know what is going on. They are suspicious that I'm not telling them everything. Those above me are also frustrated and worried about their jobs. The system is not quick. Everything stops with Jacob. No decisions are being made. Middle management has no authority. We have just become the messengers. Lots of expensive executives are making decisions that should be being made lower in the organization.

I am taking memos home to write. I spend most of my day in dialogue with other employees and my peers at other hospitals. I spend a lot of time on scheduling and managing overtime. It is not clear to me whether I can delegate these things to others, as in the past. There are no clear guidelines. I'm working forty-plus hours per week and taking more and more home.

I've noticed change at home. I'm less interested in talking about my day. My wife wants to know, but I don't want to talk about it. I'm talking more to my peers at other hospitals. I have been well.

My personal observation about how others are faring is that we are a little more distant from each other than we were before the cuts. They are preoccupied with their own environments. Every day is a challenge to survive. Work shouldn't be frustrating and bad every day. There used to be more good days than bad ones. Now there are more bad ones than good ones. There are no resources to move.

I'm anxious about the unknown, and feeling frustrated and angry. I'm playing a lot of tennis. I'm feeling left out, but no more than others. I also feel unsupported and overworked. I don't mind working hard when it is productive. It provides job satisfaction, but when you are not accomplishing anything, it isn't satisfying.

There was good general communication, but it is bogged down coming through the administrative ranks. The department managers are almost in isolation when they should be looking for a common road. Even so, I understand the need for change; no problem.

If I had the resources, this year is a window of opportunity to explore how to help others do their jobs better; to invite those areas that depend on my department to work with me; but I'm short eight people and I have lost the opportunity. Referrals to the hospital need work. We are not tapping the loyalty of those who trained here who work in the community. I can't understand how it eroded. We need more affiliations, but other institutions are greedy.

I can't tell if the change has been effective until I know what the goals are. There is no report card. We were effective up to the point of not filling the open positions below the agreed-upon cut levels. There is no direction.

I'm disappointed about the lack of definitive direction.

Word Associations

Job	Mine
Morale	Low
Efficiency	Inadequate
Cost	Getting better
Change	Frustrating

JACOB DOHRMAN, FEBRUARY 7, 1994

My title is the same and my job hasn't changed. I still report to Dr. Lewin and I have the same number of direct reports. I am working more closely with Jeri Glover because she used to report to the Director. We have about 3,200 FTEs still left on the payroll.

I don't know what will happen to my role. There is the open Director position I've applied for, organizational restructuring, and SPC. Dr. Lewin may want to reorganize. It hasn't been discussed. I don't know what his long-term philosophy is. I'm not sure he has one at this point.

My staff will be working within a different administrative structure over the next eighteen months. Some will be eliminated and departments will be redistributed among them. I don't know how those I report to will be affected. The changes will presumably support their new management philosophy.

No change of significance has been recently implemented. The reduction went well. We are monitoring the current staffing patterns closely to avoid creep. We are carefully evaluating open positions to avoid having to lay off newly hired people during the reengineering process.

The changes have been effective based on the financial indicators. The margin is greater than anticipated.

The remaining changes are of a great deal of concern at all levels of the organization—SPC and restructuring. Even with a good flow of information, the issues become very personalized; it's hard to change feelings even if employees see the positive for the organization.

I believe the changes so far have made us more competitive, but more change is needed. We have the management wherewithal to accomplish what has to be done. I have concerns about these individuals who report to me and the outcomes of decisions I may be involved with.

I feel good about the changes. We've done well and minimized their negative impacts on staff. I feel confident in my own ability to get work down through others. We are meeting our short-term goals. I'm frustrated because I'm working without the knowledge that my efforts will pay off in a promotion; however, I feel good about myself. I am continuing to work well under stress and deliver a good product.

Those who report to me are very stressed on a personal basis, and they are stressed about getting their work done. The unknown is a problem. Those above me are concerned about their own and the organization's abilities to meet goals over the next several years. They feel that through strategic planning and operations improvement they are gaining a better understanding of what it will take for the organization to meet its goals.

I'm working about sixty hours per week. I haven't noticed significant changes in how I relate to others; maybe I'm a little more impatient. I have had no illnesses of any significance.

Everyone is concerned and apprehensive but they are also willing to try new things. I have been feeling anxious, angry, left out, and unsupported at times. I haven't felt overworked.

Communication has been adequate to me regarding the organizational restructuring, but not regarding administrative restructuring, the filling of the Director position, and the reorganization of the management team. Even so, I understand why change is needed.

If it were to be done over, the changes should have been made several years ago. I talked to SPC several years ago, but the organization wasn't ready then; there was no perceived need.

I believe the changes have been effective in Phase 1. We wanted to adjust staffing levels to match the census, without restructuring.

Word Associations

Job	Good
Morale	All right
Efficiency	Good
Cost	Getting better
Change	Exciting

ANTONIO LOZANO, JANUARY 20, 1994

I'm still a Manager III. My job hasn't changed significantly. I have picked up some new projects to work on. I still report to Jacob Dohrman. My direct reports are the same, except that I picked up an additional lab. I have about the same number of employees, plus those in the new lab.

I don't know how the change will affect me. On the negative side, there may be a reduction in the number of departments I oversee. Some may be eliminated. I try to not think of the worst-case scenario. I like to believe I will be assigned more departments and that I will get involved in developing a seamless delivery system. Inevitably, there will be some consolidation of departments. It depends on SPC's approach. I don't know what will happen to those above me.

The principle change was the reduction in force. This was a significant change. In my areas it was handled through attrition. We cut ten FTEs and about $0.5 million in expenses. Morale is down. The Monday after the cuts were made, I walked through a department and there were tears. They had survived. They needed to relieve their stress. The whole thing simply overtook them.

Those in management are now getting more concerned. The grapevine is filled with stories about how cuts were made at other hospitals. It is now believed that the consulting company will work quickly to locate additional change and cuts. There is also the process of filling Wirth's position and recruiting the new Assistant Provost, both of which are unknowns.

On the positive side, the changes have created more financial stability. They also sent a signal that we could adjust and compete. It showed that we were flexible. Those who are left see that we are more businesslike in our approach, although some may be scared of this. On the negative side, we have to be careful with the workforce and the department heads. There is lots of change and uncertainty.

The employment market for hospital executives is poor. There is a general sense of having to work harder, and there is a little less morale. After Phase 2, reengineering, things will get better. The flux will end.

The department managers are frustrated. They reached their targeted cuts, and some have dropped below them but cannot fill positions. The process of filling positions is very slow since we started five months ago. [Upon reflection, he noted it was only three months, which he realized was an important slip.] It feels like five months. Decision making at the top is slow. Some of it may have to do with Jacob trying to wring out the system so that he will appear to be a viable candidate for Wirth's position.

I'm optimistic about the future. We haven't been businesslike. I'm optimistic about my role in the organization. I can't take any other line. I can't think negatively, or it will become a self-fulfilling prophecy. I'm trying to stay productive. I'm young; if something happens to me, I'll see it as an opportunity.

People are training themselves in their minds to deal with the unknown. They are rehearsing what could happen. We will eventually stop worrying. What are you going to do about it, anyway? We have to be positive for the staff. In general, I feel good about the changes; we had to make them. It was handled very well; it was positive.

I'm glad there is a lot to do. This may indicate I will be here next year. Working on the new construction project is positive. I am being recognized for my efforts. It makes me feel better. There is the hope that there will be less bureaucracy and that things will be streamlined; the organization will be flattened and people will be empowered.

My staff are feeling the same. The change was necessary. They all wonder where they will end up. Jacob is looking forward to his possible promotion.

I'm now working fifty to sixty hours per week, and perhaps fifty to fifty-five-plus thinking about it all the time. At home, we have tried to get out more because of the stress; to create a distraction. I don't believe I'm different; neither more or less nasty. I am exercising more. I haven't had any recent illnesses. Everyone else is responding to the changes day by day.

My anxieties are at a normal level. I don't need drugs yet. I have occasionally been angry, felt left out, and felt unsupported. I miss Frank Wirth. I wouldn't say I'm overworked. I expect a lot of demands.

There is little information about Phase 2 and the consulting company. The contract may still be being negotiated. Jacob shares what he feels he can. It is as though we are not trusted. It's also possible that he may not have the information either. During Phase 2 we will become more efficient and eliminate redundancy in the organizational structure. Before, we grew without a clear rationale.

If I had it to do over, I wouldn't change how the reduction was handled. I would change how we responded to the department managers during the reduction. We did not raise important issues or get clear direction regarding how positions would be filled below the agreed-to levels. Before, we were together, meeting with each other, involved, empowered, and getting things done. Now its business as usual.

The cuts have been effective. We are ahead of projections on cutting expenses, but behind in revenue. I believe the impacts of the changes were for the most part foreseen.

Is there anything else? Yes; I guess I feel exhausted from this interview. I fear others knowing what I said. I guess, overall, I'm obviously a little more frustrated.

Word Associations

Job	Security
Morale	Lower
Efficiency	Positive
Cost	Keep down
Change	Forever

MARIA MEYERS, JANUARY 21, 1994

My title is the same and there hasn't been a change in my job. I still report to Antonio and my direct reports have not changed. I still have seven employees.

We may be hooked up under another department. My guess is that all the small departments will report to a manager, who then reports to administration. This change will not be positive for my staff because we just split off. It will be a loss. We will lose our autonomy. Antonio hopes it won't happen. He fought hard for the separation. However, he is overworked and may see adding the manager as streamlining for him.

We didn't lose any positions, but since then we have lost two people—one full time and one half time. We haven't been able to refill them. This is a significant loss. This has created high stress, anxiety, and a lack of trust. I have been on maternity leave for nine weeks and just returned. I am trying to get them to open up. Our workload has not dropped, even though the census is down. Everyone is working very hard. They are overworked and we now have a waiting list for patients.

I feel apprehensive and anxious; I don't know who the consultants will be. I spend lots of time filling out forms. I filled out four sets of forms on the open positions and each asked for the same information. There is a lack of movement, low trust, uncertainty, and it is stressful. There are no answers. I speculate that not being able to fill vacancies is related to the lower-than-expected census and that the employees might not be needed.

We weren't affected much. Now that I'm back, I hear from others that no one has trust anymore. They are fearful of losing their jobs. They are more competitive for their jobs. One person who is down eight FTEs says he can't talk to his employees anymore, or communicate up the organization either.

I feel overworked; partly because I just got back and have to catch up. It is also a challenge to regroup and reopen a dialogue with my staff. They are angry, frustrated, and overworked. This is a big change. This is a striking change from when I left. While I was on leave I worked a bit and I'm worried that they thought I didn't measure up. Maybe I shouldn't have. Things have been tough; it's been hard. I had really good communication with my staff. They were a good team. Now, I feel that they are just out there and testing me. Will I really help them? Yesterday, I made a point of solving a problem to show that I will stick with it. My staff feel frustrated, stressed, fed up with the system, not trusting, and not believing in the institution. Antonio is very frustrated and stressed, but also hopeful. I think he's glad I'm back.

I usually work forty hours per week. I don't think my work is affecting me at home. I find myself using my husband to bounce ideas off of. I'm providing him more information than in the past. He's good to talk to; he has business experience. I don't sleep much now. Maybe it will take its toll.

Everyone seems to be feeling negative. I think they are trying to promote the idea that change is not bad; to educate why it is needed. It does not seem to be sinking in. Everyone is pretty negative at this point. I have been feeling anxious, angry, left out, unsupported, and overworked.

There hasn't been adequate communication. I recognize the attempts at open forums, and newsletters are good, but I don't think you can ever communicate enough. Nonetheless, I do understand Phase 1. I don't understand about not filling the vacancies that are below the targeted cuts. It's not linked to volume. I feel held back from advancing.

If I had it to do over, I would have filled the vacant positions. I guess I would minimize the busywork of filling out four or five sets of forms with the same information to fill the vacancies. I would speed up decision making and be more direct, at least with the department managers. They are metering out bits of information just like a little bird who has a crumb held up to it and can only eat so much. They may not know, but I believe they do.

The change hasn't been entirely effective. The vacancies are a problem. Around the center they did a good job. They were sensitive. I do respect and understand why, but its been disruptive. The vacancies are creating a problem. There is a waiting list and no one is happy about losing the business. I have started to pay overtime. Our productivity is at 125 percent; people will burn out after a while. They are working longer days.

Word Associations

Job	Work
Morale	Low
Efficiency	Always
Cost	High
Change	Bad

PEGGY LUBIN, JANUARY 25, 1994

I'm still a Manager II. My job is still the same and I still report to Antonio. My direct reports are the same. I have forty-three employees now.

A new section to my department will be opening March 1. I foresee that my department will have more responsibilities in the future that will contribute to shortening the length of stay and improving the profitability of the patients that we see.

My staff are looking forward to the challenge. It gives them a sense of security. The changes will give those above me more work. I keep bringing new ideas to them to improve operations.

I didn't lay off anyone because attrition took care of it. The layoffs were something we accomplished. It's time to go on. People are relieved, but still concerned about more phases; there is anxiety about the changes.

So far, people in my department are more and more willing to contribute. They are more flexible and working as a team. They are more conscious of supply consumption and not as wasteful. They seem to be more appreciative of the institution and don't take their jobs for granted anymore. There is the realization that I don't want to go elsewhere. We were able to cut our costs. It's something we had to do and we are now in a better position for managed care. As a whole, everyone is insecure and those in untouched areas are even more nervous.

I feel apprehensive about the change. I've heard so much through professional organizations on hospital restructuring. There are some horror stories about the new consulting company. I was more comfortable with the original company. I got to know them and now I have to start all over.

We're one of a few hospitals that hadn't made changes; it is time. There are some things I disagree with. When we made the cutbacks, we understood that if we had vacancies we would be able to fill them; now it's next to impossible. I'm not too happy about it. I don't want to call it deceitful. I've had the openings for three months and our volume isn't down.

I'm very busy. I've always liked challenges and I have plenty now. I'm feeling much better than before the cuts. My staff are a little discouraged at times because we can't fill the vacancies. They are sometimes overworked. There has to be a lot of flexing to make it work. They are also concerned. They are happier when the census is up. They also see other departments that haven't been touched.

Those above me are overworked and concerned. SPC flattens organizations. They are feeling as vulnerable as I am and my supervisors are.

I'm working fifty to sixty hours per week. I am relating to others outside of work much better than before. I'm back to being more sociable. I was keeping to myself. I didn't go out. I was a little depressed—no, more than a little. I was mildly depressed.

Everyone is very concerned. We are between two phases. There is greater anxiety and uncertainty, and they are more cautious about spending money.

I've been feeling anxious and occasionally angry, left out, unsupported, and overworked. Communication has not been much better than adequate. It should be better. We need to know what direction we are taking. Perhaps the top doesn't know. There are a lot of rumors about SPC. We aren't getting the facts from Dr. Maggiano and Dr. Lewin. Even so, I understand why change is needed.

If it were done again, I would have offered early retirement and communicated more with the department heads. I would have gotten them more involved with strategic planning or at least asked for their input. We have good ideas too.

The change has been effective. The vacancies are a problem. We can't move forward. We aren't recruiting for the new section and it opens in about a month. We should have opened it five years ago. I doubt we can open it March 1, without staff. I do think that the impacts of the changes were adequately foreseen.

I have a sense of reassurance about the future. I'm being trained for TQM, which is a two-year project. I wonder if that means that I'll be here in two years. We are looking for small signs of reassurance.

I'm frustrated about the politics. We lost space to another program. People don't listen to me or anyone. I'm frustrated about not being listened to. I have ideas that can save money.

Recommendations sit for one, two, or three years without action. We need to add staff to save money.

Word Associations

Job	Security
Morale	Down
Efficiency	Fragmented
Cost	Under control
Change	Frightening

TED OLSEN, JANUARY 27, 1994

My title is the same. I have a few more responsibilities. Two small departments were temporarily added. I don't know if they will be permanent. I still report to Jacob. I have the same direct reports except for the two extra departments. I think I have about 500 employees under my direction.

I don't think much will change relative to my position. It's not that I'm indispensable. Someone has to be in charge of all of these areas. I don't think I will be given more. I am more concerned about changes above me; the hiring of a new Director. It is uncertain. I will have different and fewer people reporting to me after Phase 2 and they will have broader responsibilities. This won't affect me much either.

It is certain to be stressful for my staff. They will have increased responsibilities even if departments aren't collapsed. Change is stressful. SPC will focus on middle management. The Executive I role is going to be history. I don't know if that is a wish or a prediction. His role will be duplicated by the new Director's role.

Things have become paralyzed. It's not going in the right direction. No decisions can be made at the Manager III level, which is the correct level for the decisions. Jacob is paralyzed out of fear. Dr. Lewin does make an occasional decision, but many don't get to him. It is all lip service; no one is empowered. It's a crock of shit. There are now layers of additional bureaucracy. It's not happening.

So far the result is horrible. It's devastating. Morale is bad out there. I don't have any confidence we will have any input into the changes. I was a vocal opponent to SPC. They're not the appropriate company for this medical center. We were working well with the other consultants. We had accepted them even though they had a tough job to do. The change is a slap in the face and has thrown us off balance. It's a serious mistake. There is no evidence that we need anyone as brutal as they are; after all, we are going to have a $50-million surplus this year.

The changes have been tough to make. We did the right thing. We had to do something dramatic to get people's attention about the cost issues. The subsequent bureaucratization is no good. People feel fairly worthless. This is the message from above. Jacob is part of the problem. He's afraid of losing his job. He also has delusions of grandeur that he'll be promoted. He thinks that he has a shot, but he is so distant from Dr. Lewin's style.

I'm not doing any meaningful work. I'm working hard but not accomplishing anything. It was difficult before. Now it's ten times harder. Things are not good. I know I have my head screwed on straight, but it's hard to maintain self-worth.

I try to put on a good face, but my staff are feeling pretty bad. This is a severely depressed organization, including the people way down. Jacob vacillates between fear and depression. He strikes back and brutalizes his staff when he's depressed.

I have cut back on my hours. There is no point. I'm putting in about fifty hours per week. I haven't noticed any change in how I relate to others outside of work. During the cuts I was having some difficulty, but I've brought it under control. I try to leave it at the office. My ulcer is acting up. I haven't been sick. Across the board, morale is at an all-time low.

I've been feeling anxious, angry, left out, and very unsupported. I've got a work backlog, but I'm just not doing it. I think formal communications are fine. The truth is now emerging about some of the management styles. It's not clear why things are so bureaucratic about filling the vacancies. I do understand why change is needed.

I wouldn't have done anything differently. The changes have been a financial success. The next step started with breaking promises about filling open positions. The impacts of making the changes have been foreseen. Everything has worked out pretty well. We've had to make a few minor adjustments.

Is there anything else? Yes, I hate this job.

Word Associations

Job	Don't like
Morale	Terrible
Efficiency	Okay
Cost	Still too high
Change	Okay

JERI GLOVER, JANUARY 31, 1994

My title is the same and my job hasn't changed. I have been temporarily assigned some extra departments to cover for an absence. I have requested to keep the departments to provide me additional exposure to clinical departments. This would also lighten Val's workload. She picked up extra departments when Jack left. I report to Dr. Lewin. My direct reports are the same except for the temporary departments. I have about 180 FTEs but more people. I lost about 20 FTEs in the cuts.

My position is a little different, in that I have medical center-wide responsibilities. I expect consolidations and an increase in assignments; less people, more work. During Phase 2 there will be two parallel programs, one for clinical issues and one for reengineering issues. I'll participate in the reengineering, but it may also depend on whether I keep the clinical departments. I expect the reorganization to deal with how ambulatory and the medical center are organized. The hospital's structure will change. It will be interesting to see how ambulatory is changed; we'll be better off if we merge the two. I can't foresee what the changes will be.

Plans are being developed to change my department's operations. If implemented they will affect my staff. Flattening may or may not occur. We have three shifts, seven days a week. We have to have supervisors over all of these people. I expect it to be flattened. The big challenge will be to do lots of things but with fewer people.

I don't know how the change will affect Dr. Lewin. He is attending more of the hospital's meetings. He has a new management philosophy—self-directed work teams that involve staff at all levels. They get to participate in problem solving. There are two major unknowns, the new Hospital Director and the Assistant Provost position. This is challenging change. Dr. Lewin's role is stable.

Vacant position review is a recent change. We established a committee to review requests to fill vacancies. What is significant is that the previously agreed-upon staffing levels were based on a 76-percent census and it has been lower; in the 60s. Managers feel that we owe them these jobs despite the lower census. It is a difficult process for everyone. How do you justify a job? There are no data or records to do it, and in our group we have been trying to figure out the appropriate questions to ask. It has been hard challenging and questioning each other. The requests then go on to Jacob who asks more questions and then up to Lewin and Maggiano who ask more questions. Now we have a process in place. Some requests have been pending since October. It has taken its toll on department managers, even though the reduction went very well in October.

I think we have very frustrated supervisors who don't know who to blame for not being able to fill their positions. There are layers of people who ask questions. We weren't always clear about the questions that needed answers. They aren't sure we aren't just trying to aggravate them and make their lives difficult. They have to consider all their options. It is smoothing out now.

I missed the meeting on Friday where future changes were discussed. I don't know what the process is or the targets. I'm in the dark on Phase 2, but I'll support it, whatever it is. Until Friday, the senior staff didn't know and this didn't help their buying in. Phase 1 was run mostly by the hospital. Phase 2 is being run by Dr. Lewin or Dr. Maggiano, I'm not sure which one. This isn't good or bad, it's just interesting. Changes are needed; they're necessary. Staffing is down to census levels. Some did small changes within departments. Phase 2 begins major change.

There are two parts. I'm the least senior of the hospital's senior staff. I was concerned about losing my job in Phase 2. Now I'm feeling better and I have an opportunity to participate in Phase 2. Everything is uncertain. In Phase 1 we could help others adjust; in Phase 2 we are all affected and it's hard to work outside of oneself to be supportive of others. I've had much more illness the last six months than I've ever had. There is a lot more stress and I'm feeling it.

My staff are stressed and frustrated. Prior to Friday, there were many rumors about SPC. People were stressed out about the likelihood of having them here. Not filling vacant positions is also frustrating. Those above me are feeling pretty good. He knew about the plans and how SPC will work here, and he knows the targets. He may not feel great that the organization has to go through this, but it has to.

I'm probably working around forty-five hours per week. I don't take lunch, but I do go to the gym sometimes. I haven't noticed any changes outside of work. I have had more colds—bad ones.

People are very nervous. At the management level, they are calling peers at other organizations that have been through the SPC process. The feedback has made them very nervous. I have been feeling anxious and left out. I haven't felt angry, unsupported, or overworked. Communication hasn't been good but I do understand why change is needed.

During Phase 1, even though a small group was working on the reductions, rumors were rampant and often close to right. I wonder who was irresponsible enough to communicate what was going on. The rumors were difficult to dispel. An example was a rumor that people would be escorted to the auditorium by security guards. People wondered why they weren't being treated with more trust. We need to be more sensitive about the leaks in Phase 2. Jacob is the only person in the hospital who has seen the SPC contract.

So far I think the changes have been effective and their impacts were foreseen. Unforeseen was the position-review process. It wasn't discussed as a part of Phase 1.

I think I can see direction from the top to make change; and then there are the open positions—the Hospital Director and the new Assistant Provost role. They will start in the midst of all the change and won't have time to get oriented; they'll have to implement the restructuring without experience in the organization.

Word Associations

Job	Security
Morale	Mixed
Efficiency	Needed
Cost	Control
Change	Necessary

CHRIS REGAN, FEBRUARY 1, 1994

My title and job are the same. My reporting is the same. As of Monday, the supervisors which have reported to my assistant manager will report directly to me. The assistant will then work on projects. I have eight direct reports and eighty-six employees. We only lost about 1 FTE.

I don't know what will change. I don't know if it will be brought about by the redesign or the new Assistant Provost. Staff won't be affected. Their positions are needed, regardless of who they report to. If the supervisors report to a nonprofessional, it may cause them some anxiety. Those above me are more affected than I am. I'm not sure about Ted. He'll probably be happy if he loses us or keeps us; he'll probably be happier to keep us.

The change in organization structure is known to everyone. We have relooked at scheduling and doing with less staff. So far, it hasn't compromised anyone. There is concern about what the vision is for the future. We are running at 103 percent efficiency and we are in a slow season. There is a problem with filling vacancies.

People are working more efficiently. They are willing to take on more tasks. Anxiety was down after October, but is building again. Staff believe I'm trying to get the vacancies filled, but they aren't sure I'm doing a good enough job of selling it to the people who make the final decisions. I'm keeping them informed of my progress.

I don't know what's coming. It's an interesting end to my career. I'm not as anxious as others; I'll retire this year. I have picked up some feedback on SPC from other organizations, but I still don't know what they will do here.

The changes that have been made are alright. I've heard some things about the cross-training of nurses. There is dissention and passive aggression. It has done the job on morale. I wouldn't like it if it was thrown at me. There is lots of specialization and new staff coming onto units who aren't going to be as good as the ones that are there.

My job is getting more interesting all of the time. There are more time frames; things are wanted in a short time. You need to be able to generate information; a lot is going on at one time.

The supervisors are feeling okay and some are bonding. Some of the staff below them are good and some are apprehensive. Those that are new are adjusting more easily than the ones that have been here forever. Those above me are feeling worse than I am. One department is in a tizzy. They are trying to accomplish a lot of things and they have to deal with over a thousand people. Ted is interested by it all. He doesn't seem to feel threatened by it.

I work forty-five to fifty hours per week. I'm trying to be good to myself. I haven't noticed any change in how I relate to others outside of work. I am enjoying them more. I haven't had any health complaints either.

Others are responding in different ways. It depends on where you are in the organization. Senior management is excited by it, but also stressed by what has to be accomplished. It is on the tip of everyone's tongue. People took some of the examples at the Friday staff meeting the wrong way—their departments weren't shown. This is a very complicated organization, and I will be amazed at who will take the Director's job, given the reporting arrangements here.

I haven't been feeling anxious, angry, left out, unsupported, or over-worked. Communication has been adequate. I receive good communication from Ted. They have also used other vehicles. I understand why the change is needed.

The way the sequence of events unfolded, there wasn't much that could have been done differently. We needed to get started earlier. There was a short time frame. It was fairly humane.

The change has been effective for the bottom line. We have to believe it was. A reorganization needs to take place, except for adding the extra layer. I don't understand Dr. Lewin's role. I don't know if the impacts were foreseen. Some of the problems being encountered have always been here. When volume and staffing were high they weren't much of an issue. But when the volume dropped they were still there. We haven't gotten to the meat of the problems yet.

Word Associations

Job	Work
Morale	High
Efficiency	Better
Cost	Money
Change	Okay

Chapter 6

Case Interpretations
and Overview

The story that emerges from the interviews in Chapter 5 is one of major change accompanied by the development of a demoralized group of hospital employees. This chapter provides the second set of independent interpretations by the three consultants.

INTERPRETATION BY HOWELL BAUM

Themes

There is no point in mincing words: Things have gotten worse, much worse, perhaps worse than feared. All units lost positions; some units lost many. Between firings, resignations, and budget cuts, some managers do not even know how many people they have authority over. Top management resists requests to fill vacant positions, and middle managers and their staff work overtime in increasingly futile efforts to do their jobs. Not only that, just as all this was happening, top managers fired the consultants who recommended all these changes and brought in a second group with a well-circulated reputation for savagely cutting organizations. Without a moment's hesitation, the people interviewed routinely say they and their staffs feel frustrated, angry, anxious, and depressed.

Significance and Hypotheses

It doesn't take any special psychoanalytic sensibility to see or understand these reactions. However, what deserves special attention is just how deeply these people are wounded. It bears repeating that a hospital is supposed to be a place of healing. "Lots of other organizations have gone through it," Stan Pittman notes, but "It's different here because we have been a caring organization." This hospital has a national reputation in the miraculous field of organ transplants. It has literally given new life to the dying. Yet now, the hospital's managers have repeatedly acted in ways that take life from its own staff. Describing a perversion of the hospital's mission, staff talk as if their organs have been removed. Tom Frey says plainly, "Supervisors are disheartened." The organ of caring is gone.

Any talk of organ removal is, to be sure, only metaphorical; but, unconsciously, people experience such metaphors literally. They feel real. While many at the hospital have lost heart, the organ about which fear seems pervasive is the genitals. Over and over—numbingly—people refer to being cut. There can be no pretense this is a neat surgical incision. To understand what this means to hospital staff, we must completely forget what "cutting" means in management. In the unconscious, "cutting" is cutting—nothing less.

To Cynthia Winston, it is a "slash." She fears the new consulting firm is "cutthroat." Chris Forbes says work relations have become "cutthroat." Pittman says the new consulting firm has "cut off [other organizations] at the ankles." Unconsciously, "throat" and "ankles" may only be attempts to disguise the real body part in danger. Ed Mills, also referring to the throat, says the ancillary areas are being "strangled," and he is "totally paralyzed." Ted Olsen fears everything is "paralyzed," including Jacob Dohrman.

"Frustrated" is how people describe themselves. They try to get their work done, and they cannot, because they do not have enough staff. They try to fill vacant positions, but they cannot because top management will not authorize new hiring. Whatever they try to do, circumstances are overwhelming. "Nothing I do will change anything," Judy Harris laments for everyone.

On its face, frustrated is an understandable term for this condition. But connotations and associations with the word reveal still more of the experience. One colloquial meaning of frustrated, for example, is sexual: someone cannot get any satisfaction. Impotence would be one cause. Indeed, frustrated sounds strikingly like "castrated," even though the words have no etymological kinship.

It is speculative to suggest that some who call themselves frustrated mean they feel castrated. Still, Nugent offers supportive evidence when she talks about the overall situation. "Morale is rock bottom; very, very low. We can't fill vacancies. In some areas they have lost a third of their staff below the original agreed-to levels for the cuts. . . . No one knows what to do. They are very frustrated and short tempered." She says the "cuts" have "frustrated" people and made them "short." But she says much more. Using the same language as nearly everyone interviewed, she says "morale" is "low." Only two persons consider morale unqualifiedly positive. But, more significantly, only a handful of people evaluate morale in terms of "good" or "bad." Most assess it vertically, whether it is "high" or "low," or, as Peggy Lubin says, "down." At the least morale refers to people's spirits. Still, staff members use morale so often to connote their sense of efficacy that "low" morale seems to describe becoming impotent.

It is useful here to look more closely at the expression downsizing. It is terrible English and only too obviously, and thus unsuccessfully, a euphemism for firing individuals; but it also suggests castration, particularly in its more colloquial cousin, "cutting down to size." Again, this is more than a play on words; it is an effort to understand how organizational members experience restructuring.

In this connection, "flattening" is every bit as terrifying as "cutting." In managerial language, flattening refers to reducing the number of hierarchical layers in an organization. Yet if we forget that esoteric usage, we cannot avoid recoiling in horror from the prospect of being in an organization that will be flattened from above. In the unconscious, being flattened sounds very much like being knocked impotent. Kasman favors flattening but acknowledges it is "a big nut to crack." While we should hesitate to attribute unintended meanings to her comment, we should, nevertheless, ask why she chose this metaphorical way to say "difficult."

Nearly as often as people worry over past or pending cuts, they complain of the urgency and difficulty of "filling vacancies." As Nugent suggests, they mean they must have additional workers to carry out their missions. They must have help before they drop of exhaustion. Still, if we forget the managerial meaning of this phrase too, we can explore its unconscious meanings.

Frey, for example, says, "It's been tough to keep morale up. We signed a contract to cut, and now we have vacancies we can't fill." Chris Regan reports, "Anxiety was down after October, but is building again. Staff believe I'm trying to get the vacancies filled, but they aren't sure I'm doing a good enough job of selling it to the people who make the final decisions." When vacancies are unfilled, people can't keep morale up and they become anxious. To be sure, these concerns are related to work. But the words convey other meanings. Unconsciously, "filling a vacancy" could describe undoing the work of castration by replacing the genitals. It could, as well, refer to satisfactorily performing an act of intercourse—no longer being frustrated, and reassuring that one is not impotent.

The transcripts do not tell us enough about these individuals to enable us to be certain what they think unconsciously. This analysis is

speculative, but it is consistent with what people have said. People
are not speaking literally of their own genitals. Both men and women
use this language, suggesting many share a common metaphorical
framework for their sense of potency. Again, the purpose of this analysis is to explore the unconscious meanings of these organizational cuts
for the people living within the organization—to understand how the
cuts feel to them.

It is difficult, if not impossible, to read the transcripts without becoming anxious. My own organization went through cutting and restructuring two years ago, and the interviews evoke all the anxieties I
felt then. Even though our President declared no one would be fired,
many of us worried about what we would end up doing in order to
continue to support our families. That anxiety is so debilitating, it
seems hardly necessary to say there was more. And yet there was.

People's anxiety, rage, and sense of impotence concerned whether
they could control what they would do, whether what they would do
would express what they valued in themselves, and, worst of all,
whether they had anything of value in themselves to express. Even in
a situation where there was a safety net of no firings, people had difficulty reacting and acting on their own behalf. Two years later, many of
us, even when we succeeded in keeping our old positions, do not feel
sure we will not be put through it again, this time coming out worse.
How much worse the situation is in this hospital, and how much more
deeply these people seem wounded.

Hence, one reason why a reader might want to reject this discussion
of cutting and impotence is not that it is so far fetched, but, to the
contrary, because it may be right on the mark. That, after all, is why we
push such thoughts into our unconscious, trying to keep them from
troubling us. That, after all, is why we speak of throats or ankles rather
than a vital organ.

For a child who feels anxious about these matters, castration is both
an unconscious potential reality and a metaphor. It is the child's way
of understanding death—ceasing to be. Castration means the loss of
the possibility of love and, thus, annihilation. None of the adults interviewed really believes he or she will be cut bodily. And yet the
metaphorical, unconscious concern about castration offers still another
clue to how staff are thinking and reacting.

For an adult to think in the ways children think is regressive. It is a
defense against adult reality that follows this logic: If I am a child, rather
than an adult, this horrible thing cannot be happening to me, because
I have not gotten here yet. And if I am a child, I cannot be responsible
for what is happening to me. Not only am I not responsible for causing
it, but I do not have to be responsible for fixing it. If I am a child,
someone else—a powerful, caring adult—will make things better.

This line of psychological defense does not seem to be working. There are no powerful, caring adults arriving on the horizon. Jacob Dohrman, whom most see as the "good" top manager, in contrast to the "bad" Arch Lewin, feels "anxious about promotion," and "doesn't feel empowered" (Kasman), and "is paralyzed out of fear" (Olsen). Dohrman, who earlier said his morale was "good," now reports it is only "alright." He says he doesn't know what Lewin's long-term philosophy is, and even he feels left out and unsupported.

As a result, people still feel anxious. "People feel fairly worthless," Olsen reports. Speaking for many, he says, "I'm not doing any meaningful work. I'm working hard but not accomplishing anything. . . . I know I have my head screwed on straight, but it's hard to maintain self-worth." What he says is understandable on its face. The rules of the game at the hospital are so in flux, and so much attention must be given to the change process, rather than patient care, that it is difficult to do something that connects in any obvious way to patients. Not only is it difficult to see a meaningful result of personal effort, but the laws of cause and effect seem so suspended, it is difficult to see any results at all from personal effort.

At the same time, widespread feelings among the staff that they have lost their worth reflect a still more regressive, unconsciously infantile reaction to the hospital situation. Feeling unable to express caring, people feel unworthy of being loved. An infant must be confident of having the mother's love before he or she can separate from her and begin his or her quest for autonomy, initiative, accomplishments in work, and so forth. For the moment, these staff members, who are adults and have adult accomplishments in the rest of their lives, have been so deprived of supports in the hospital that they psychologically feel like the most vulnerable infants.

Put most simply, they do not trust the world of the hospital to support them in any way. Winston "feel[s] a little betrayed." Meyers reports "low trust." Mills says, "There is no trust in the organization at every level of management." Bob Ryder notes "a lack of trust in the organization." On and on it goes.

Loss of love and castration are ways infants and children unconsciously think about annihilation. Adults understand death more realistically. It should be unnecessary to note that, whatever happens in the second phase of restructuring, no one will literally be killed. Yet talk of death and killing is pervasive. Antonio Lozano reports, "The Monday after the cuts were made, I walked through a department and there were tears. They had survived." Mills, as noted, says the ancillary departments were "being strangled." Ryder explains, "Everybody is waiting for another axe to fall." Winston and Forbes expect the new consultants to be "cutthroat."

Pittman, whose mother died recently, says, "I can't separate my mother's death from this." Not only are the hospital cuts and his mother's death linked in time, but they feel the same. It is as if he can no longer rely on a caring institution. "I'm physically and emotionally exhausted; worn out. It's like classical depression," he observes. It's also like an infant would feel if he lost his mother—both devastated and worried she went away because he was not worth enough to her.

Rosetta Shelton, who was described as agitated and unwilling to be interviewed in the first round, now talks, and she says, "Being interviewed is like a reporter coming up to someone who has just lost a child and being asked how does it feel." Though she speaks as a psychological adult, someone who could be a parent, she talks of the most tragic loss possible. As many others, she had put so much of herself into making hospital programs into what they were, and now they were taken away—killed.

The depth of workers' depression, the extent to which they feel they have lost control, and, perhaps, their identification with the aggressors are signaled by talk of suicide. It is almost as if the only freedom people have in a murderous situation is to take active control over the inevitable; to do themselves in. Brenda Early, asked how she is feeling about her work, says, "There is a big pool of water, and we are getting in deeper and deeper and it's hard to stay afloat. Work is almost overwhelming. . . . You can't squeeze a turnip." When she is asked how many hours a week she works, she says she tries to control her load: "I'm not going to kill myself." This is a common expression for talking about work, and it should not draw special attention, except in this context, where it follows a description of drowning in deepening water. If the water were real, as it may seem in the unconscious, it might be easiest to get it over quickly by doing the worst deliberately. She sounds as if she is telling her unconscious mind not even to think about it.

Frey, on the other hand, after he has said "It's been tough to keep morale up," "Things have stagnated," and "Supervisors are disheartened," reports he and his staff are "killing themselves" working to get things done. Again, it is hard to hear this as just everyday talk. He complains his boss "bites," and "In many cases we've hurt patient care." At least in fantasy, it would be easier to kill himself than endure all this, including guilt for hurting patients.

What is important about listening to these people is to understand that much of what they say involves fantasies, but that these are not "only" fantasies. They express real thoughts, many unconscious, that influence not only how they feel, but how they act. Mike Payne describes a representative sample of the consequences of the cutting: "One person is out on a leave of absence with depression, and another has had a heart attack. People are calling in sick who never used to. The pressure is causing people to buckle."

Doug Lofgren laments that cutbacks mean reduced services and reveals, "I hurt my back at home, cleaning." A fantasy might be that he has been punished at home for neglecting his work at the hospital, or else he punished himself by taking on work he knew he could not manage. In any event, the reality is that he tried to do at home something he could no longer do at work and hurt his back.

How could all this have happened? Certainly it is nothing David Maggiano or Arch Lewin wanted. One might argue that they were unable to anticipate the depth to which their reorganization would hurt people. Yet it is striking how insulated they are from subordinates. What has happened in recent months is only a worsening of what happened earlier. Even a relatively unempathic observer could have seen how changes were affecting people. Absenteeism, for example, is noticeable and recorded behavior.

Not only did these top managers not see or listen to staff members, but they also made decisions without consulting others or even giving explanations. How scary it is for staff to find that even the consultants whose recommendations led to firings were themselves fired, to be replaced by a firm with a reputation for still greater severity.

Both staff and readers of these interviews are left to guess what top managers have in mind. Maggiano and Lewin, perhaps, are anxious about the financial condition of the institution and anxious about keeping control over everything—even though these interviews show the futility of such a wish. Perhaps they believe (or wish to believe) staff are either resilient or replaceable.

Yet it is hard to imagine that so many people who think and feel so much about death, and who so deeply mistrust top managers will simply pop back "once things settle down." Moreover, it is difficult to assume that even new recruits, who were not part of this devastation, will be able to walk in and take over responsibilities without being affected by the feelings and culture the reorganization has engendered.

Assessment and Suggestions

It is harder now than earlier to think of consulting interventions that could improve the situation. Maggiano and Lewin keep to themselves, divulging nothing of what they want, with or without advice. They give no sign of being concerned about staff morale or patient care. They have done nothing to dispel their new consultants' well-traveled reputation as cutthroats. They betray no glimmer of thinking that management and subordinate staff have common interests.

Suggestions that staff formulate alternative restructuring proposals at this stage would be quixotic. Instead, those who want to stay and provide good service should think in terms of organizing to advance those interests with, or against, top management. Interviewed staff talk almost exclusively about what goes on in the hospital, without saying much about whether those events matter, or might matter, to outside groups such as professional associations or labor unions, the news media, elected officials, or community activists. Staff could benefit from consultation in political organizing and public relations to enlist whoever might be concerned about patient care, the hospital's services, or the hospital's staff. Without such an initiative, the prognosis looks negative.

INTERPRETATION BY MICHAEL DIAMOND

Themes

Effective institutional downsizing requires internal commitment and collaboration, job security, mutual trust and respect, relatively clear timelines for completing various phases, and transformational synergy. In the case of General Hospital, not only are these conditions absent, but a serious crisis of leadership is emerging that may be recognizable to all but the leaders themselves.

Significance and Hypotheses

As I noted in response to the first set of interviews, the level of participation in decision making is suspect. Despite the consultants' efforts to structure the downsizing phase in a manner that required management to carry out the percentage of agreed upon cuts in their units, the hospital employees were not sufficiently involved in the process. In fact, the executive- and consultant-driven process for downsizing—that included two noteworthy meetings discussed in my response to the earlier set of interviews—depersonalized human relations by structuring a "clean way" to eliminate people's jobs. While this process may be less painful for the executives and consultants, it may have serious and far-reaching consequences for hospital morale and membership. Survivor guilt among remaining hospital employees at General Hospital will fuel anger and aggression that might further polarize group and interpersonal relations (aggravating regressive psychodynamics such as splitting and projective identification) between the executive team and the hospital management and staff.

In fact, based on the second set of interviews, a highly significant number of managers and staff at General Hospital are feeling angry and possibly becoming cynical about change. After meeting the required level of cutbacks in staff during Phase 1, they did not anticipate the threat of additional cutbacks. According to many workers, hospital management and staff carried out their side of the downsizing agreement. Proposed reengineering and structural changes have not occurred as yet. Hospital employees do not see a real shift from the first phase to the second, they express their frustration and diminished support for change. Many workers feel betrayed.

Four months beyond the first set of interviews, they continue to feel anxious about their future with General Hospital. Moreover, Maggiano and Lewin's hiring of a new consulting firm (SPC) with a reputation for laying off large numbers of employees and their apparent unwillingness to fill position vacancies has left hospital managers and staff feeling hopeless, powerless, and quite angry. Executives appear insensitive to workers' anxiety, as evidenced by minimum information sharing and inadequate participation in the strategic planning and structure of institutional change.

Nevertheless, in the case of General Hospital, everyone seems to appreciate the need for change in an environment of managed care and decreasing census. However, the hospital executives and consultants have not taken advantage of that fact. And although Maggiano and Lewin espouse the values of empowerment and participation, their actions, according to the staff interviews, directly contradict what they say. There is no evidence that they acknowledge this fundamental agreement with their employees. More important, downsizing is a top-down, unilateral process at General Hospital that is rendering hospital employees powerless and depressed.

The irony, then, is that the hospital administrators treat their staff as if they (employees) are resistant to change, and the workers who understand the need for change experience conflict with the executives. The nature of the conflict is quite personal. It is experienced by employees as an intimate attack on their self-competence and self-worth (or self-esteem). Organizationally and psychodynamically, conflict in General Hospital is the result of change inflicted upon employees in an aggressive manner. Consequently, workers feel they are being blamed for the problems that led to downsizing in the first place.

I believe (based on the interview data) that Maggiano and Lewin are unwittingly abusing their staff and acting as if they need to coerce them to change. The escalating mistrust between hospital executives and staff is symptomatic. Maggiano and Lewin are not adequately sharing information nor sufficiently involving employees in the change effort. Consequently, they mistreat hospital staff, unconsciously viewing them as (psychoanalytically speaking) "bad objects" rather than members of the same team. Workers assume the role of containers of Maggiano and Lewin's persecutory anxiety about change. Thus, remaining employees are sent home when there is little work to do. They are expected to do more with less and, consequently, feel attacked and demeaned. Their organization no longer cares for or about them. Thus, workers turn around and project their bad feelings on Maggiano and Lewin, and additionally upon Dohrman, the Director of Hospital Operations.

A severe chasm is produced separating executive management (Maggiano, Lewin, and Dohrman) from hospital staff. Intergroup splitting and polarization occurs and drives a wedge between them. Primitive fight and flight unconscious actions surface as a manifestation of regressive psychodynamics produced by collective anxieties. Consequently, executives perceive hospital workers as the enemy to be gotten rid of or dominated and made loyal; hospital managers and staff see either the executives as the enemy they must flee from or, in some instances, they identify another unit as insufficiently sacrificing and view them, consequently, as the enemy. In short, scapegoating is alive and well. This rift threatens the human and operational core of General Hospital, and will continue to do so as the staff's anxiety increases and goes unaddressed by the hospital executives.

Fractured relations between leaders and followers at General Hospital means poorer quality healthcare for patients and customers. Based on the interviews, hospital staff are currently observing this trend. They are saying that costs may be down, but the quality of service and care has diminished as well.

Assessment and Suggestions

Something must be done. Hospital employees cannot work in an environment of persecution, victimization, and terror. Repairing the devastation of an ill-informed organizational change effort would require profound changes in organizational leadership and culture at General Hospital. The university and/or its board must intervene.

INTERPRETATION BY HOWARD STEIN

> When the existence of the Church is threatened, she is released from the commandments of morality. With unity as the end, the use of every means is sanctified, even cunning, violence, simony, prison, death. For all order is for the sake of the community, and the individual must be sacrificed to the common good.
> —Dietrich von Nieheim, Bishop of Verden.
> Quoted in Arthur Koestler, 1961, p. 89.

Introduction

"Raw" is the first feeling word that comes to mind as I read the second set of interviews. In these interviews, there is much less guardedness in expressing feelings, including the emotion of anger (and its close linguistic cousin, "frustration"). As I read the transcripts, I feel as if I am watching a war movie with battle scenes, deathscapes, and regroupings to prepare for defense against later assault by forces that promise to crush them. I am surprised by my conflicting emotions. I am revulsed by the bloodless carnage at General Hospital, but I also strangely revel in it, then feel guilty, then righteous again. Waiting for death feels worse than death itself. Violence feels like relief against the fear of waiting for violence to be visited upon the hospital, only it is followed by no relief, only more oppressive waiting. I want something to happen, and I do not. The grief I feel is overwhelming and without promise of end.

The ostensible attack is coming from the seniormost administrators, Maggiano, Lewin, and Dohrman, with the new consulting company, SPC, as their ruthless henchmen. A great deal of symbolic blood is being shed on behalf of a downsizing forever awaiting, Phase 2. The interviewees bring a far less buoyant optimism and "can do" attitude to these interviews than they had in the first set. There is effort, sometimes forced optimism, but these are enshrouded in dread and resignation. Some have a sense of relief that the "cuts" of Phase 1 are over, but the relief does not last. It is of little comfort to people who feel utterly out of control of their organizational lives. One anxiety is over, only for another if not greater anxiety to arise now from different sources. "Phase 1 was run mostly by the hospital. Phase 2 is being run by Dr. Lewin or Dr. Maggiano, I'm not sure which one," says Jeri Glover. Administrators feared losing their job in Phase 1, but could at least "help others adjust." "In Phase 2 we are all affected and it's hard to work outside of oneself to be supportive of others," Jeri Glover continues. One moment the speaker is "feeling better" for not having been fired; in the next breath, she talks about uncertainty, more illness, and more stress. It is next to impossible to fill open positions, yet there is more work to do, and the interviewees feel responsible to get the job done. With the mass firings of Phase 1, there should now be less bureaucracy, but there is not; instead, there is more (as in how positions are to be filled).

The emotional tone of this second set of interviews should forever put to rest the widely held notion that people have strong affiliative and dependency feelings associated with units such as family, religion, ethnic group, and nation, but have no such strong feelings toward "mere" workplaces.

As I read the second set, I look for continuity and discontinuity with the themes, feelings, and fantasies I had read in the first set. I am asking myself, "What does it feel like now to be these interviewees (for instance, the theme of endless waiting)?" "What does General Hospital's future as a group, and individual interviewees' futures, feel like, especially now that the consulting company has been changed to Strategic

Planning Consultants?" "What developmental stages, conflicts, and vulnerabilities, together with defenses against them, does the current configuration of events conjure?"

Part of my emotional background and homework (preparation) for this second set of interviews is my attendance, so far twice, at Steven Spielberg's 1993 movie, *Schindler's List*. As I watched that movie about the World War II Holocaust against the Jews, I kept asking myself, "Why is this theme (and this movie) so popular now? What responsive chord does it strike especially among Americans, and not only among American Jews? To what terror and wish does it speak?" The answer I begin to come up with is that the movie is a parable of our time in America; it is about "us" (Americans) as well as being more immediately about "them" (Jews, Nazis). It is about the experience of catastrophe in our midst; a "back to the future," long a subject of Spielberg's movies.

It is, among other things, about the cultural ubiquity and ferocity of downsizings. Who, we ask in terror, is an "essential worker" (a recurrent phrase in the movie) to any organization these days? We are all, in a sense, homeless or imminently homeless Jews who fear a common fate—and who hope for a fatherly Oskar Schindler who will rescue us, or at least try to rescue us (Stein, 1994a), from abandonment and annihilation.

The list and litany of disposable, superfluous people grows: street people, people with HIV and AIDS, the poor, the elderly, juveniles who commit crimes, people without health insurance, people out of work, people who smoke cigarettes, ethnic minorities, and workers and executives alike who are "reduced" from the workforce. If I am even approximately accurate in my interpretation that *Schindler's List* is a metaphor for what it feels like for many people to be an American at this time, it follows that these in-depth interviews with General Hospital administrators can be read as a parable not only for other hospitals, but for virtually every workplace where profit and competitiveness have come to be the paramount values. If we are all at risk, or at least feel that we are, the interviews recorded and interpreted here are mirror and drama of what is occurring everywhere.

As a consequence of this line of thinking, a theory of workplace culture and identity (General Hospital, for example) must also be a theory of personality and society. Likewise, any intervention (such as consultation) must be formulated in terms of knowledge of what is local and unique about this hospital and its university, and in terms of broader personality and social theory and problem-solving approaches.

My second context, tied to the first, is the question, "Whatever happened to the fantasy/fear of 'nuclear winter'; of the end of the human race by nuclear war between Americans and Soviets?" Throughout the 1980s, it was a relentless topic in the scientific as well as political and lay press. Part of my answer comes from reading the transcripts of the first, and now the second, parts of these interviews. It feels as if, through the fact and dread of corporate-industrial downsizing, we as a nation (not only as individual companies, hospitals, and universities) are recreating upon ourselves the nightmare we feared our outside enemy would heap upon us. We are the bomb exploding upon ourselves and our workplace–neighbors; our metaphoric nuclear war, with psychological "fallout" everywhere, is on the home front. Or to use a different, more conventional metaphor: We all live in Bosnia. Nowhere and no one is safe.

That is where we are in the interviews as we await Phase 2, as the appointments of the Hospital Director and the Assistant Provost still have not occurred, as little direct information is forthcoming from the offices of Maggiano, Lewin, and Dohrman, and as SPC has been brought in as the new consulting firm rumored and nationally reputed to be brutal in its cuts. Death is all around; there is nothing one can do to avert it or to know whether one will be survivor or casualty. The war is on the home front; one of its battlegrounds is General Hospital, between inpatient and ambulatory. It has just spread to the wider university, the new president of which recently announced fiscal retrenchment and layoffs in response to the loss of revenue from the hospital. In at least one interview, there is a stark blurring (identification) of traumatic past and present. Stan Pittman says, "I can't separate my mother's death from this. The holidays are also a factor." Symbolic death consumes more and more space and time.

I wrote in my introduction to the first set of interviews that I read them as I would watch a movie, read a novel, or listen to an opera. My emotions and fantasies are active participants in understanding. As I read the second set of interviews, the sheer brutality of the situation at General Hospital, and the magnitude of the brutality, is what seizes me. Here are men and women struggling for their emotional souls and trying to remain compassionate and civil under trying circumstances.

I wonder as I read: Will the tortured become themselves torturers? Will the brutalized become brutal toward their direct reports? Is there a "Faustian bargain" shaping up, wherein the interviewees, tormented by their roles and acts, hope they will be spared by joining league with upper administration, but even they cannot be sure? It is as if some inner battle lines are now drawn between resisting heartlessness and joining the wider organizational brutalization.

Themes

First, I remind the reader of thematic categories I inferred from the first set of interviews. As I read the second set, I ask myself whether these categories remain constant, whether they change, which ones change, and so forth. I suggest that the reader take on this task for himself or herself as well.

Main and Subsidiary Themes   The atmosphere of the interviews is leaden with waiting and almost motionless stagnation. There is the wish to move and the inability to move. General Hospital as a hospital is anthropomorphized into a living but paralyzed organism: It is immobile; immobilized by the downsizing and by the expectation of worse. Dread is the most prevalent mood in anticipation of Phase 2 of the downsizing and restructuring. I can almost feel the oppressive weight of time and lack of clear direction or decisiveness.

Here enters some version of the subsidiary theme I noted in the first part: leadership, present and absent. We hear that three of the highest administrators (Maggiano, Lewin, and Dohrman) are now "communicating" (that word again) little with those beneath them, except largely and silently through the new consulting firm, SPC; and that two crucial leadership positions (Hospital Director and Assistant Provost) have not yet been filled. Frank Wirth is still sorely missed; those emotional roles and administrative tasks he filled, and for which he was admired, are now replaced by voids and the experience of virtual existential nothingness.

Metaphors   Here, as before, I present some of the key metaphoric words, phrases, and sentences as if they were the core of the interviewees' narrative.

Change to get with the 90s.

Too many walls between departments.

Cutthroat.

Lack of protected access to keep them [employees] out of the rain and cold.

My department is being assaulted.

"Business" versus "people."

I'm totally paralyzed.

There is no game plan.

Spinning our wheels.

Everything stops with Jacob [Dohrman].

Every day is a challenge to survive.

There is no report card [goals].

Everybody is waiting for another axe to fall in Phase 2.

We're overloaded.

There are too many plates spinning.

There are a lot of pots boiling on the stove and there is no cook in the kitchen.

In Japan there is a lifetime of employment so it is safe to make suggestions that eliminate positions.

People don't listen to me or anyone.

It's a crock of shit.

[The change to] SPC [as] a slap in the face.

I try to put on a good face.

It's a time bomb.

Every organization has to stay alive.

We're still making money like nuts [$50-million surplus].

Two major unknowns, the new Hospital Director, and the Assistant Provost.

The SPC process.

The rumor that people would be escorted to the auditorium by security guards.

Jacob [Dohrman] is the only person in the hospital who has seen the SPC contract.

Everything is locked up now, dead, zip.

Stagnated.

Dramatically wrong.

SPC is coming to flatten the organization.

It's a disaster.

Everyone in denial.

People are holding things tight to the vest.

A lot of dead wood.

Horror stories.

Got rid of [people], others got cut off at the ankles.

No one at the top is listening.

There are no birthrights.

[Identity of] medical center [as a whole, versus] split apart into hospital, ambulatory, and the schools.

People are territorial where there used to be flexibility.

Catch-22.

Reality has hit them in the face but there is worse to come.

Blaming the reductions.

All of our ducks are still not in order.

Workhorses.

Older employees versus younger employees.

I inherited the staff.

There is a big pool of water, and we are getting in deeper and deeper and it's hard to stay afloat.

You can't squeeze a turnip.

It seems like things are rudderless.

Unfreezing.

"No margin, no mission" [statement of Dr. Lewin, uppermost value on business].

No direction from the top [of General Hospital].

A big nut to crack.

Hospital as the golden goose and getting everything and fat [feeling about Dr. Lewin and ambulatory's view].

[My job is] up for grabs.

A lot of foot dragging.

Dragging their feet.

Chaos.

I don't look back.

My assumption here, as with the first set of interviews, is that metaphors examined alone can reveal conscious and unconscious feelings, fantasies, and anxieties in organizations. They are here unfettered by the real-world business being discussed; they are, in a way, the most real, ultimate, "business" and "work" of the organization. The emotional impact of reading these metaphors is much more overwhelming and exhausting to me this time than with the first set of interviews.

Control versus Out of Control   There is the sense of people desperately trying to do their jobs, not knowing any more precisely what their jobs are or will be, while they and their organization reel in a sea of uncertainty and dread. One manager spoke of "rehearsing what could happen"; a frequent way of dealing with uncertainty over the future is ruminating or actual acting out, as if one might moderate the future's anticipated terrible effect by anticipating it beforehand. It reflects an attempt to turn the intolerable experience of being a passive victim of circumstance into being its active architect. The trouble is that this often takes the shape of magical thinking and doing.

Another form the conflict over control takes is chronic grief and anticipatory mourning of self, of roles, of others, and of the organization. The chronic grief can be expressed paradoxically through the inability (or the refusal) to mourn, the insistence on business as usual, and a shifting of responsibility to the reified institution or to the reduction in force (as though all motivation and responsibility were external).

Expected versus Unexpected Story Line   There was a widespread sense of relief that the downsizing of Phase 1 was now past. Overall, interviewees had expected a restructuring and building of a new organizational normalcy following Phase 1. Instead, there is dread and stagnation. Some wonder whether anything was really accomplished by the downsizing, and there is widespread fear over what the new consulting firm will do to them next. The future seems even more uncertain than before the downsizing, which they had expected to clear the path to the future. Over and over again, interviewees expressed a sense of rupture with whatever institutional story line (narrative structure) they had known or expected.

"Us" versus "Them"   From these interviews, the dichotomy between us and them, inside and outside, is now both horizontal (hospital, ambulatory, and schools) as it was in the first interview set, and vertical, that is, the uppermost administration (Maggiano, Lewin, and Dohrman) in relation to everyone else beneath them, and the administrators interviewed in relation to those who report to them and to those still further down the chain of command. The social distance in all directions seems and feels enormous, increasing, persecutory, and unbridgeable. A new, related, and ominously looming "them" is the new consulting firm, SPC, who are depicted as the executors of the will of upper management; the cognate term executioner likewise comes immediately to mind.

"Communication"   If during the first set of interviews communication already loomed large, here it dominates every category. (Interestingly, I made a typo as I began this paragraph and wrote "community" instead of "communication": My "Freudian slip" reveals, I believe, the wish I unconsciously infer and feel from the interviews. The wish for [lost] community pervades every utterance.) A number of quotations from the interviews will illustrate the paramount role communication, its absence, its style, and the experience of it plays at General Hospital. Likewise, Jacob Dohrman's name, role, and style appear everywhere in the interviews: He is the focus both of reality and of fantasy. I suggest that the reader read this list in the same spirit as the collection of metaphors in the first two sets of interviews (I stopped note-taking halfway through the interview set).

I don't know.

There is little information about Phase 2 and the consulting company.

No communication. Everything is unexpected.

Nothing is changing for the moment.

I want to get going.

Apprehensive, anxious, fearful.

No one has trust anymore. Overworked.

It is also a challenge to regroup and reopen a dialogue with my staff [past vs. present].

I had really good general communication with my staff. They were a good team. Now I feel that they are just out there and testing me.

Everyone is pretty negative at this point.

The rationale for not filling the positions is not being shared top down, from Maggiano. Something is not in synchrony. There is an absolute break between the top and the rest of the organization.

Dictates versus explanation. If we are supposed to be a team, the top isn't participating.

The system is not quick. Everything stops with Jacob [Dohrman]. No decisions are being made. Middle management has no authority. They have just become the messengers.

We are a little more distant from each other than we were before the cuts. They are preoccupied with their own environment. Every day is a challenge to survive.

There was good communication, but it is bogged down coming through the administrative ranks. The department heads are almost in isolation when they should be looking for a common road.

There is no feedback.

I don't get any information back . . . no targets or goals.

There are a lot of rumors about SPC [the consulting company]. We aren't getting the facts from Dr. Maggiano and Dr. Lewin.

People don't listen to me or anyone.

Things have become paralyzed.

Jacob is paralyzed out of fear.

It is all lip service; no one is empowered. It's a crock of shit.

Slap in the face.

Brutal.

Bureaucratization is no good. People feel pretty worthless.

Jacob [Dohrman] is afraid of losing his job. He also has delusions of grandeur to be promoted.

I try to put on a good face, but my staff are feeling pretty bad. This is a severely depressed organization, including the people way down.

Jacob vacillates between fear and depression. He strikes back and brutalizes his staff when he's depressed.

No one knows.

No one can think anymore.

There has been inadequate communication. How can supervisors reassure others if they don't know that they will be here?

How do you justify a job?

Many rumors about SPC.

Rumors were rampant and often close to right.

Boundary Uncertainty   The ambiguity voiced in the first interviews continues here. It is worse. Now even the wider university makes cutbacks, presumably in response to the hospital's fallen revenue. The question of the boundary of trust pervades everyone and everything. People at General Hospital trust no one, yet they are expected (and expect themselves) to function as wider, interdepartmental, trusting teams.

Functioning versus Feeling From reading these interviews, I sense abundant and diverse feelings being expressed in contrast with more of a retreat-into-task performance in the initial interviews. Some express a numbing of empathy toward others in the hospital, or at least an attempt to deaden it. There is much free-floating anxiety and anger. It is as if people are frozen in their feelings, unsure of how to feel about themselves and their situation.

A variant perhaps on the theme of functioning versus feeling is "business" (e.g., "our positioning in the marketplace"; or Dr. Lewin's motto, "No margin, no mission") versus "people." According to the former, people are mostly or altogether means to corporate ideological ends (e.g., increasing organizational competitiveness, profitability), while according to the latter, people are ends in themselves.

The Experience of Change Massive, traumatic change seems to have been followed by a time of changelessness and motionlessness, and by a waiting for the next invasive change to sweep any accomplishments away. The words used by interviewees come across to me as deeply felt physical, bodily, almost preemotional experiences; preverbal, not merely "verbal." Brutal, decisive action vacillates with ominous waiting. There is a sense of foreboding and helplessness in the face of change and time. There is no boundary to change during this time, no sense of when it will all be over, and no sense of how it will turn out. Amid this, there is a leadership vacuum with respect to appointing the Hospital Director and the Assistant Provost, and a second void with respect to filling any open positions. Put metaphorically, there are more and bigger holes and fewer and fewer sealed holes.

A variation on the theme of change is the change in the style and self-image held by members of the institution about "the institution" ("we," "us") itself. In turn, this is a meditation on the experience of time and of radical discontinuity between the current sense of personal and corporate self and the past self. There is now the sense of vast vertical (up and down the administrative hierarchy from Dr. Maggiano to interviewees' direct reports) and horizontal (hospital, ambulatory, schools) splits. The prior sense of wholeness is gone. Words associated with the past General Hospital are "caring," "open," "flexibility," and identification with having "worked for the medical center." Now the words include "indifferent," "brutal," "mistrust," "divisive," "territorial," "split apart into hospital, ambulatory, and the schools," "self-preservation," "business oriented," "control," and "survival."

New Themes   Trying to keep an upbeat attitude, to think positively and to remain optimistic while the overall mood is of resignation and dread, comes across in such expressions as "I try not to think of the worst case scenario," "I can't think negatively," "Every organization has to stay alive," "I try to put on a good face, but my staff are feeling pretty bad," "I want to get going [movement, decisive action, direction]. I guess I have to trust it will get done," "We're a trusting lot and we are trying," and "I used to be sympathetic to those going through rough times." These feel like a willful effort to keep on task; to fend off feelings of loss, depression, and anger; and to deaden fears of the future and feelings about what has already taken place in Phase 1. In the vernacular, they feel as if the speakers are struggling to "psych themselves," to be "cheerleaders," and to talk themselves into positive thinking, while not much deeper down they do not really believe it. The themes feel like a mask they wear for themselves and for others so their real faces will not show.

Another new theme is the relation between empathy within the workplace and outside the workplace. I begin to sense less empathy and patience at work, but more empathy and patience at home. This surprises me; I had expected it to have been the reverse. The relationship between inside and outside General Hospital is evoked by the following excerpts from the interviews:

I can't separate my mother's death from this. The holidays are also a factor [the interview was held in early February].

[I was] being short and abrupt at home [at the time of the first cuts]. Now I'm more aware of it and working on it. . . . I know I can't treat my family that way.

My new relationship has turned me around. I'm more empathetic now, which may be helping my staff. I'm better able to calm them down and get them centered and proactive.

I find myself using my husband to bounce ideas off of. I'm providing him more information than in the past. He's good to talk to; he's an asset; he has business experience.

Another new theme is increase in illnesses, or at least in the reporting of illnesses: colds, high blood pressure, heart attacks, sore throats, diarrhea, abdominal pain, waking up in the middle of the night, depression, "buckle," "strain," "tired and getting sick," "increase in sick time, tardiness," and "tired and getting sick." Perhaps the thematic and adaptive opposite of this internalizing (somaticizing) response is indifference, fatalism, and withdrawal, as, for instance, Judy Harris replied to the question of how she felt about the changes that will be made: "I don't know what the future changes are. Frankly, I don't care that much now. Nothing I do will change anything. If I can't go with the flow I'll leave."

Deep involvement to the point of sickness contrasts with a pulling back, if not a preparation for exit. This might in part relate to the degree of commitment and expectation of future longevity by the interviewees at General Hospital. Chris Regan, for example, replies with detachment to the question about her feelings about the changes that will be made: "I don't know what's coming. It is an interesting end to my career. I'm not as anxious as others; I'll retire this year." Regan conveys a serene sense of distance others do not psychologically or financially possess. Or is it bitterness disguised as loftiness? At any rate, the relationship between personal life cycle and organizational cycle are surely part of the perception, experience of, and response to the threats at General Hospital.

Significance

What do all these themes mean? I am struck, almost physically, by how much task, fantasy, and effect overlap, if not intersect, throughout the interviews. The reader here does not have to work very hard to hear profoundly personal and disturbing emotional material that, in more ordinary times, I would expect to be far better disguised (defended against by repression, splitting, and various forms of riddance from the self) in the interview materials. For example, "We are operating at dangerous levels of low staffing and there is decreased morale." Phenomenology, that is, the narrative account of conscious experience, comes increasingly closer to unconscious feeling and fantasy: The interpretation is closer to the surface.

Further complicating adaptation to change is the fact that, at times, multiple competing values must be acted upon at once (and, perhaps, as though there were no conflict). For instance, the newer, multidisciplinary team concept involves greater responsibilities. It implies greater "lateral" autonomy and more fluid, task-based work groups. Yet no one can seem to make decisions, horizontally or vertically, and everyone is waiting for more ominous, capricious decisions to be enforced top-down, either directly or via the consulting company.

Hypotheses

As with the themes section, I begin here by summarizing the hypotheses I drew from the first set of interviews: university, hospital, and departments as symbolic objects; downsizing and the problem of aggression;

assault on interviewees' narcissism; magnitude and relentlessness of change deepens the suffering (metaphors of war, death camps); leadership succession; social change and the inability to mourn; and organizational metaphors as expressions of shared intrapsychic social reality.

In the current set of interviews, I find abundant evidence for these seven again, but they are now far less discrete hypotheses or interpretations, as they are facets of what feels like a more unitary, regressed, mental world. In fact, I confess that if this second set of interviews were my only data, I would not have inferred the original seven distinct categories from them. The world expressed here feels to me as if I have entered a developmental mode that precedes differentiation of self from environment or to which deeply disturbed people regress. It is a world dominated by projected "world-destruction fantasies," except that to those experiencing them they feel terrifyingly real. They do not feel like fantasies; they feel like the end of the world. The fate of the body becomes the fate of the world; internal rage is played out on the stage of the social world.

To put it differently, under massive regression the enemy becomes more and more dehumanized (from zoomorphism to becoming a dead thing, a piece of shit). Among the interviewees, what is the fate of aggression? Who is the enemy? It changes; it vacillates; it accumulates: upper administration; lateral, competing organizational units; and one's very self and body (disease, sleeplessness, depression). There is neither a stable "us" or a stable "them" (the enemy); the search for reliable displacement and containment is continuous.

To my ears there is great and disturbing similarity in dynamics between the proverbial backward-hospital schizophrenic's private world-destruction fantasies, those of the interviewees at General Hospital, and our own; that is, the delusion that the external world is being annihilated and an externalization of the inner experience, including powerful feelings, of the dissolution of the self. The differences are that the interviewees and we other cultural "normals" are able to preserve (via a vertical split in the ego) more intact, reality-oriented ego functions that are sufficiently well isolated emotionally from the regressed parts, and that cultural defenses such as institutional membership, ideological rationalization and intellectualization, and the ritual of work tasks and routines can temporarily divert attention and emotion from the experience of annihilation. The backward schizophrenic is, ironically, less dangerous than the normals who can agree on a shared worldview and can muster technology, communication, bureaucracy, and other facets of reality to validate and fulfill fantasy.

In this context, the categories I first described in separate hypotheses now feel indistinguishable and collapsed, even though we might heuristically label and isolate them as distinct. Was I wrong in my first assessment or diagnosis? I do not think so. I think that the outer and inner worlds of the interviewees have dramatically changed under this sense of siege. General Hospital (as any institution) can be viewed alternately as a Kohutian "self-object" (something that exists in the real, external world that is taken and incorporated into the self, obliterating distinctions between outer and inner [Kohut, 1971]), and a Kleinian (or object relational) symbolic object of projective identification (an externalizing and imposition of the inner world upon the outer, inducing in the other person or group behavior that complies with and confirms the inner fantasy [Klein, 1946]). In organizations, both processes complement each other; they have stabilizing and equilibrating (defensive and adaptive) dimensions. Together, they consist of the core of a sense of "we-ness," of psychosocial identity (Erikson, 1968) over time.

That former sense of wholeness associated with the inner and outer worlds of General Hospital is now being demolished, if it is not entirely shattered already. Libidinal object constancy (the ability to hold a continuity of perception and feeling toward a person or thing) is gone. The symbiotic tie with the institutional object (symbolic heir to the mother–child "dual-unity," as Mahler and Furer [1968] called it) has been broken. The role, the sense of place, the sense of pride, and the sense of future, to name only a few parameters all bound up intersubjectively as part of one's identity, are gone with the downsizing. Now, the dread (and reality) of vulnerability, at once contemporary and filled with feelings reawakened from infancy, contends in mighty struggle with the wish for dependency and, in turn, with the struggle against the wish. Interviewees frequently cope with the experience of massive change by a split in the experience of time: idealizing the past and past leadership as good and whole, and demonizing the present and anticipated future of General Hospital and its leadership.

At an even developmentally earlier level, physically more primitive than separation–individuation, it is as if one's very social skin (more abstractly, boundaries) has been punctured, pulled away, scored, flayed, and scraped off (Ogden, 1989). Through the merger of self with group, it feels as if one is bleeding to death as a "body politic"; as an institutional organism. The uncertainty, stagnation, and sense of being stuck all make healing of the punctured social skin difficult, if not impossible. Raw, primitive rage is *deneutralized, reprimitivized,*or *unbound,* to use some psychoanalytic terms. People have been stripped of their familiar defenses, outposts in reality, and adaptive modes, and developmentally ancient defenses and feelings come pouring out. The absence of these is associated with and expresses, among other things, annihilation anxiety, death anxiety, persecutory anxiety, separation anxiety, abandonment anxiety, and castration anxiety. In groups as in individuals, the deeper the regression, the less the disguise of primary process (that is, instincts, wishes, unconscious fantasies, and unconscious feelings) and primitive defenses. In terms of the topographical model of mental functioning (the dynamic unconscious, preconscious, and conscious thought), there is less distance between psychological "depth" and "surface."

Over and over again in the interviews, we are witnessing a catastrophic emotional reaction and an attempt to cope emotionally with that ongoing sense of catastrophe, all the while maintaining an "on-task" dedication. As an additional hypothesis, I suggest that twin symptoms of the breakdown of General Hospital organizational identity are increased physical and emotional symptoms (internalizing, somaticizing) and increased outwardly directed rage and suspicion (splitting, externalizing, projecting) toward foes and scapegoats. Self-traumatization (for instance, the abuse of one's closest associates or subordinates, as by Jacob Dohrman; and somatization) in the wake of endless trauma is a form of reversing the intolerable position of passive victim into the more acceptable position of active agent; it achieves at least a magical anticipatory mastery over the dreaded future. My further guess is that the defense of isolation helps to keep the interviewees functionally productive on the job, even as they await further catastrophe from the consulting company and upper administration.

To these I would add a further hypothesis: the use of RIF itself (an abstraction of and euphemism for firings, riddances, or symbolic killings) as a projective target. For instance, in Mary James's words, "People are blaming the reductions for not being able to do anything." The RIF is at once a fact and a fantasy, a virtually personified, reified object, or an entity that can be invoked to do less in job performance, which, in turn, would increase and confirm the stagnation of the hospital. This represents an externalization of superego functions ("It's not my fault, it's the RIF"). Clearly, all these individual hypotheses are facets of the overarching hypothesis; namely, organizational regression and the effort to reorganize and restore the inner mental world from the regressed position.

Metapsychological Considerations   Every writer and every consultant has regret for what he or she wished to have thought of earlier in the analysis or consultation. Let me voice one. A hotly debated concept in psychoanalysis is that of *metapsychology*, namely a wider framework of assumptions that contain specific propositions or interpretations. Building on Sigmund Freud, Heinz Hartmann, David Rapaport, and many others, I would suggest (and wish I had thought of earlier) a metapsychological grid or matrix in which each set of interview material can be situated and assessed. This schematic consists of multiple "points of view" for understanding the interviewees accounts. Among them are the following:

Topographic (the status of the material in the vertically organized dynamic model of the mind—unconscious, preconscious, and conscious)

Structural (the relationship of the material in the model of the ego, the super-ego, and the id)

Economic or dynamic (the form the biological drives take and where they are expressed, as in repressed and displaced rage at the sense of stagnation)

Psychogenetic (the developmental point of view which situates current responses in relation to childhood fixations or regressions to childhood traumas and conflicts; obviously, thus far in the two sets of interviews we have been given no free associations to very early fantasies, experiences, or memories)

Adaptive (the relation between the internal fantasy, wish, and defense and interpersonal relations and the wider social–natural reality)

Dual instinct theory (for instance, love versus aggression, life versus death, equilibrium, preeminence of one, or fusion of these polarities)

These metapsychological viewpoints can be understood as complementary interpretive frameworks.

What Would I Do as Consultant?

From this second interview set, I would continue the approaches outlined at the end of the first set: using my own emotional reaction as a key to organizational data; persisting in abiding with and uncovering the "communication" issue (What is real? How do I know? What does it feel like to be stuck?); listening for slips of the tongue (metaphors) to learn about feelings, fantasies, and wishes at General Hospital; creating a safe enough interpersonal environment (holding environment) in which more of the story and feelings could emerge, facilitating integration; and serving as ego support, ally, and advocate, while at the same time listening for and interpreting resistances.

To amplify the first point, I would try to be as honest as I could be (with myself and with them) about how overwhelmed I feel and, I infer, they also feel. I would not make promises to fix things. If I promised anything, it would be to be with them, to persevere, to keep talking, to keep listening, and to acknowledge my limits even as I acknowledged theirs together with their transference wish for me to have no limits and their rage toward me as I confront them with my own constraints. It would be within that intersubjective net that any concrete suggestions or recommendations would be made.

Let me expand on this point, based on the emotional intensity and rawness of the material in these interviews. The consultant's role of empathic listener, container, and holding environment helps interviewees to diminish fragmentation and depersonalization, and in turn to accomplish their interpersonal tasks with greater empathy. In American biomedicine (and in our wider culture) we often distinguish between "just talking" or "just listening" and "doing something" about a problem. In all areas of life we almost exclusively value doing, activism (Kluckhohn and Strodtbeck, 1961; Spiegel, 1971), and interventionist strategies as if we were waging a war to fulfill a task; as if not *doing* something were a sign of passivity, dependency, weakness, and yes, femininity (as we imagine it culturally). We overvalue reengineering and restructuring as forms of relatedness in which we "get things done."

We underestimate the value of being able to speak one's mind and heart safely and being heard as worthwhile and genuinely transmuting. But the extent to which we hunger for this ability is illustrated in the interviewees' poignant stories told in Dr. Allcorn's presence. The interviewees keep coming back for more, even though Dr. Allcorn is not, strictly speaking, performing an "intervention." He is, so to speak, "just interviewing" or "just gathering data." Yet his questions, his listening, and his note taking are themselves interventions from the interviewees' viewpoints. He is giving them back a precious and besieged part of their very selves. He is not merely gathering data. Stated differently, that very process of data gathering is profoundly therapeutic for the interviewees (and, I suspect, also for the interviewer). Dr. Allcorn is providing an intersubjective space in which interviewees' profoundly painful, dysphoric feelings and fantasies and experiences can be safely placed and contained outside the self by the relationship; a far healthier, less defensive way than externalization or projection. We should never forget that those rich, wrenching, "native" narratives Dr. Allcorn records do not and could not exist apart from the interviewees' relationships (including [transference] fantasies about those relationships) with Dr. Allcorn.

What Ira Stamm writes in an article on "Countertransference in [Psychiatric] Hospital Treatment" also describes a key function of the consultant:

According to [W. R.] Bion [1959], the work group is continually buffeted by three kinds of unconscious forces or needs that may influence it at any point in time: security, self-preservation, and salvation. . . . The therapeutic task of the treatment team and its leader is . . . to provide Winnicott's stable and secure "holding environment" where optimal psychological work can take place.

The sine qua non of teamwork is to create a climate where staff members feel comfortable enough to risk self-disclosure, not so much to use the group as a forum for personal psychotherapy, but to use it for understanding one's personal reactions and thus for helping the patient. (Stamm, 1987)

Harold F. Searles similarly writes as follows:

In my experience, frequent and informal meetings of the various staff members who are involved in the care of [profoundly regressed and fragmented psychiatric inpatients] are of inestimable value, for at least three reasons. First, they provide an arena for catharsis of some of the powerful feelings which have been engendered, so that the emotions in the over-all social group [i.e., staff] can be kept within manageable bounds of intensity, thus avoiding the total fragmentation of the group. Secondly, they help the various individual members to go on functioning *as* individuals in their work with the patient—as individuals who are relatively free to act upon their own particular feelings about the patient. Thus he [the patient] is presented with genuine people of various kinds, with whom to identify constructively, rather than being faced with a staff group which is struggling to preserve some pseudo-harmony, some ostensible unanimity of attitudes towards him, in order to hide their sharply divergent true feelings about him. . . . Thirdly, these personnel meetings enable, again as part of the same process, a genuine collaborative integration to develop within the working group an integration of different attitudes towards the patient. This is a process which . . . must take place outside the patient before integration of his own diverse personality fragments can occur *within* him, through constructive introjection of the well-integrated staff group which is working with him. (Searles, 1965, emphasis in original)

Stamm's and Searles's comments about the often neglected emotional dimensions of staff meetings in psychiatric hospitals apply without modification to how a consultant can help in working with General Hospital's administrators. Such meetings allow and facilitate the emergence and sharing of our common core of human experience. This process in turn diminishes the fragmentation and increases the integration among participants, inspiring practitioners to treat others more as whole, complex human beings. It accomplishes it by allowing intense, painful, internal material to get out so that it does not have to "get out" projectively and be deposited in others, by subterfuge, in administrators' day-to-day work with supervisors and direct reports. The style of consulting or facilitating described by Stamm and Searles draws more from the object relations "holding environment" viewpoint of Donald W. Winnicott, Michael Balint, Ronald Fairbairn, Wilfred R. Bion, and others than it draws from the more strict interpretivist position of classical psychoanalysis.

Here I add one of my own countertransference reactions; that is, what I am emotionally drawn and tempted to do. The second set of interviews stimulate a rescue fantasy in me: Surely there is something major or dramatic I can do to redeem General Hospital from the ravages of downsizing; actions that range from "whistle blowing" to the press to talking directly with upper administration. My own magical thinking is a would-be shaman's omnipotence induced by the feelings of impotence induced by the group and sensed by the consultant. If acted upon, the consultant would become the interviewees' doomed missionary of magical control.

My countertransference feelings vacillated wildly from "There is nothing I can do" (helplessness) to "I can, I must, make a decisive difference. I will be the one to come up with the solution." (Here, id and superego join in common cause to rescue failed narcissism and the hospital.) I emphasize that both these extremes, and my vacillation between them, are not entirely my own. They are the resonance between my unconscious and that of the interviewees. Their projective identification provokes me to feel like them and like the parental redeemer who would step in and take over.

Likewise, I have a second countertransference response: the fantasy of flight to somewhere better and safer, or that I could somehow take them there as a new, better, parent–leader. Both of these fantasies are mine, but as evoked by the pressure upon my own unconscious of reading the material. My task is therefore to sit on, as it were, hold, or interpret these fantasies as important organizational data, not to act them out; to avoid joining the splitting (for instance, between upper administration and staff) and thereby the dehumanizing of some group at General Hospital; and to help interviewees feel their grief, and not only their rage. Can it be genuinely empowering to people to help them to feel how truly vulnerable and helpless they actually are, and from that position, not from false hope, to formulate options, decisions, and action plans?

The issue is, "What will the interviewees (and the wider General Hospital) allow me to do?" versus "What do I wish to do?" and "What are my motivations?" With narcissism-based therapeutic ambition, for instance, I might be tempted to try to direct and control the interviewees, just as they are struggling to control their future. On the other hand, with better boundary delineation I might be able to serve as a comforting, safe, reflective "holding environment" in which catharsis and insight and some working through are possible. But these are all my viewpoints and wishes: As consultant, I am also a fantasy object of the interviewees and of their wider vertical and horizontal network. If, for instance, I am identified with the repressed and split-off contents of their unconscious, and, via projective identification, come to be a repository of these, my presence and effort to make the unconscious conscious (among other tasks) will induce considerable resistance on their part, including efforts at suppressing my ideas, oppressing me personally, and inducing repression within me so that my defenses correspond to theirs as the price of my continued belonging. The question is this: Will they allow me to do my work? And further, what precisely is my work as consultant? Who defines it? Finally, will I even recognize the projective identification as it occurs?

The Consultant as Culture Critic   I wish, hesitantly, to add a further topic to what I would do. The basis for this additional role is my recognition of the suffering being experienced and the suffering being induced. On the surface, the very idea is an oxymoron. For instance, how dare a consultant hired by a company or hospital to help them deal with downsizing question the very validity, the motivations behind the downsizing itself. One could get fired for less. But is "the bottom line" the only bottom line? What values deserve to go without question (which, of course, is a separate issue psychodynamically from why people do not question certain values, such as are embodied in "bottom line," "downsizing," and "managed care" policy thinking)?

This raises several other questions, among them the following: Can entire cultures or organizations be themselves dysfunctional, regressed, and pathological? Is not dissent sometimes healthy (in the sense of individuation or differentiation from an enforced consensus as described in Irving Janis's celebrated work on "Groupthink" [1982])? For whom does a consultant work and how subtly can the consultant be co-opted emotionally (e.g., by intimidation and identification by an organization) to do what he or she would not do "personally" (precisely the public–private split among the Nazi physicians in the death camps [see Lifton, 1986])? Is the refusal to participate within the repertory of a consultant?

I am continuously out of breath as I read the interviews and write the commentary. It is difficult and demanding enough, both for treatment and theory, for a psychoanalyst to work with an individual patient who has experienced waves of trauma and who has woven early experience, feeling, and fantasy into an indomitable character structure. How does one translate this theory and practice into working with individuals and large whole groups who are dealing not only with recent past assaults upon their identities, but who live in wait of the next while all the while strive to get a job done? If, as organizational consultants, part of our self-appointed task is to help groups work toward acceptance and grieving of past tragedy to transmute it emotionally into unavertable necessity, is it our task to help these groups to accept, to resign themselves to, or to protest in advance future anticipated tragedy? For organizational executive, mid-level manager, worker, and consultant alike, what is the nature of the ego from which we ask these things to deal with ongoing emergency reactions of the ego to recurrent trauma and expectation of further trauma?

Conclusions (For Now): More Questions

From where comes personal and organizational resilience (Diamond, 1993) under these relentless conditions? If all I have here described, interpreted, and imagined (myself serving as consultant) has distant, indelible childhood roots in wishes and defenses against dependency, independence, separation, Oedipal conflict with the parent of one's same sex, and the like; and if all these are unconsciously played out and rekindled in contemporary workplace events; does that in any way relieve our responsibility for creating something less than a hell on earth for those with whom we work and with whom we consult? Those of us who work with the unconscious life of organizations have, I believe, a special responsibility to be aware and to awaken in others that awareness of the peculiar human vulnerability that comes from having a prolonged infancy of utter helplessness and dependence on the good will of others (La Barre, 1954, 1972). If part of our task is to help organizations to understand their group dreams and nightmares, still another part is to help them (and ourselves as well) have the courage and love to awaken from these dreams, even if this is not part of our official, original contract or job description. It is one thing to help organizations to have emotional catharses and let go, if only partially, of emergency ego reactions; it is another to foster organizational climates in which these recurrent emergencies do not take place. Finally, for now, the magnitude of events at General Hospital, and nationally in healthcare reform, reminds me of the limits of what any individual consultant can do, irrespective of the sense of dire urgency he or she might rightfully feel and wish to do something about. I must keep asking myself, "Whose anxiety am I treating, mine or theirs, or worse, mine through theirs?"

I feel my theory and practical skills to be stretched beyond their limits. "What consultant has a right to more questions than answers?" I ask myself. I wish to know so much more than I can, or perhaps ever may. Yet as consultant, like the interviewees, I must act even in a void of knowing. To my imagination and to those of the interviewees, Maggiano and Lewin, and even Dohrman (who was interviewed) as well as the new consulting company, remain utter stick figures. They are one-dimensional "bad guys" who are "doing something bad" to General Hospital; the interviewees and I know so little about them. They are remote, mostly silent, and responsible for major decisions about General Hospital's future ingredients sufficient to inspire terror, regression, and primitive, persecutory anxiety.

Specifically, I would wish to know the Dohrman behind the public rages he has. In the interviews he speaks mostly abstractly in "organizationalese": positions, restructuring, reorganizing, long-term philosophy, the organization's ability to meet goals, strategic planning, operations improvement, and adjusting staffing. He seems far more comfortable with the impersonal than the personal; "deliver[ing] a good product" seems to be his highest value, and people's feelings get in the way of "see[ing] positives for the organization." Yet he is also very dependent (without ever directly saying so) on decisions and those who make decisions above him, especially on Lewin. In the interviews,

Dohrman is more projective target than real person. Even as I type these interpretive notes, I often make mental "Freudian slips" (parapraxes) and think to type "Doorman" and "Doormat," which are at once an image of a kind of gate keeper and a disparaging fantasy of someone who lacks (rather than possesses) considerable authority and power. Identifying with the victims of downsizing and with the victims of his wrath (children at the mercy of a bad father), I imagine myself doing (counter-Oedipally) to him what he symbolically has done to others: walk on them as though they were mere "doormats." To take the heroic fantasy further, I would rescue the maternal organization and the mother–child symbiosis from the evil father. If this is all partly my own wish, it is also partly a wish induced from reading the interviews. Lack of clear communication and reliable information and the lapse of a sense of community lead to an inflammation of fantasy to fill the void, my own included. If only I knew more.

I wish we could humanize the upper administrators better by knowing more; for instance, why they were chosen for their roles, by whom, and the nature of the fit between their personality and the emerging top-down social structure. How, for instance, does Maggiano and Lewin's friendship affect institutionwide policy making? The uppermost administrators are not a kind of Aristotelian "Prime Mover"; presumably, they also report to someone else. They accrue the magical power of deux ex machina when they act so forcefully, yet we do not know why or in whose behalf.

I am dissatisfied by even more: The two sets of interviews challenge any strictly mechanistic stimulus-centered or psychophysical theory of social change (popular "stress" theory) on the one hand, and any hermetically intrapsychic, one-person-at-a-time theory of the unconscious and reality on the other. If I may modify Jean-Paul Sartre's (1956) famous declaration in his play *No Exit*, "Hell is other people." Hell is the feeling and fantasy world in which we weave and entrap ourselves and one another (as "internal objects" via projective identification). Clearly, from these interviews, reality (at least social reality) is analyzable, both as an object inducing defense and adaptation, and as an introject, an inner, unconscious representation that serve as defense and adaptation, and that in turn shapes future reality.

As symbolic heirs to their original maternal (and wider caretaking) figures, people have symbiotic attachments to their organizations; they use workplaces to complete or patch up their psychic and bodily integrity. The internal life of General Hospital is no exception. What makes for tragedy inside the ostensibly sound economic streamlining is how exploitable the human animal is, even within the protective bubble of culture. Natural disaster occurs from impersonal nature; social catastrophe comes as often from human callousness as from anything rational. Persecutory anxiety is an irrational regressed response to chronic, emotionally terrorizing situations, but it is hardly surprising.

Normal separation-individuation is made far more difficult under chronic conditions of assault upon identity. Institutions, which is to say, networks of human relationships and emotions, are now routinely ripped apart (by hostile takeovers, corporate mergers, alliances and competition run wild, and silk suits and ties nattily at war via computer printouts, bottom lines, and board rooms). We have created a latchkey society of mutual abandonment. What McDermott (1991) calls "corporate society" increasingly rests upon the for-profit corporation as virtually the fundamental unit of life (and upon which even family, child rearing, and religion now rest). What developmental tasks, then, are not dashed upon the societywide fantasy of profit, greed, deficit, and the fear of greater economic loss? How much profit, how wide a margin, and how much leanness and meanness are enough? (And, of course, why are these our guiding stars?) Capitalism, we Americans say, has triumphed over the now-fallen Communist ways of the Soviet Union and its dependent camps. The world is free to become more like us. We are left to wage economic and symbolic, if not bloody, war on each other; "free to hate" (as Hockenos [1993] says of a Europe liberated of the Communist empire) via, among other things, medical corporate alliances and conglomerates that seek to "capture patients" and undermine if not destroy "noncompetitive" clinical entities, as in war.

Over the long haul of human history, discontinuity is more the cultural rule than continuity. At the level of tribe, nation-state, and corporation alike, unfairness is more rule than exception. Do we not secretly admire the sociopathic extremes of those nineteenth-century industrial marauders we call "robber barons"? "Tradition" is usually more wished-for legend and projectively constructed past than established fact. Large-scale social change migration (technological, political, ideological, religious, and economic) has long wrecked the settledness of our human symbioses. Social reality is not a "good enough" mother, let alone an idealized breast.

In our increasingly hermetically sealed, vertically integrated, corporate and 24-hour computer-linked world (Moore-Ede, 1993) that is run like universal shiftwork, society has become (again) virtually a company town. We are even beginning to turn to our workplaces for all our health insurance and child care. Are we secretly trying to create the conditions ripe for a Theodore Roosevelt to be a superior parental "Rough Rider" and put voracious corporate executives in their place? For healthcare, job security, and sense of identity, the workplace and "work" (in the sense of wage earning) have accrued the heavy burden once the dominion of family, religion, art, and other institutions that served as containers of longed-for symbiosis and love. In human history nothing is permanent; displacements of population and of identity are common. General Hospital is, by this measure, no exception.

To make it more complicated yet, our era is dominated by an increasing sense of social entitlement, not only on the part of numerous minority groups, but of virtually everyone. Entitlement and limitation are on a collision course (as in, for example, the American Disabilities Act of 1993). Thus, when an entire workplace and not only a single job is threatened by layoffs, it feels as if there is nowhere to turn since everyone is downsizing. Perhaps rampant entrepreneurship is the wave of this future. It is hard, under these circumstances, to "let go" and grieve the loss of work, virtually the only sure thing left of American institutions. And then even work fails to be a holding environment. In some respects, American biomedicine is an even more complex and regulated social environment than many other modern institutions. With the movement toward cost containment, regulation, and profit since the early 1980s (DRGs [Diagnostically Related Groups], HMOs [Health Maintenance Organizations], PPOs [Preferred Provider Organizations], IPAs [Independent Practice Associations], and PROs [Peer Review Organizations] to limit inpatient and outpatient "consumption" of services), hospitals, clinics, and insurance companies have actually added layers of nonclinical, administrative, mid- and upper-level managerial roles to "police" healthcare. So we are now "delayering" what only a decade or slightly more ago we layered, in order to try to control healthcare costs.

In this brave new corporate world, persons cease to exist; there are only institutional goals, roles, objectives, mission statements, and impersonal strategic plans—and this, of course, in America, where we avowedly prize individualism and self-determinism most highly, with an almost protest quality. We also collude in believing that organizational strategic plans and mission statements, for instance, are truly autonomous and impersonal; as if real people with their own motivations, values, and group dynamics did not decide upon one course instead of another. Often, "corporate" is a cop out. Still, we must somehow grieve the lost world that could no longer be, and our own powerlessness in the face of a world whose course we could not avert or reverse. And still again, despite the elevation of unfairness (and its narcissistic counterparts, shame and entitlement) to virtually a current social reality principle, social reality is at least potentially capable of compassion, of empathy, and of values vanished and banished from our downsizing frenzy.

If we know that people are vulnerable to exploitation (in the Freudian sense of exploiting the residues of all our childhood fears, losses, wishes, and rages), does that not place a special responsibility of consciousness and conscience upon all those who participate in radical social change such as is occurring at General Hospital, and not only upon a category of persons called consultants? Were I a consultant at General Hospital, I would try to voice such an advocacy role with all clients and in all client groups. Or, in the collective wish to act out, to virtually disgorge ourselves of our own ideals and consciences, do we seek to repress all we have learned in the past century from the Freudian revolution?

Further, we hear repeatedly in the national news and at corporate meetings that the 1990s and the distant future are "multiple policy environments" and "multiple agenda environments" rather than the unitary, long-lived work worlds of the industrial age that lasted in America for a century and a half. "We must learn to adapt in creative ways," or "Adapt or perish," we are constantly enjoined, as if by comparison the coal, coke, iron, and steel era of mining and manufacturing was itself not also exploitive, inconstant, adversarial, competitive, often inhumane, dangerous, and even deadly. It is easy to idealize the familiar past and demonize the uncertain future. The disturbing question is how much we are adapting to the current chaos and the new social structure, and how much we are unconsciously colluding with others to create and perpetuate it, only later to suffer from it (for example, to receive punishment for guilt, to give vent to hatreds, and to express violent Oedipal or pre-Oedipal impulses with impunity). Were I a consultant to General Hospital, I would share my questions and misgivings with my clients and listen carefully to what they do with my speculations.

The interviews force me to reexamine the relationship between psyche and situation: Which structures which, or how do they structure each other? What is the relationship between the stress induced by a situation such as mass firings; the meanings brought to that situation (e.g., the meaning of work and workplace and of workplace relationships, and the effects involved); the characteristic defenses and adaptations people (such as employees of General Hospital, the interviewees in particular) make to that situation; the role of a consultant; and, certainly not least, the feelings, fantasies, defenses, and adaptations all these induce in the consultant?

I leave this second set of interviews with questions I do not yet know how to answer: How does a consultant work within such a system as General Hospital without being co-opted? How does a consultant leave, or even imagine leaving, following a consultation, without abandoning those who remain behind to a living hell? Can consultation, itself the very act of listening rather than dictating, serve as a form of protest against human disposability, as an encouragement of resilience, and as a form of resistance (in the sense of lifting the veil of the unconscious, the very opposite of the psychoanalytic connotation of resistance as repression)? Are all human expectations and hopes ultimately chimerical, to be dashed on the implacable rock of social reality? If so, then where does that social reality come from? Is its existence not of our making, and therefore not our ethical responsibility? Does the "Reality Principle" have any room for notions of evil, oppression, betrayal, and compassion? Can a psychoanalytically informed consultant say, "Yes, this is, but it should not be"? If yes, then to whom? What does a consultant do with the almost cosmic sense of unfairness and injustice the General Hospital situation provokes?

Finally, the consultant is also a member of the wider society, in which mass firings have become an unquestioned routine way of doing business. We must, as responsible citizens, ask what we are to do when there is nowhere within the society, not only within the organization, to escape. Can the consultant somehow become an agent of social change vastly different from the prevailing regression and acting out? And from where does the insight, the heart, and the sheer stamina come?

OVERVIEW OF INTERPRETATIONS

The three case consultants poignantly describe an organizational situation that has grown much worse. Those interviewed express many disquieting feelings, such as guilt, betrayal, anger, fear, dread, lack of support, powerlessness, hopelessness, worthlessness, depression, futility, frustration, and almost limitless anxiety. Their organization (their leaders) has stripped them of their competence, empowerment, and self-esteem (cut them off from being effective). They are unable to make the most elementary of decisions. They also experience themselves as being unmercifully subjected to a change process imposed from above and from without (the external consultants), while simultaneously they are told that they are participating and empowered when they clearly are not.

Communication seems to have also failed. Senior management now minimally shares information. Maggiano, Lewin, and, to some extent, Dohrman have become remote and uncaring authority figures. Senior management is tacitly understood to be blaming those who have run the hospital for the downsizing and restructuring. In effect, they are getting what they deserve for being bad managers. It seems as though, despite the staff clearly acknowledging the need for change, the assumption being made by top management is that they will not voluntarily change and must, therefore, be driven to change. The staff have become bad objects, just as senior management have become bad objects in the hearts and minds of the staff. Senior management has made it clear that if the staff do not like what is going on, they should get out (my way or no way; management by intimidation). The result is that a vast chasm of dehumanizing interpersonal distance has opened between the staff of the hospital and senior management, and to a lesser extent between the hospital and other organizational components. It is also clear that psychological defenses, such as the splitting and projection of bad feelings, reinforce these dynamics by promoting the development of all good and all bad perceptions of others.

The result of these organizational dynamics is that morale has plummeted to an all-time low. Staff are feeling unsupported and uncared for. Their sense of worth and well-being has been lost. They ultimately fear the loss of their work life, and what amounts to accompanying self-annihilation. A few are not waiting to be killed off by the process and are, in a sense, exercising the only remaining option that they control over their work life, that of ending it and leaving General Hospital. An additional implicit loss is any thought of caring for patients, which seems to be lost in the sea of change.

The case consultants have clearly found themselves to be confronted with a scene of horrific organizational violence, seemingly (they hope) unintentionally perpetrated upon the members of General Hospital by top management (Maggiano and Lewin) with the tacit approval of Dohrman and the support of outside consultants. The case consultants have had their sensibilities assaulted by the insensitivity to the mass psychic and organizational destruction being visited upon the hospital's staff.

The interpretations of the case consultants led me to recover several memories (associations) that relate to the unfolding scene. The first memory is that of a movie I saw twenty or more years ago. Its plot was based upon the wish of a newspaper reporter to develop a better understanding of what it would be like to be on death row. Suddenly, the character finds himself accused and convicted of a murder and sentenced to death. During the reporter's stay on death row he learns that the state has changed its law against the death penalty and criminals will now be executed. A prisoner is then dragged kicking and screaming to the gas chamber and, because of his resistance, is injected with a drug that totally numbs his consciousness so that he continues the walk to his death without awareness. Subsequently, a personal vendetta conducted by the head guard places the reporter next in line for death. Most assuredly, the executioner comes for him. Frightened to the point that he can barely walk, he rejects the mind-numbing drug. He is placed into the chair and all of his limbs are strapped to the chair. A black hood is placed over his head. The camera focuses in on his head. The hood is being sucked in and out of his mouth with a power and frequency that only can be created by terror. The camera's gaze is directed around the room to a view of the witnesses and there, in the observation room, are his editor and colleagues. The viewer now understands that the reporter's wish to learn more about death row has been fulfilled beyond his highest expectations. The camera then moves back to the hood, which is no longer moving. It is removed and the reporter is dead.

The second memory is of a primordial scene from a nature program, in which a gazelle is singled out of a herd by a pack of wild dogs. Hopelessly cornered and outnumbered, with dogs hanging from most body parts, the gazelle freezes. It then has its chest and belly torn apart and eaten while it stands. A close-up of its head shows a great round terror-filled eye seemingly staring into eternity.

What do these images have to do with General Hospital and the work of the case consultants? I suggest everything. The experience of those interviewed, as expressed by the consultants, is in most ways consistent with waiting in terror for what will happen. They are helpless before the attacking pack (top management and consultants) and experience themselves as frozen in time and space and being torn apart emotionally. They are powerless to act. Their experience of themselves as effective, valued, and loved human beings is being extinguished. They (and by extension the organization), like the reporter and like the gazelle, are helpless and frightened and unable to help themselves or escape. They now seemingly wait to read their name and epitaph on the list of those departed from General Hospital. Being self-destructive and terminating one's job (self) may be preferable for some to passively sitting in their chair waiting for possible annihilation or, as one interviewee put it, pulling the trigger of the gun held to one's head.

These images and those offered by the case consultants underscore what is perhaps the primary underlying theme of the second set of interviews and the unilaterally imposed and threatening change process. The issue raised is around the notion of the fight or flight response to excessive chronic anxiety. The existence of an ongoing and seemingly almost interminably painful and threatening life experience can be expected to promote considerable anxiety and accompanying physiological arousal (more illness is reported) as well as the psychological need to cope with it. Two common responses are to resist and fight back against the source of the threat, or to remove or change it or to flee from it and be rid of it. What seems clear in the case is that the members of the organization, while experiencing themselves to be under attack, are not able to exercise either of these options (fight or flight) and are, in a psychodynamic sense, being torn apart from themselves and each other while they are eaten alive by the situation and their anxieties.

Leaving an organization and finding a new job are highly stressful and usually avoided. Those who have worked for General Hospital for a long time (some since it opened) also feel a sense of loyalty and trust that they will ultimately be taken care of. Some also fear that they cannot find as good a job elsewhere or that they will suffer a major inconvenience in relocating their families. Leaving, therefore, is often not an easy option and is often one that is felt to be a last resort. At the same time, the interviewees are helpless to change, resist, or fight back against what is going on. All the shots are being called at the top, and organization members are seemingly expected to suffer through their disempowerment and the considerable threat to their jobs like good soldiers—silently and obediently. Top management's position is simply that everyone has to adjust to change.

Of equal importance, the question is also raised about those who will survive. They are pitted against their friends and colleagues and win (survive) at their expense. The thought, "If but for the grace of God go I," comes to mind. Thus far, however, there are no survivors, only victims.

The consultants are hard pressed to find what they feel will be effective intervention strategies to change these organizational dynamics. Reading the case provokes feelings of wishing to be able to rescue and heal the staff at General Hospital. Anyone wishing to intervene would have to guard against acting out these fantasies. It seems clear that intervention must occur from a level above Maggiano, such as the President of the university or the governing board. Maggiano and Lewin seem to be well defended by the consultants, the layers of management below them, and their willingness to manage by intimidation. Organization members have been disempowered to such an extent that they are unable to effectively advocate for their interests. The prognosis also seems a bit grim in that even new recruits will be adversely affected by the exceptional nature of the damage to the organization and those who create it every day they come to work.

The Larger Social Implications

Last, Dr. Stein points to the significance of the case in terms of understanding our society at the close of the twentieth century. He asks several questions: "Are the horrors of Nazi Germany and the potential horror of a nuclear holocaust being visited upon the employees of our downsized and reengineered organizations?" "What does a period of national downsizing and reengineering say of our culture, and what does it portend for the future?" "What of the notion of a loyal workforce, when the employer shows no loyalty to anyone?" "What of the notion of devoted workers, when the environment created by downsizing and reengineering creates an individual as well as social paranoia which focuses attention upon oneself and one's survival more than one's work and organization?"

The case thus far raises the question of whether it is possible to kill an organization from the inside out by destroying the spirit of those who work for it. It has long been said that human resources are the greatest asset of an organization. However, they now appear to be the greatest expense and must be cut out. In the process, employees become expendable. One can only wonder what a workforce traumatized in this way will feel in the decades to come.

Part IV

Waiting for the Hammer to Fall

It is now eight months since the first interviews and a year or more since the first consultants were hired and the downsizing was announced by Dr. Maggiano. Many of the trends noted in the introduction to Part III continue. In particular, refilling open positions is still a slow but improved process. When supervisors or managers leave, the positions are now often not requested to be refilled (in anticipation of flattening and reorganization), which for at least one area left forty employees without an immediate supervisor.

The new consulting company has proceeded to go to work and many large committees (thirty to fifty members) with diverse membership have been developed to examine hospital operations. No significant changes have been made as a result of the product of this work; however, as will be observed in the interviews, a general concern has developed that some key people have been excluded from participation in the committees while others, who are less experienced, have been included.

The new Hospital Director and Vice Provost started work in July. Many of the interviews were completed prior to their arrival.

The hospital's census continues to remain low (aver-aging in the low 60-percent range during the summer, which is 10 percent or more below original projections). It is hoped the autumn will bring an influx of admissions. Also worth noting is that actions to improve the census via more aggressive managed care contracting or the development of a network of affiliations has not borne fruit.

Formal communication, often through Signals, has focused on several concerns. Full employee participation in the restructuring process has been stressed. The goals of all of the change has been explained to be the development of a flexible organization that can readily adjust to variations in census, and the creation of a self-managing workforce that seeks continuous improvement (doing the right thing the first time, every time) of hospital operations. Others items discussed have been the need to close wards when volume is low and the development of practice guidelines that reduce utilization of hospital resources and length of stay. The strategic planning process was completed in June. Strategic goals were explained, as well as an operational reorganization process that involves twelve major committees that include a wide assortment of physicians and staff. Managed care contracting progress has been regularly reported. It has also been announced that a formal advertising and marketing initiative will begin and that the medical center campus has been formally separated from the university.

Other events include the loss of physicians in one important clinical program and accompanying media coverage that made it sound like the hospital had lost the entire program, which was not true. Matt Towner left the hospital in June to take a position in another hospital. His responsibilities were reassigned to the four remaining Manager IIIs. Some now have as many as fifteen departments reporting to them. The university also announced that it met its targeted reduction for the first year. One additional aspect of the case is that the local healthcare delivery marketplace continues to consolidate into large networks. The fact that the center has thus far not begun to create its own network or moved to join a developing network is of general concern to many employees who are informed about events in the marketplace.

One other noteworthy event is a story told by Dr. Lewin during a meeting with the management staff of the hospital. He explained that everyone in the room was standing on a train station platform holding three tickets. One would be for the train on which he was leaving; the second would be for leaving the hospital, and the third permitted him or her to stand on the platform a short time before deciding which of the other tickets to choose.

Last, the interviewing process was interrupted for the month of August due to the first author's absence, and a few interviews were completed in September.

The reader is reminded that the first six interviews have been selected as representative of the case in the event all twelve are not read.

Chapter 7

The Third Set of Interviews

VAL KASMAN, JULY 20, 1994

I'm still a Manager III. I'm responsible for a number of ancillary departments, clinical services, and program development. I still report to Jacob. I have about a dozen departments that report to me and around 800 employees. I've just added a number of departments.

I imagine that the scope of my role will expand to cover responsibilities for the matching ambulatory programs for my inpatient services. If you want to really know, I've had absolutely no communication about this issue, which is frustrating. It ticks me off about being involved in the change process. The SPC committees are an exercise in tolerance. There is no information or meaningful involvement.

If we are flattened, I think some who report to me will be laid off. I may lose some administrators. I don't know how it will affect Jacob.

Nothing has been implemented. There is only extreme anxiety, frustration, anger, distrustfulness, and negative attitudes. Two people are being constantly blamed, Maggiano and Lewin. People believe that they don't know what they are doing. They are letting SPC run over the organization.

I feel that our ethical foundation is eroding. People who speak out are told to be quiet. Those who seem to be responding positively are those who are quiet and passive. They are doing and saying what they are told. Speaking out for me is becoming a disservice to me. Independent thoughts are dangerous. You don't question the establishment. Everyone and the physicians see that they aren't playing a role. We know what to do, but our voice isn't being heard. Be quiet or else. I'm not intimidated, but I'm getting very angry about it. I'll do my best even if no one appreciates it. I guess I might take that other ticket and leave.

I have no idea what the changes will be. It's a very scary thing. Everything I do, I have to hope I'm making the right decision. Recently I lost all of my supervisors in a department which has forty staff members. I didn't know whether to recruit or perhaps wait for the possibility of decentralization. I ended up appointing an interim manager.

There haven't been any changes to discuss. Penny Hill, the new Hospital Director, just started. She brings some freshness and will hopefully create a bridge between us and Dr. Lewin, who is still oriented toward ambulatory. She'll serve as a liaison.

I feel overwhelmed and disempowered. I never felt so unable to control most minor things. Every requisition for even a two-day temporary has to be approved by Dr. Lewin. It's so hypocritical. He says he wants to push decision making down into the organization.

I feel good about myself. You know why? It might sound a little cocky, but I feel very confident I know what I'm doing. This process has validated that. I probably should be more cautious about what I say and that doesn't feel good. In one committee a colleague kept speaking out and SPC put in a stronger personality to chair the committee, but he didn't quiet down then either.

My staff are feeling anxious, depressed, frustrated, disempowered, distrustful, and, all in all, pretty rotten. Jacob feels better now. He didn't get the job and life goes on. He seems relieved. He is better than in the past year. He needs to decide if he will stay or leave.

I'm working at least fifty-five to sixty hours per week; it's hard to do any more. I just realized I've lost three weeks of vacation. I hadn't taken any vacation for the past eighteen months. I went last week. I reached my maximum accumulation almost a year ago. I worry about everything else except me. Maybe that's a female thing to do, or maybe I'm just stupid.

I don't see any change at home; I'm still crabby. Yesterday my husband confronted me about taking my attitude out on him. I have been well; just stress-related headaches and backaches which have gotten worse. I used to have them occasionally; now it's every day. I didn't realize how all of this has affected me until I took the week's vacation.

In general, everyone is responding very poorly. I wonder how much damage control could have been done to avoid this. I'm so disgusted. I was optimistic when it started. One of the consultants described our culture here as coercive manipulation.

I have been feeling anxious, angry, left out, and overworked. I feel very supported by Jacob, but not by my colleagues. Communication has been poor but I understand why change is needed.

If I did it again, I wouldn't have brought in SPC for sure. I would have been more honest and direct with our employees, even if I had to tell them things that might distress them. The analogy is to a bad marriage with children. Is it better to keep it together for the children even if there is constant fighting, or is it better to dissolve the marriage? Is the dishonesty of keeping it together worth it. I don't know; I feel manipulated.

The change hasn't been effective. There hasn't been any change. The impacts were not foreseen.

I don't think there is much else to say. The positive side is that this has been a growth experience. It's been interesting and will lead to a book. I had hoped it would be a better organization, but I'm not sure now. I have no confidence it will end up better; the way I had hoped. I thought that we could be efficient and provide patients better quality and user-friendly care. I thought the employees would settle in, but that is not happening. Some good will come of it, perhaps in several years when you look back.

Word Associations

Job	Frustrating
Morale	Low
Efficiency	Pathetic
Cost	Unchanged
Change	Good

The interviewing was a benign experience. It took an hour of my time. It was kind of nice. I had a legitimate chance to unload. My headache is better now.

STAN PITTMAN, JULY 11, 1994

My title and job are still the same. I oversee the development of policies and procedures. I'm a resource to others for professional and personal development. I also function as a change agent. I report to Jacob. My direct reports haven't changed. There is no position control, so it is hard to know how many employees remain. We count paychecks. There are 1,700 to 2,000 left. We have cut about 300 more since the start of the year.

My position will probably be eliminated. This has probably already been decided between Dr. Lewin and the new Assistant Provost. If it isn't, my role will probably be downgraded. Those who report to me are also likely to be eliminated. The cuts have probably already been decided and will probably extend down to the level of Manager II. They want them out.

I have no idea how this will affect Jacob. My department is being taken out of the hospital. Either it hasn't been worked out or it must be none of my business.

There are fewer staff. Acuity levels are as high as in the past and possibly higher. The sense of disempowerment is absolutely remarkable, especially when everyone is speaking of empowerment.

I am in the process of resigning to make way for the new Assistant Provost. I am negotiating my departure package. I am concerned about leaving the department in good shape, no matter how angry I am. We were an outstanding department.

I feel awful about the forthcoming changes. It appears like the individuals [Dr. Maggiano and Dr. Lewin] responsible for all of this are deriving their satisfaction from what is going on. They are getting what the want—one way, my way.

The biggest recent change was the downsizing. Some was inevitable. There is a great amount of anger from the doctors. People are leaving and other good ones are looking to leave. It seems clear no one really cares. Only two people are important [Dr. Maggiano and Dr. Lewin]. Things are very negative and physicians are staying away from the center. It doesn't look like the hospital will be the same quality organization it once was. The best may leave. If you don't like it, you can leave, seems to be the attitude. Others can be hired to replace you.

How am I feeling about my work? It's over. I'm looking either to retire or I will look for another job. I am proud of what I accomplished here. I am ambivalent and very, very angry. It's frustrating. Sometimes I would like to swipe everything off my desk.

Those who report to me are frightened; very, very frightened. They are realizing they had freedom and security and lots of control over their work. They had autonomy, which will be removed. They will lose power. I let each of them use their own style of doing things. They will lose that. We've been together a long time. My departure will be like a death. They will wonder who will protect them now.

Jacob is as frustrated as I am. We have been two allies. We only have each other to talk to. We didn't get the promotions because, we were told, we had too much baggage. The new Director and Assistant Provost, however, have less experience than we do.

I have cut back dramatically on my hours; less than forty per week. I'm depressed, I guess. Hopefully it will change when I get out. I haven't had any health problems. I've actually been feeling a little better.

How others are responding depends on their level. There is lots of uncertainty. Loyalty is falling apart. Staff are concerned about themselves. The low raise didn't help either. They have to handle larger case loads. There is lots of frustration, anger, and disillusionment.

I have been feeling anxious, angry, and left out. Jacob has been very supportive. He is very ethical. There is lots of mickey mousing around and we are having a hard time getting the work done. TQM is a bunch of crap. It slows decision making down. We also went through an exercise of setting goals with our customers in mind. The methodology was something I have used for years, but a consultant had to be hired to direct the work. I don't think there has been adequate communication and I only understand the need for it to some extent.

If it were done again, Dr. Maggiano and Dr. Lewin should have taken the time to find out what is going on here and get to know the organization. There was absolutely no dialogue with those of us who were here before they started making changes. Dr. Lewin sits in lots of meetings, which makes everyone anxious. No one knows why he is there. Its seems like he is evaluating people. No one asked, they just assumed the hospital was bad.

The change has been effective for what they are trying to do. For the betterment of the organization, no. The impacts of making the changes haven't been foreseen. There is a lot of negativism among the staff. The so-called open forums don't provide any real information, and everyone is afraid to ask the tough questions.

Word Associations

Job	Work
Morale	Low
Efficiency	Getting things done
Cost	High
Change	Never ending

The interviewing was comfortable and not threatening. I believed in the confidentiality; I trusted you. The questions were nonthreatening. Hopefully, some good will come of the interviews. I'm happy to think someone will read about what happened here.

JOSEPH GREENE, SEPTEMBER 1, 1994

My title and job are the same, however, my responsibilities and the organization of my department have become confused. The new Assistant Provost may take over my department. She was responsible for my department at her last two institutions. My department might also be divided up based on product lines. I just don't know. I'm not sure what will happen. I do think it has probably already been decided. There is a lot of confusion now about who is on first. I still report to Val. I have one clerical person and two half-time managers who work the other half. I have lost what amounts to 1 FTE of a supervisor. I have 31.2 FTEs and about forty people. This is about the same as before.

We are working to implement self-managing teams. We are making progress. This anticipates the possibility that we will be decentralized and my position as well as the two part-time managers will be cut. I'm also holding open communication meetings and all staff are invited to participate, even those who do not report to me. The new teams report their work during these meetings. No one is talking to me about the reorganization.

It's hard to say what will happen. I'm preparing my department for decentralization and self-direction in the belief that my position may be eliminated. More staff may be cut. The census has been in the low 60-percent range for a number of months. It may go back up in the fall. There has been a shift to ambulatory, same-day surgery, and same-day admissions. I don't think that my department will continue to report to Val. Her position may change too. She may get to stay because she is a woman.

We are moving toward self-managing teams. We are trying to adjust to subtle changes in the organization and the staff reductions. We continue to develop innovative programs, but we don't get any recognition for our work. I think our program is still good for the hospital.

Nothing has occurred yet. I think everything is a prelude to a major change. I feel anxious about the center and that it has lost ground. We keep waiting for a change that will improve things. There haven't been any affiliations; no new directions or stronger managed care contracts.

All the changes have been losses and everyone is grieving. We lost Wirth, Dohrman, and Pittman and some Manager IIIs. It is sad.

I still feel challenged in my work to adapt, but a part of me wonders if I can really do it or do I really want to do it. I am learning to use the computer and doing my own typing now. I feel anxious and have mixed emotions.

My staff are stepping back and just doing their jobs. They are waiting to see what happens and not making waves. So far we have been able to maintain a pretty healthy balance within the staff. They haven't been too much affected by what is happening yet. There is, however, a general attitude of being unsure and depressed.

Those above me are just as confused. I don't know if they will be here. They aren't saying much, but I think that they are running scared. They are also overwhelmed with work.

I'm working more hours. I come in earlier and stay later. I'm probably putting in fifty hours per week now. Outside of work, I am talking more of retiring. Before, I had a strong identification with the hospital, but not anymore. My attitude has changed. I haven't had any recent illnesses.

Everyone here is affected. They are anxious about their jobs; they have no security. They don't know how things will change. They are anxious, apprehensive, depressed, and fearful of the unknown. There is also lots of anger being expressed.

I have been feeling anxious, angry, and left out. I haven't felt unsupported or overworked. There has been lots of communication, but it is all just words. I do understand why change is needed.

We had a good team here that made the place what it was, and I think that they would have been willing to reexamine their process. Now we have three people from the outside, Dr. Lewin, the new Assistant Provost, and the Hospital Director calling all the shots; or perhaps more accurately just Dr. Lewin.

I don't know what the changes are to say whether they have been effective. All I have seen is tearing everything apart. There haven't been any increases in the census or patient satisfaction. We are losing patients and doctors and we don't have any new affiliations. It still remains to be seen if the impacts were foreseen.

Word Associations

Job	Very precarious
Morale	Lower than ever for me
Efficiency	Better
Cost	Reduced
Change	Adapting

The interviewing was good and you were easy to respond to. Trust was built over time and I felt comfortable that the information wasn't going to be used for internal purposes. I identify with the project. It's a nice thing to do to chronicle what has happened here. It was an opportunity of the moment. It has been fun to be a part of it.

BRENDA EARLY, JULY 21, 1994

My title and job are the same, as are my direct reports. I take care of personnel, budget, capital requests, and administration. I still report to Ted Olsen. I have about 62 FTEs, which has not changed recently. We increased by nine a year ago, when they were transferred to my budget and direction.

The new Hospital Director will probably redefine many roles. People in key positions have left or are leaving and the remaining positions in senior management are overloaded. It might be logical to assign some of their work to others, such as me, which I really don't want. During the next two years there will be a lot of reorganization of patient care to develop a patient focus, which is supposed to drive down decision making to the lowest levels. I would get more empowerment to manage my service line. All of these traditional concepts are talked about.

My staff are trying to define the organization structure and reexamine how care is delivered. This may have a lot of impact on people. I'm also trying to cross-train people. The lower skilled people are feeling more vulnerable than those with technical skills. There are pluses and minuses to the change. I'm not sure about how the roles above me will be changed. These roles might be eliminated or end up with less responsibility.

We have been working on cross-training for several months. I have a lot of vacant positions. Things have become stressful in the last few weeks. The doctors are leaving; we have lost several groups, but in one area we have recruited one new doctor and they are as busy as ever. The doctors have low morale, which has impacted the staff and I think quality has suffered. Recruiting is also tough; we don't pay enough and we don't have a reputation now for being a stable employer. People don't want to transfer either, because they don't want to be the last one hired for fear of being laid off.

The result is that we have got a lot of stressed-out people. Some days are worse than others. Everyone has a work overload. We got used to the lower volume and now it is back up. We just got some additional space, which has been a positive sign to the doctors and staff. There are lots of different dynamics going on. Some doctors worry about what is going on and are even perhaps afraid for their jobs.

There was no choice but to make the change. We had to survive. I am hoping that they can respond more quickly. There are lots of old ideas being surfaced, but there is too much talk and no action. It's all group process. I'm a little concerned that the process is moving along too slowly. There is lots of waste and inefficiency that we could be dealing with.

It is interesting that they replaced the Hospital Director. Now it seems that they don't need all the remaining layers. There is no place for Jacob. They probably had to bring neutral people in over Jacob and Stan. The committees get a large cross-section of people on them, which generates some ideas but nothing much has happened. They are skeptical that they are not being told everything. People want to know where the beef is. There is communication, but no one trusts they are being told everything. Sometimes it seems like overkill.

There is not enough time to do my job now. I'm afraid to answer the phone or open my mail for fear of getting another deadline or assignment. I'm not real excited about it. The work is unmanageable. There is a lack of coordination to all of the requests. I don't have time to do my job because it seems like I'm always doing something for someone else. I feel comfortable with myself and who I am. I'm just stressed and I feel bad about all the stuff that is not getting done.

There is lots of paranoia and stress among the staff. People are overly sensitive. Everyone wants it to be them who gets something. Some are very rigid and don't want to change. They overreact. Others are threatened. Their job might be done by others, but some accept things and get on with the work. They work well together as a group, which has helped.

Ted is stressed. I see him less and less because he is so busy, but he is now trying to meet with me regularly. He has a good nature, or maybe he just hides it from us. Dealing with Jacob is difficult. Jacob is a micromanager but not a decision maker. He's intimidating in his approach and can be rude. He lacks an appreciation for what others can contribute. He has no sensitivity to what is going on.

My hours have increased because of the projects. I'm putting in about fifty hours per week and I'm working on some weekends, which I promised myself I wouldn't do. Outside of work I don't get the time to see my friends because I'm too tired. I have been well.

In general, I see a lot of stressed-out people and very low morale. People are very unhappy and frustrated. I feel anxious some days. I have to do a lot more to support myself because my staff can't do it. I'm angry some days, especially when there are deadlines that conflict with each other. I haven't felt left out. I'm too included. I'd like to be forgotten. I'm not intentionally unsupported. My staff just don't have the skills to support me. Ted is supportive though. I have been feeling overworked. There has been overcommunication and I understand why change has been necessary.

Some things have been good. If it were done over, some training should have been optional. I would like to see things happen faster. Lots of people here haven't been through a process like this. I have seen other models where people were assumed to be intelligent and able to think for themselves, which is missing here. My biggest gripe is with the control over filling positions. We are wasting a lot of time by not responding faster. I'm close to not having enough staff. Requests go to a committee that always approves the request, then to Jacob, and eventually to Dr. Lewin. Why do it at all? If we agree on the numbers of staff, why wait?

How has it gone? It depends on the goal. We have saved money. There hasn't been a lot of change. I don't think the impacts of making the changes were foreseen. The cuts were okay, but the control over filling positions wasn't foreseen. Those making the decisions are disconnected from operations. The 2.5 percent raise was devastating. Morale is in the subbasement. Some people are very angry and absenteeism is up. I'm looking for a new job; maybe out of healthcare.

Word Associations

Job	Oh, God
Morale	Bad
Efficiency	Poor
Cost	Controlling
Change	Inevitable

The interviewing was very pleasant, nonthreatening, and open. It was a positive experience.

ED MILLS, JULY 8, 1994

My title, job, and staff haven't changed. I have 64.8 positions, but only 57 are filled. I am in the process of recruiting. I have also had a number of recent resignations. I think they are leaving both because of the situation here and because they have a better offer. I still report to Val.

I have a more active role, especially in multidisciplinary teams and networking. The institution is not bringing in more patients. There is no incremental progress. We have paid our dues at the department level, though. I am really concerned that there is no progress; no motion. We have all but lost our referral base. They are concerned about their jobs due to the lower workload and reorganization.

I'm somewhat concerned about the future. I'm having a great deal of difficulty identifying the role I should play. It has changed from the past, and the future is uncertain. I'm in a transitional state. It is hard to know what I am supposed to be doing. There is insufficient information to know. I am troubled about the organizational changes, the management style, and the attitude from ambulatory. Do we have a fundamental change, or new nomenclature to justify another fiefdom? Dr. Lewin is trying to impose his philosophy on the rest of the organization. We don't know where we are going. Those in ambulatory have been through the program and they are now trying to exercise it over the whole organization. There is a sense of conflict. Five years ago, the hospital was considered to be power hungry and not supportive and now it is the reverse. The whole process is kind of interesting. People are skeptical and suspicious and appropriately so. There has been no educational effort associated with imposing the new philosophy; we are using lots of language and acronyms but not making much change.

They are asking more questions about where we are headed. They read the information that is available, but one thing overshadows everything, and that is the sharper awareness of the lower census, which has recently been in the 50-percent range. Everyone is worried about the downsizing and more reorganization seems to be inevitable. Overall for last year, the census was around 70 percent, which is 6 percent below projected.

Those who report to me are experiencing significant emotional, morale, and stress effects. They are all becoming visible.

The operations improvement and redesign process is new [Phase 3]. There are now many more committees to deal with, regarding clinical resource management. There have been some positive outcomes. The doctors are cooperating and even asking me about information on their use of resources. This is very positive. We can make the organization competitive, but it will take time to see the benefits.

The result is mostly positive. More people are willing to change. The work so far may not translate into immediate change. There are lots of committees at work, which is a good start. It is sometimes hard to act on all of the ideas that are being generated. We need a game plan. We need to know if we are supposed to support primary care in order to figure out how to do it.

We are so fragmented and specialized. Part of us has to reach out for the primary care environment. We also have to support the remote sites. It is hard to see where we will be in a year. There is no game plan in place. Where is the direction? We will have fewer resources, but we are going to have to support new initiatives, goals, and objectives. They are poorly defined. There is nothing to latch onto. We need to know what will be expected. We are behind the curve on marketing. We are playing second fiddle to other area hospitals.

I am only certain that we are going to have to change, but I haven't seen the changes spelled out. Some changes add more questions; like the new Hospital Director—did we need one? The new executive roles have not been publicly defined. I feel uncomfortable, not just for myself but also for my staff who ask questions. We need to know what needs to be done. We are getting some collaboration. We are placing our hope for survival in the hands of the consultants, which makes me a little nervous. They seem to be thinking for us. They write the minutes of our meetings and say things in them I can't recall saying. The consultants are doing the whole thing instead of us taking over the work. People recognize SPC is driving the organization rather than the organization driving SPC. Ideas that are surfaced that the consultants don't approve of are nicely discounted or diffused or redirected. They have a plan and are following it.

I feel reasonably good about the change process. It is inevitable. I am uncomfortable about the process to date; it has not brought in more patients. We don't know where we are going. My peers in other hospitals have already made commitments to a direction. The troops are all over the place and we haven't figured out where the war is.

It is much more stressful than last time. I thought six months ago that we would have the new direction. Now, six to twelve months later, there is no direction regarding our external targets. We are on the right track internally. We need to know where we are going as an institution. What are the programs? Not knowing adds stress to what my department ought to be doing or will be asked to do.

Those who report to me are feeling the same or possibly more so than I am. They are younger and have lots of commitments. Many are asking, "Will I have a job?" Before they wondered about it. Now they ask about it. I try to be reassuring. The open forum a few months ago involved no layoffs, but restructuring. At a recent forum they were less certain and many in the audience were asking about layoffs. Things aren't as good as before. People are reflecting on the situation.

Those above me are feeling the same kind of stress I'm feeling. They are seeing the census drop and dealing with the consultants and the need to cut back costs. Now people come to work the ask about the census. Before they worried about whether they would be able to meet the demand for their services.

I'm working fifty hours per week and I'm taking work home. I'm definitely spending more time on work than before. Meetings are killing me and everyone else. It seems like we are talking to others more about healthcare and reform, the job market, and the economy. All of these things have a real meaning to me now. I haven't had any recent illnesses, but I certainly recognize I am working under more stress.

Everyone is going through a lot of what I am going through. I have been feeling anxious, some anger, and left out, especially regarding the change in the management philosophy. I have no problem with feeling supported. Those above me don't get any better support either. Everyone is getting good at CYA [cover your ass]. We seemed to be much better organized to do it. There are three players: Dohrman, Lewin, and Maggiano. Dohrman doesn't move out of fear of making waves. Lewin is busy talking TQM, but doesn't talk to the department heads. Maggiano is insulated from what is going on by Lewin's position. They aren't getting the job done. Where are the patients? The President of the university is also getting involved talking to people. I don't think he appreciates that the cash cow [the hospital] can no longer subsidize the campus, but he has all of these big plans. I have been feeling overworked. I'm doing more, but I don't see any outcomes. Much of the time, work seems like an exercise in participation.

Regarding communication, good use has been made of available media. I think we did pretty good preparing everyone for change, but there are no details on what we are going to do. I am comfortable with my understanding for the changes. The employees aren't, but they are more informed.

There isn't much I could have done differently. All the decisions were made without my input. I try to work with it and keep the casualties down. The staff understand the need for change. The census keeps on going down. The question is, "Where is the substance?"

Whether the change is a success depends on what they want to accomplish. We prepared ourselves in a positive way to deal with change, but it is hard to see improvement. Most of the impacts of the change were foreseen. There has been good communication, but it comes up short because it lacks specifics. There are no new contracts to bring in patients.

I don't have anything to add. We are all experiencing the same thing. We have to understand it and find a role to become part of the solution.

Word Associations

Job	Mine
Morale	Low
Efficiency	Average
Cost	High
Change	Evolving

My experience of the interviews is that they were informal, at ease, and comfortable. The questions were reasonably probing. I wasn't intimidated.

JACOB DOHRMAN, SEPTEMBER 21, 1994

I'm the Executive I. I'm responsible for the daily operations of the hospital. I now report to Penny Hill. My direct reports are the senior management team of the hospital. We have just about 3,000 FTEs now.

The Executive I role may be diminished relative to the Director's role; her role may be diminished as a result of the way it was defined by Dr. Lewin. This may lead to my role being redefined or eliminated. Also, nursing no longer reports to the hospital's administrator, which is a significant diminishment of my responsibility. The process of organizational redesign may also eliminate the next level of administrators below me, or some might have expanded duties.

Those who report to me feel that, although those leading the organization claim to foster empowerment, just the opposite is happening. They feel disenfranchised.

Penny Hill has been here two days. The greatest change over the past few months is the lack of varied input from multiple sources to best define, understand, and resolve operating problems. They are doing more in isolation. They are inadvertently isolating themselves from information and others on the staff.

Since we spoke last there hasn't been much change; however, significant change appears to be looming on the horizon. It's not defined or being communicated.

There is great frustration at all levels of the organization. They were at a point when some major changes could have been made last fall and that was missed.

This organization is like others. It must foster an environment that accepts change to accommodate constant change. I feel very positive about the early cost-restructuring process a year ago. I'm not sure or comfortable with the process being undertaken now nor the course of action that may be laid out for the next year. In the absence of a Hospital Director, I initiated and directed the initial cost restructuring, which was successful. I haven't been at all involved in planning and implementing the next phase.

I've been thinking about my job. I have concluded, based on past performance and recognition from others other than Dr. Maggiano and Dr. Lewin, that I am prepared, ready, and willing to leave, and I have, in fact, accepted a senior-level management role in another hospital. I am feeling very good about myself; self-confident.

My staff are concerned about their roles and the future of the organization. They feel that they have lost a significant amount of their influence in guiding the organization. They feel very much separated from Dr. Maggiano and Dr. Lewin and ambulatory care administration.

Dr. Maggiano and Dr. Lewin feel good about what they are doing. They believe that now that they are in the driver's seat they will be able to more than surpass past successes and overcome their past inertia in positioning their organization for competing in an already consolidating marketplace.

I'm working about the same—fifty hours. Outside of work I have tended to maintain my close relationships, but I have been discussing the organization and my personal frustrations more frequently. I have been well. I believe everyone is very anxious and frustrated and concerned about their roles and the new management philosophy of Dr. Maggiano and Dr. Lewin. I haven't been feeling anxious. I have been feeling angry and, more recently, left out. I have been provided a lot of latitude regarding operating the hospital, which would seem like I am being supported, but at the same time, Dr. Lewin has not expressed any interest in the hospital and what I do. I haven't felt overworked.

Communication hasn't been adequate. I understand why change is needed in general but not recently. I don't understand much of what is going on now; for example, why certain people have been assigned to key committees. If I had it to do over, I would have relied more on individuals, myself, and the senior management team to support the next phase of change [restructuring] since significant work and operating benefits will be derived.

The changes in the fall were effective and continue for the most part to be thought of as positive. They had a favorable impact on our finances. Since then nothing of significance has changed, although we continue to reduce the number of staff.

The impacts of the early changes were foreseen. We knew morale would be adversely affected and would have to be dealt with over time.

Word Associations

> *Job* Frustrating
> *Morale* Lower

Efficiency	High
Cost	Concerned
Change	Exciting

I enjoyed the meetings and working with the interviewer. I felt positive personal benefit. The interviews provided me a chance to pause and reflect.

MARIA MEYERS, JULY 8, 1994

My title and job are still the same. I serve on a variety of committees and I also do some clinical work—four to eight hours per week. I still report to Antonio. Everyone in the department reports to me. I have nine people and about 7.72 FTEs and some registry staff.

I expect my job to be reabsorbed or eliminated in the redesign. This would terribly affect my staff. They will be angry with the loss of our autonomy. How it affects Antonio will depend on what the restructuring is. I could decrease his work if I report to someone else, or he might end up with even more departments.

We are working on automating our documents for charting, which saves a lot of time. I lost 1 FTE last year and one has recently converted to part-time. I have been able to fill two positions, which is exciting and I feel positive about it.

We have been able to decrease the outpatient waiting list and we are better able to meet inpatient demands as well. We have actually got about an additional 0.5 FTE.

The change has been necessary. I believe it will affect a lot of people. They are willing to do it but change is difficult. Everyone is apprehensive, uncertain, and they don't know how it will impact them. If I lose my job or have it reorganized, I won't like it.

The changes have been necessary. I feel for those affected, but there has been some good too. We are really busy and improving performance has been positive. There is an unbelievable amount of work. I can never get caught up. It's frustrating. I feel overworked, which doesn't feel good. I have got to do it; get it done. I don't communicate how I feel to my staff. I don't complain. They are uncertain. They don't have a grasp of the next process and how it will affect the department. There is communication but no details. They are skeptical. Antonio is frazzled and overworked beyond control.

I've been working forty-five to fifty hours per week; more than in the past. When I am incredibly busy, I take it out more at home. I have been well.

Everyone is skeptical. They feel that they aren't as informed as they could be. Everything is unknown about the redesign. There are lots of rumors. I think they trust that the right decisions are being made and that people care. I have been feeling anxious and overworked but not angry, left out, or unsupported.

Communication has been adequate, but we are not getting all of the details. Information is being withheld. I asked Dr. Maggiano if there would be more cuts. He said no, but I don't believe it. He said they were not anticipating a layoff and they are looking at redesign. They are clever and bright and are just not using the word layoff. They don't know how the organization will look after the change. I understand why change is needed.

What would I have done differently? I'm on the fence on this one. The hospital supports an open-door policy for indigent patients, but it is beginning to cost us. I also think other hospitals are beginning to try to dump on us by rejecting indigent patients. The process is so long and drawn out. I don't know if it could be done quicker, but speeding it up would be a good thing. Getting it over quick reduces uncertainty and the anxiety about what will happen.

The change has been effective. The impacts were foreseen.

Word Associations

Job	Work
Morale	Low
Efficiency	Fair
Cost	High
Change	Good

As an interviewer I think you were here to gather data on a sensitive subject. You were well prepared and easy to talk to.

TED OLSEN, JULY 14, 1994

My title is the same and my job has grown a bit. I have a few additional departments I picked up when Matt Towner left. I have maybe thirty more employees than before. I still report to Jacob.

I see us being folded in with outpatient center administrators. I may pick up some ambulatory responsibilities and they some hospital responsibilities. I may have a reduction in some areas because of the new Assistant Provost.

My staff will report to different people as will different people report to me. I don't see Jacob staying here much longer. I will probably report directly to the new Director.

Matt Towner leaving has been the biggest change. There are a bunch of committees. Nothing is going on that is meaningful to save money.

The clinical resources management initiative is the key. Whatever it can't cut will be accomplished by layoffs. The restructuring will also create layoffs.

So far, the result right now is just attrition. People are choosing to leave. I am aware of others planning on leaving. I'm still here, but still not satisfied and I'm still looking. I recently turned down a great job offer because it didn't fit the needs of my family.

Clinical resources management [Phase 3] is good and will payoff without impacting care. Operations restructuring means cuts. Some will end up leaving that we should have tried to keep. I am less supportive of this initiative. SPC's process is not believable. It's like mental masturbation; busywork. There is lots of talk and no action. Nothing has changed in the last six months. We are talking about stuff that is not meaningful. The committees are too big to do work; forty people many times. They are called together to bless the work of the consultants and decisions made by top management. Just like rubber stamps. I feel manipulated. Soon the talk will be over and people will be cut.

There haven't been any changes. It's been a total waste of time. There is lots of anxiety that we aren't doing anything. There isn't much I do that contributes much. I just hold the ship together. I have more responsibilities, but my effectiveness is way down. Those who report to me feel about the same. They are frustrated and left out. The sad part is that they are getting used to it; feeling unempowered and waiting. They are getting comfortable with it. Jacob is feeling disenchanted, unempowered, and almost certainly looking for a new job.

I'm putting in fifty to fifty-five hours per week. I've fallen back to just doing routine stuff. There is no point in busting my chops. I haven't noticed any changes outside of work. It's not affecting me as much. My health has been okay.

Everyone is feeling about the same. My peers, the few who remain, do talk about it. We are on the same wavelength: frustrated, disempowered, waiting, and anxious. Maybe half of them are looking for new jobs.

At times I feel anxious. I also feel angry, left out, unsupported, and sometimes overworked. Has there been adequate communication? This is a tough question. Yes, because I know what is known is getting communicated because I'm on the communications committee. But really no, because Dr. Maggiano and Dr. Lewin don't know what they are doing. I still understand why change is needed.

If I had to do it again, I wouldn't have hired SPC. I really couldn't affect what happened here. I also function sort of as the conscience of the organization to point out wrong. I would have sent a clear message on everyone's employment status; a message of commitment to our people. Morale would be different. Instead, we have ambiguous answers and employees aren't buying in. They want to know if they will have jobs. We can afford an answer like that. We can retain them and make adjustments through attrition and retraining.

Last year, the layoffs were a wake-up call that we could survive, but the last nine months of doing nothing have been a big mistake. We could have healed up and got on with the work. We waited too long. Good ideas have been put on hold. We needed to let the remaining people know that they are very valuable to us. This didn't happen and the disempowerment is also a problem.

After the cuts, our effectiveness was lost. There hasn't been any change after the cuts. I don't know if the impacts were foreseen. I guess it was adequate. Who could have seen the disempowerment and arrogance?

Word Associations

Job	General Hospital
Morale	Poor
Efficiency	Not here
Cost	Too high
Change	Pluses and minuses

I felt the interviewing was positive. It was a cathartic experience. I trusted you to keep it private.

PEGGY LUBIN, JULY 14, 1994

My title is the same but my job is diminished. I have lost a number of my departments and functions to other areas. I now have less responsibility than when I started seventeen years ago. I still report to Antonio. I have two supervisors and a secretary who report to me. I have 37.5 FTEs, which is down 10.5.

I feel that my entire department will change. Rumors have it that we will move to a satellite-type approach. There are many different models. This will eliminate my role; that's the sense I have. No one seems ready to say it though; Dr. Lewin may be waiting for the new Director. I think they have already made the decision and not told me.

My staff are feeling very anxious, upset, and there are lots of rumors. Antonio was a part of it. I feel I didn't have his support. He is a weak person. The change diminishes his responsibility.

Reduced responsibility is the only change I see. Everything is in transition. I haven't seen the final outcome. They changed the program. They took what they wanted and ignored the rest, and my guess is that it will come back to haunt them. But they may ignore problems anyway. The physicians are very frustrated.

If I could, I'd walk today and never come back; this would be fine with me. I'm beyond feeling angry, I just don't care. They are losing

someone who is very loyal. They don't deserve my loyalty. I feel the
same about the changes that have been made. I feel that there is no
challenge. I'm still busy, but there is no desire to plan or do anything.
I don't think it will change. I think it is best that I leave. I am ap-
proaching them for a buyout. It's not good to have someone around
here with as negative attitude as I have. It all started with my needing
more staff. In return, I was asked to find ways to avoid adding staff.
This led me to believe my department would continue to report to me.
It wasn't fair to my staff. They learned about the change when it was
announced in a meeting in another area of the hospital.

Antonio is a fake. He told me this information was not true, so I told
my staff. Two months later is was true. I lost all of my credibility. Also,
a person from ambulatory was selected to chair a committee I should
have, mainly because these are Lewin's people.

I feel betrayed by Antonio. My staff are feeling betrayed. Some are
feeling as angry as I am. They're very upset. We built everything and it
is now all being torn down. It was like your child. I am being nice to
others and not angry. Every day is difficult. Antonio has no feelings.
He thinks he did good to bring me through this process. Its delusions.
It was easier for him that I leave. I am a strong person and outspoken
and I know a lot of people here including the physicians. I think he
thinks it is a victory, but it really is a total defeat. This restructuring is
out of sequence with the phases of the plan. Others are thinking that if
they can do this to me after so many years, they can do it to them.

I have cut back to thirty-eight to forty hours, never over forty. My family
and friends are concerned about me and what will happen to me. I am
single and alone. I've been on an antidepressant for the past six months.
I have insomnia and I wake up throughout the night. I'm anxious.

Everyone else is very upset and concerned. I just heard another key
person is going to resign. But the people in ambulatory are very happy
these days, and Dr. Lewin consistently shows a preference for them. I've
been feeling anxious, angry, left out, and unsupported, but not overworked.

I don't think communication has been adequate. I don't think they
are telling the whole truth. They tell us what they want us to know.
I'm a party to this and I'm not pleased. I don't agree with what they are
doing. It's change for change's sake.

If it were done over, I wouldn't have hired a new Director or the
Assistant Provost. I would have investigated SPC a lot more. I would
want more input from key personnel. Jacob was not promoted after
fifteen years. General Hospital has always been a family [many family
members work at the hospital]. I wouldn't have made as many changes
as quickly, but some changes should have been made more quickly.
People have lost any sense of security. The physicians are very upset
and some of the top doctors have left. This year we had eighty-five
leave and only fifteen new ones. The word is out. We're not giving out

the right image. I don't think I would have changed anything in my department; nothing is under my control.

I don't think that the change has been effective unless you are looking for destruction. People are starting to wonder what the goal is. Is the goal to destroy this place by running it into the ground and then sell it off? The impacts of making the changes were not foreseen.

Word Associations

Job	Security
Morale	Down
Efficiency	Lost [in a personal sense]
Cost	Up [in terms of the human toll]
Change	Upsetting

At first I was concerned about a breach of confidentiality during the interviews. This is not normally a part of my personality. People are no longer at ease here and they are unwilling to discuss their true feelings. Now I don't care.

CHRIS REGAN, JULY 18, 1994

I'm still a Manager II and I still report to Ted. I'm responsible for fiscal and personnel administration and clinical issues. I oversee a registry and supervise my staff. The only change is that I have a position that I won't be filling any time soon. The shift supervisors report to me, which is new. They used to report to the Assistant Administrator, who now only handles special projects. I have about ninety-five employees and 60 FTEs. There hasn't been a recent change, although I'm down about fourteen positions.

I don't know what changes will be made. I absolutely don't know. There is no need for two administrative positions. I don't know how it will change. Perhaps the new Assistant Provost will have something to say. I might become her direct report.

If they continue to report to me there won't be a change. I don't know though. If there is change and I report to the Assistant Provost, Ted will have less to do. There is also a new Physician Director for my service who has a new vision for it. We have redesigned our work flow to absorb the cuts of eighteen months ago, and we continue to redesign as needed.

Morale is lower. There are peaks in our work that are extremely hard to handle. We are not able to give all the attention we would normally be able to give to patients during these times. There is less time and sensitivity for patients. Some who have subacute conditions have longer waits during peak times.

I don't know about future change. I believe we are doing what other organizations have done, and I've been through this before and I'm not particularly distressed. I hope there is empowerment to make some of the changes we need to make. There hasn't been progress in some areas. I will be pleased to see some changes made.

Other than the workforce reduction and ongoing planning, I'm not sure what changes have been made. The level of activity in TQM and all the committees that have been formed is stimulating, but they take a lot of time, some of which is taken from patient care. I have this feeling all of the major decisions have already been made and that the groups and committees are just meeting to approve the decisions. It seems manipulative. It just doesn't ring true.

I'm just back a week from being out two and a half months for surgery. There is lots to do, but it's not unmanageable. I have to put in longer hours. There are so many things to do relative to all of the committees. If you have a few fires, you get behind. I'm personally feeling wonderful. I'm the only person I can control.

My direct reports feel overwhelmed. They are doing a good job of keeping morale up. They're pretty positive and they support me. However, at the next level down their support is more questionable. They don't feel as threatened as a year ago, but they do feel burdened from the reduced staffing. They see these problems as my causing them. Those above me are probably under more stress than I am. They have lots to do.

I'm working about fifty to fifty-two hours per week. This is more than in the past. I haven't noticed any changes outside of work. I'm very happy. As for my health, I had surgery for a chronic condition.

My staff are adjusting and responding. I think the staff are calling in sick much more often, which is a red flag to me. I haven't been feeling anxious, angry, or unsupported. My direct reports and Ted are very supportive. I haven't felt left out. I'm planning on retiring early next year. I'm feeling pretty neutral, but I would also like to see things through. It depends on how I'm feeling as to whether I feel overworked. I don't feel particularly overworked. I feel managers should work more than forty hours anyway.

I think communication has been adequate. I don't believe it, but it has been adequate. They are doing their best. There is an aura of inauthenticity about it. More decisions have been made than are being communicated. But maybe the decisions shouldn't be communicated. There is so much mistrust between workers and management in the workforce in the United States in general. I also don't think I'm entitled to know, although many of those who are younger think they should. I feel that the change has been necessary.

If it were done over, they should have started sooner. It should have been taken more slowly, say over three or four years. It could have been more gentle that way. So much is going on in a short period of time. I always had the impression, since I arrived five years ago, that we don't know where we are going or what we want to be. There is too much fragmentation. There is no coordination or focus.

The change has been effective in terms of fiscal management and lowering costs. We still aren't in tune with the market; our volume hasn't gone back up. We haven't done anything except pursue managed care contracting. I don't think the impacts were foreseen. Most anticipated what would happen when you work with less.

Word Associations

Job	Work
Morale	Low
Efficiency	Adequate
Cost	High
Change	Good

The interviewing was interesting, low key, and comfortable.

JERI GLOVER, JULY 18, 1994

I'm still a Manager III and my job is the same. I recently added a new department to my responsibilities. I report to Dr. Lewin and now the Manager III of ambulatory. I have about eight direct reports, two staff, and 300 FTEs under my direction.

A lot is changing, but I don't know what it is. I haven't seen or heard anything. How it affects my staff depends on whether they report to me or someone else. I expect I might report back to the new Hospital Director, at least until the reorganization. I'll still report to ambulatory for outpatient.

I have had additional departments added, which is to my liking. I haven't seen much else. The result is that, after the cuts last October, we have been expected to wait, which is frustrating. We waited for the new consultants and we are now waiting for the new process. Some areas did small changes. People are learning to tolerate whatever they've got, because we thought we knew we were supposed to wait. It seems like an unspoken expectation to wait. We were then asked by Jacob why we were waiting. If we had ideas for improvement, we were supposed to act. That was two months ago and no one has really done anything. Given the information we have about the consultants and the change process, it still seems like we should wait so that we are coordinated when we act.

As an organization we need to make some significant changes. I don't know if significant is the right word, but it will be hard to do. We'll be better off in the future for it. It's hard to go through change and hard to move everyone along.

Since October, we have had a waiting period. Everything since October has been minor. We have learned to live with what we've got. We know more is to come, but nothing has happened. We should have used the momentum we had after October to move ahead. Now I can't see how we are going to reinvigorate our people to change. There are no comments on presentations in meetings. There is only apathy. No one wants to participate; we waited too long. The public forums are not well attended and people don't ask as many questions. All people seem to care about is their job and whether they will keep it. Most managers are not participating in the new consulting company's phases of work. No one knows what is going on. There is apathy and fear.

I would like to take the summer off. Baring that, work is going well. I'm happy to have acquired clinical responsibility. I'm okay too. Not knowing what will happen when the new Director and Assistant Provost arrive makes me anxious. I don't know how well I will or won't fit into their style of doing things.

Those who report to me are moving ahead. They continue to plod along. They are anxious and want to participate more. They know as much as I do.

I never see Dr. Lewin. Jacob is anxious; he has a new boss. I'm sure he must be disappointed and nervous. Neither Dr. Lewin, Jacob, or the manager of ambulatory show their feelings. This tends to block the discussion of feelings in the hospital, but the ambulatory manager holds open meetings where people can and do express their feelings. I think Jacob's management style is inconsistent with where they want to go.

I'm working about fifty hours per week, which is no real change. I haven't noticed any changes outside of work. I banged up my knee several times recently. I guess I'm accident prone.

I see more people leaving or at least looking. In a way, I think that by dragging our heels on refilling positions, employees have come to see us as unable to act. The question for them is, "When is enough, enough?" The delays have impacted them so negatively. There is such a contrast between talking about empowering people and having to fill out forms ten times.

I have been feeling anxious and left out. I haven't felt angry, unsupported, or overworked. Communication has been inadequate, but I still understand why change is needed.

If I did it over, I would have done a couple of things differently. I would have started Phase 2 sooner. The current hospital management style is not conducive to the process. How we have managed ourselves in the past won't work. In the past, some were participative and some weren't. We need a transition to get to the new program. We can't seem to get TQM going. We need training on how to manage in the new system; how to operate in support of the new process.

The change has been effective from the point of view of keeping expenses down and not letting them creep back up. It has been ineffective as it relates to the organization's health. We aren't as healthy as we were. People are afraid and anxious.

The impacts of the changes were foreseen but they weren't addressed. For example, we knew we should do some work on grieving for those who remained and we didn't do anything. I wish we could get things over with and move ahead. We keep waiting for direction.

Word Associations

Job	Keep
Morale	Tentative
Efficiency	Needed
Cost	Keep
Change	Coming

The interviewing was a good process. The warm-up before the questions was good. There was trust that my opinions would not be shared.

ANTONIO LOZANO, SEPTEMBER 19, 1994

My title hasn't changed. I'm still one of the survivors. I have more responsibility now because people left. I also now report to the Manager of ambulatory and the new Hospital Director. My new ambulatory responsibilities are providing new things to learn. I have two new direct reports and a total of about 300 employees I am responsible for.

It is a little clearer what will happen. It's close to getting better in terms of what we understand about our positions. We are moving toward product lines, although I'm not sure how it will affect my role. I'm not concerned anymore. There isn't much I can do about it.

In time there will be more change, but I can't tell to what degree. Cutting down the barriers to horizontal communication will cut down on the amount of communication that has to flow up to senior levels of management, which will mean that they have less to deal with.

One recent change is that Jacob left. I frankly feel better now, because he could be controlling and not always respectful of me, which seemed to get worse with time. I now sit in on meetings with ambulatory staff, and the center looks like it may merge with another local hospital.

The result is that I'm more relaxed now and more positive, although everyone doesn't share my opinion. There is too much rigidity among some, but I'm feeling much better able to adjust to change now. In the center, employees are nervous. They wonder how the changes will affect them. They have yet to get used to change.

I don't exactly know what they will be, but I think that they will have a positive impact. There is a willingness to try something and a willingness to listen. We aren't waiting to be told what to do now and we have some input. I am less afraid of change because I'm part of it, although this may be a naive attitude. I think my career will now move forward. The effect so far is positive. Change was necessary.

I feel good about my work. We are cutting unnecessary tasks and simplifying work. The new Director has an attitude of "Let's make it happen." My staff are apprehensive. They are tending to see it as more positive, but they are also concerned about more change. Some people are coming to terms with change or leaving. Those above me have a lot of work ahead of them. They are making progress.

I'm working fifty-five hours per week, which hasn't changed. I do think that I am more productive now. I'm getting focused and there are fewer crises. I'm doing much better outside of work. I'm more positive now. I have been well.

Everyone has a wait-and-see attitude. They are being cautious. They understand what is happening, but some are still resistant.

I have been feeling anxious to a more normal degree; there is less stress. I haven't been feeling angry, left out, unsupported, or over-worked. We learned from a survey that only about two-thirds of the department heads have communicated with their employees, which is disappointing. We are not answering the question, "What will happen to me?" I still understand why the changes are needed.

I have no real regrets. I wouldn't have done anything differently. It's somewhat early to tell about the effects. I'm optimistic, including whether the impacts were foreseen.

Word Associations

Job	Security
Morale	Mine is improved, that in the center needs improvement
Efficiency	Getting better
Cost	Still an issue
Change	Rapid

You were a good listener, patient, and willing to let the conversation go off on tangents. You were respectful.

Chapter 8

Case Interpretations
and Overview

The interviews in Chapter 7 underscored the negative effects of the trends described in Part III. Staff morale is very low and there now exists clear evidence of disillusionment and distrust of the leadership of General Hospital.

INTERPRETATION BY HOWELL BAUM

Themes

Much at the hospital is the same, only worse. It hardly seems to bear noting. Top managers tell subordinates little about their intentions or actions. Staff continue to worry about cuts and bemoan low morale. People feel powerless, anxious, suspicious, angry, and betrayed. And on and on it goes.

And yet there are differences—developments, though decidedly negative ones. Jeri Glover notes that staff do not discuss their feelings about what has happened and what they fear. The tone of these interviews is more subdued than in the past. People say they are waiting to see what will happen. One might call it the calm before the storm, but it is more like the calm in the eye of the storm. People have been shaken terribly already, and the death-like calm only gives them time to worry about the inescapable devastation coming next.

Staff members have described others or themselves as depressed before, but more seem depressed now. The flatter affect of many interviews does not mean people are apathetic. Rather, people do not discuss their feelings with others or with themselves because they cannot: Some feelings are so frightening, people keep them unconscious, out of their awareness. Fearing getting cut, they may be terrified, they may be enraged, and they may want to cut—kill—those who threaten them.

These are scary feelings. They can seem unmanageable. How could someone do his job if he kept thinking about killing his boss? It is only a fantasy, though newspapers periodically report revenge shooting sprees by fired workers. With these impulses, it would be better to keep quiet, not risking even dangerous words; and, better yet, to repress even the thought of attacking.

But these feelings do not go away. Judy Harris and Joseph Greene offer two typical examples. Asked if she has been feeling angry, Harris says, "It's over. Every so often I am indifferent. What good does it do? I try to keep focused on facilitating change. Let's get on with it." But a moment later, asked if she has any concluding comments, she remarks, "I'm a little angry today. I want to be indifferent, but I have been so committed to the hospital." She is angry. She tries to be "indifferent"— to suppress her feelings—but she cannot.

Asked how he is feeling about his work and himself, Greene says he feels "anxious and have mixed emotions." He catalogs the mixed emotions when describing others: "They are anxious, apprehensive, depressed, and fearful of the unknown. There is also lots of anger being expressed." Two of the most definitely mixed, conflicting emotions on this list are anger and fear: going on the attack and holding back from fear. The real fear of getting fired takes on many unconscious meanings, including retribution for any aggressive action. It would be safer to lie low and try to repress all feelings. And yet Greene notes that having these mixed emotions makes people anxious. They cannot avoid worrying, not only about being fired, but also about being punished for being angry. We will look in a moment at what happens to the feelings that will not go away.

Significance and Hypotheses

In these interviews, there is a striking change in people's language. Earlier, staff talked about organizational structure and patient care, drawing as they could on conceptual frameworks to make sense of things. When describing their jobs and interests, some made use of theoretical language. They talked about their work in a way that mixed concrete and abstract. Those who complained that people were losing sight of a big picture asserted the importance of seeing the particulars in a larger perspective.

Now, people's mental maps are constricted; they speak more and more about mainly themselves. Still more, they talk about survival. But their metaphors have changed. As before, perhaps because they work in a hospital, perhaps because it performs organ transplants, they speak in bodily language. But now they do so more frequently and desperately.

Bob Ryder observes, "If the department goes down or if my position is cut, two people get screwed." But, "If this is what they want, screw them." "People," he notes, "are pissed." Tom Frey, asked at the end how he experienced the interviews, explains, "By the second interview I was pissed off and frustrated and more open. Now I'm so pissed off, I don't care, and I'm really open." Ted Olsen criticizes the consultant's process in these words: "It's like mental masturbation. . . . I feel manipulated." Stan Pittman, referring to a different organ, says Total Quality Management "is a bunch of crap."

Several points about this language are important. One is that these everyday phrases, about getting screwed or being pissed off, for example, are not just expressions. Unconsciously, people experience them literally. A metaphorical bunch of crap is really a bunch of crap. People mean exactly what they say.

At the same time, these particularly aggressive bodily expressions reflect staff members' growing concerns about literal bodily integrity. Peggy Lubin takes antidepressants, but she still has trouble sleeping, and Frey wakes up anxious. Val Kasman has headaches and backaches. After mentioning a coworker who had a heart attack, Frey explains that he himself "recently collapsed in a restaurant. I've been vomiting, and my back has hurt."

Chris Regan notes that staff are calling in sick more often. She mentions she recently had surgery. Her condition was chronic and one might wonder why she had surgery now. Perhaps, besides making medical sense, it was a convenient way to get out of the bad work situation. Perhaps, mixing metaphor and reality, it would make it easier for her to walk out. Perhaps it is a way of using sick leave to prepare for the retirement she plans for next year. Perhaps the situation brought to a focus for her, as for others, concerns about bodily integrity.

Glover has health problems that force a question that might be asked of many of these others. "I banged up my knee several times recently," she reports, "I guess I'm accident prone." Some of us have friends who are so accident prone, we cannot help thinking they bring their "accidents" on themselves. To put this differently, unconsciously, people may intentionally injure themselves. One motive may be to get others' sympathy.

Another, which may go with the first, is to stay or get out of situations that arouse anxiety. For example, someone who is uncertain whether he (or she) can do enough to keep his job might unconsciously get sick or injure himself so that he could blame any failure on his bad health, not his job performance. It is hard to forget that Doug Lofgren hurt his back at home. Or someone who is angry at bosses that talk about cutting jobs, who wants to hurt them, but who unconsciously fears they will punish him for any aggression against them could unconsciously retreat from the situation by getting sick or hurt—both conditions calling for sympathy rather than retaliation.

Finally, there is a variation of this last possibility, one psychoanalysts call "identifying with the aggressor." A worker who feels powerless to protect his job against the decisions of distant bosses might unconsciously turn that helpless passive experience into an imaginary active one by identifying with the bosses and doing what they would do—hurt him. By taking their place in fantasy (by doing their dirty work for them) he inflicts damage on himself (in this case, bodily injury rather than firing), but he has the unconscious satisfaction, dubious as it is, of being in charge of his fate. And, perhaps, in this magical thinking, an "accident" is enough of a "gift" to the bosses to persuade them, after that suffering, not to cut his job.

In other words, many health problems are more than "simply a result of stress." They involve complicated unconscious psychological dynamics. And that is one place where, to return to the earlier question of what can happen to repressed anger at bosses, aggressive feelings can end up. When people feel angry but powerless to act angrily toward others, they may end up turning their anger against themselves in some of these ways. Thus, beneath the overt calm can lie a stormy depression.

Another observation about staff members' bodily language is important. Earlier, bodily metaphors, especially those of "cutting," seemed to refer to castration. In other words, unconsciously people seemed anxious that organizational downsizing would affect their ability to engage in genital activity. In the latest interviews, Julie Nugent implies the top managers are still sexually active. She describes the new Vice Provost in ways evoking stereotyped images of relations between doctors and nurses: "She is young and attractive. There is the belief that Dr. Lewin likes to hire sweet, petite, attractive, and young women who are bright. She commented on this when I had a chance to talk with her. She knows she is young and attractive. . . . Dr. Lewin is a charming, intelligent, and warm person."

In contrast with such a liaison, the "screwing" that Ryder talks about is a one-directional loveless assault. "Mental masturbation" is two steps removed from sexual intercourse. Getting "pissed off" is only a show of bravado, usually by someone not ready for sexual relations. These are successively less mature forms of development.

Finally, there is the "bunch of crap." Developmentally, children begin with a focus on eating and the mouth; psychologically, they are concerned about whether they can trust the world. When they are satisfied the world is trustworthy, they can take part in toilet training, with bodily concerns about excretion and mental concerns about whether they can act autonomously. Crap, it should be clear, is a subject of great interest at this stage. Normally, children move on to become aware of their genitals, to examine and display them, and to be concerned whether they have the power to take initiative. If reassured, adolescents move toward mutual sexual activity and concerns about intimacy, followed by the various turns of adulthood.

Thus, in normal development, a child who at one time is concerned about feces goes on to take an interest in sexual relations. Alternatively, if at some moment an adult finds sexual activity frightening, he may "retreat" to an earlier, more satisfying, safer stage and set of concerns, such as urinating or defecating. This is what psychologists call "regression." This appears to be what many hospital staff, individually and collectively, have done. Unconsciously, anxiety about genitality seems to have driven them back to interests in defecation. "Crap" is only one of many such references. "Everyone," Ed Mills reports, "is getting good at CYA [cover your ass]."

Staff still speak of jobs being "cut," but increasingly they use a new bodily metaphor in these interviews: "elimination" of jobs. Harris, Cynthia Winston, Maria Meyers, Pittman, Lubin, Greene, and Rosetta Shelton all speak of their position being "eliminated." Meyers, who seems especially concerned about linguistic precision, clarifies that she expects her "job to be reabsorbed or eliminated." Those are the decisions made in the bowels.

It is unclear whether elimination is a new euphemism promulgated by top management or the consultants, or whether it was subordinates' formulation, but its widespread use indicates it has meaning for staff. The word has many connotations. Whether in the human body or in complex organizations, what is eliminated is worthless waste. Meyers conjures up a vivid image of being digested matter in the hospital's bowels, waiting for the brain (certainly not the heart) to decide whether to reabsorb it or eliminate it as dregs. It goes without saying that the image is degrading; it is also one of complete passivity. It is virtually impossible for people who imagine themselves so shamefully to act.

If one thinks about hospital staff, their language, and associated unconscious concerns in a developmental framework, one might speculate more frustration will push people even further in a regressive direction; back toward being concerned about food, thinking about situations in mouth-like language, and worrying whether anyone can be trusted. In fact, from the start, a reality in which people withheld information and lied contributed to reasonable mistrust. At this point, mistrust seems rampant, spreading from those who were found to mislead to others who are regarded with suspicion as a matter of course. One indicator is how people thought about the interviewer, initially a stranger to all.

An interviewer who is a stranger inevitably arouses fantasies about his motives; fantasies built on workers' experiences, memories, and unconscious assumptions about people who have authority, ask questions, and so forth. Some workers see this stranger as an enemy to be thwarted; others see him as an ally who can publish and validate their merits. What is striking in the hospital is how many begin with negative assumptions about the interviewer (Baum, 1994).

Their answers to his question about how they had experienced him and the interviewing process reveal how their experience of organizational restructuring has led them to think about people in general. "I wasn't intimidated," Mills insists. "Not threatening," Pittman says. Why should they be? What assumption about human nature even raises the question of intimidation and threat?

Harris speaks for many when she says, "It was scary, it is hard to trust." Ryder explains, "I wondered if I could trust you. I didn't know if you were really doing it for them." Lofgren elaborates, "At first, I didn't know whether to trust you. I was concerned that you would report what I said." Lubin notes her surprise at her own, similar reaction: "At first, I was concerned about a breach of confidentiality. . . . This is not normally a part of my personality. People are no longer at ease here, and they are unwilling to discuss their true feelings."

In other words, though most interviewees say they came to trust the interviewer, even to see him as an ally in telling their story, they talk about how recent experiences in the hospital had led them to assume the broader world was untrustworthy. This is different from simply becoming cynical about individual top managers, and it more deeply contaminates relations with others.

Harris says it all, simply: With things as they are in the hospital, it is hard to have faith in anything anymore, and without faith, life itself is in jeopardy. What is so touching about what she says—what is so piercing about her implicit accusation—is the association with childhood upbringing. It is something deep inside children in their families.

In an earlier interview, Shelton said changes in the hospital were like losing a child. Now Lubin echoes her: "We built everything, and it is now all being torn down. It was like your child." She says the hospital "has always been a family [but] . . . people have lost any sense of security."

Kasman—and it should be clear it is the women who speak this way—goes on to ask a decisive, troubling question about the health of this family. She begins as Harris did: "I feel that our ethical foundation is eroding." Then, asked what she would have done differently in reorganizing the hospital, she declares, "I would have been more honest and direct with our employees, even if I had to tell them things that might distress them. The analogy is to a bad marriage with children. Is it better to keep it together for the children even if there is constant fighting, or is it better to dissolve the marriage? Is the dishonesty of keeping it together worth it?" Her analogy is not fully clear. Staff in this case, not programs, seem to be the children, but it is uncertain who is married to whom. Still, her comments have two important meanings.

First, as others who talk about family and children, she speaks metaphorically of unconscious issues. Language of "elimination" reflects regression from adult mental concerns to those of childhood. Anxiety about trust suggests some have moments when they are no more secure than infants. Yet finally, "family" talk raises questions whether the hospital can support life at any level. Harris implicitly passes judgment when she seems to associate the changes with a baby: "The nine months of limbo have not been good." What good is a body that can eliminate waste but not bear children? And how must workers feel who think of themselves as stillborn?

In addition, Kasman's remarks must be taken, as they were meant, as a question whether, to put it bluntly, the hospital can be saved as a healing institution or whether it should be closed down. There is no reason to doubt David Maggiano and Arch Lewin mean to keep the hospital in business. Their strategic concern has been how to do that. Instead, staff ask what the hospital can be maintained for and whether the accumulating human as well as economic costs justify further effort.

This is an awkward moment for us to take leave of the hospital, because Maggiano and Lewin have not implemented the restructuring they promise. Perhaps, as they wish, they will keep the hospital solvent and staff morale will eventually improve. In the absence of information from them, these interviews give no basis for speculating on the hospital's financial future. Regarding morale, these interviews only confirm the earlier negative prognosis.

Assessment and Suggestions

At this point, it is hard to imagine consultation to either Maggiano and Lewin, who seem ensconced behind thick castle walls, or subordinate staff, who seem incapable of collective action in their staff roles. Perhaps organizational reforms will provide a new foundation for re-creating the hospital, but no quick or easy improvement is likely. For those who can leave, this is a good time to go.

What these interviews show most clearly is how organizational change that does not involve participation of staff members can have harmful personal, psychological, consequences that will cripple virtually any structural design. To say this is not to prescribe any specific method for staff participation, nor does it assume participatory planning will inevitably lead to consensus and avoid hard or controversial decisions. But this hospital presents a graphic, irrefutable case for planning with the intelligence and authority of staff of all kinds, as well as patients and community stakeholders. The personal and organizational costs of top-down restructuring are manifest everywhere.

Whatever one may think about Maggiano or Lewin, this is not a simple story about villainous top managers. It describes what happens when a handful of people think they know enough on their own to change a large institution, when they conceive of an organization as consisting of abstract roles rather than people, when they assume an adversarial relationship with subordinates, and when they react defensively to criticism. Organizational change is not just change of an organization; to be effective, it must also be change by the organization. That recognition may be humbling to top managers, but it should also encourage them: No one is in it alone.

INTERPRETATION BY MICHAEL DIAMOND

Themes

Persistent Stress and Uncertainty at General Hospital The medical center and hospital are in critical condition and without intensive care. At this time, it is unclear whether the organization can be psychologically repaired or structurally and functionally reintegrated. General Hospital employees are working under severely stressful conditions.

These conditions produce psychologically regressive behavior that manifests itself in overly simplified forms of thinking and fantasizing. Psychodynamic processes of splitting and projective identification emerge, thereby causing fragmentation of interpersonal relationships, which become categorized into polarized opposites such as "good and bad," "accepting and rejecting," or "allies and enemies." Feeling psychologically distraught and hopeless, hospital employees unwittingly produce an unconscious, intersubjective structure of working relations—embodied in the organizational identity.

The nature of this common identity (or identification) is based on the pattern of shared emotional attachments of members to the organization, and the unconscious meaning of this attachment. In the case of General Hospital, the emotional bond has become fragile and riddled with anger and disappointments. Hence, work dysfunction and operational paralysis may be around the corner and, to some extent, seems already to have occurred. For example, one manager claims, "There are increased patient complaints. Response time is down. They [staff] are described [by patients] as angry and ugly. They are wondering about how they can continue to deliver good care. . . . We are already pretty flat here." Thus, it is unclear whether General Hospital can return to the reparative mission of providing quality healthcare to the community.

Hospital physicians, nurses, and staff below Dohrman's position (as evidenced in the interviews) are feeling victimized and under constant attack. Their anxieties, stemming from uncertainties, excessive ambiguities, and lack of clarity, are high. Relationships between and among staff, within and across divisional boundaries, are strained and emotionally loaded. Survivor guilt, as noted in the last interpretive response, persists. Workers feel bad about themselves and share a malignant, negative identification with their employer, General Hospital. The organizational structure of accountability is in flux and unclear. Many employees either do not know to whom they report or have inherited a new manager or, in the case of managers, have been given new sections of responsibility. Feelings of mistrust and paranoia are the norm rather than the exception.

Ineffective Leadership: Contradictory Theories in Use   The leadership at the medical center and hospital is in serious trouble. Maggiano and Lewin continue to espouse the philosophy of participation and self-managed work teams. Hospital managers and staff, interviewed after eight months of transition, consistently report that Maggiano, Lewin, and Dohrman, collectively manage in a top-down fashion. This contradiction infuriates employees and aggravates the aggression and hostility many of them feel toward Maggiano and, in particular, Lewin.

Lewin has not been well thought of, and this certainly jeopardizes his ability to lead. For example, one section head, referring to Lewin's hiring of a new Vice Provost, stated, "There is the belief that Dr. Lewin likes to hire sweet, petite, attractive, and young women who are bright."

Lewin was generally mistrusted and disrespected from the beginning of his tenure as Assistant Provost for Health Services. There is no evidence from the interviews that he has gained much respect since that time. In many instances, the level of resentment toward him has accelerated. His superior, Maggiano, seems unaware of this factor and the reasons that employees in general are demoralized and uncommitted. In fact, in order to more deeply appreciate the nature of ineffective leadership at General Hospital, I would need to interview and observe Maggiano and Lewin. Leadership performance is evaluated on the basis of their actions as reported in the interviews and, thus, interpreted by the organizational identity they have created.

General Hospital as Paranoid Organization   Brenda Early, reporting on how workers feel who report to her, observed, "There is lots of paranoia and stress among the staff. People are overly sensitive. Everyone wants it to be them who gets something. Some are very rigid and don't want to change. They overreact. Others are threatened. Their job might be done by others, but some accept things and get on with the work. They work well together as a group, which has helped."

Some employees can work, but a "psychology of comparison" and the concomitant "zero-sum" thinking is contagious under the stressful circumstances. At General Hospital, psychological defenses among hospital management and staff are often stretched to their limits; horizontal management among departments and between managers is breaking down. The same administrator describes her relationship to Dohrman as "difficult." She states, "Jacob is a micromanager but not a decision maker. He's intimidating in his approach and can be rude. He lacks an appreciation for what others can contribute. He has no sensitivity to what is going on." Consistent with other accounts, it appears that Dohrman mirrors the style and attitude of his superiors, Lewin and Maggiano.

One basic feature of a paranoid organization is what Bion (1959) called a fight–flight basic assumption culture. At General Hospital, leadership is more than simply ineffective; it is deeply mistrusted and disrespected. Speaking of Maggiano, one interviewee said, "Information is being withheld. I asked Dr. Maggiano if there would be more cuts. He said no, but I don't believe it. He said they were not anticipating a layoff and they are looking at redesign. They are clever and bright and are just not using the word layoff. They don't know how the organization will look after the change."

Regardless of whether this is true, the leadership (Maggiano and Lewin) is leaving much to the imagination of the employees and thus increasing their anxieties and insecurities. Consequently, hospital workers feel persecuted and victimized, which produces primitive psychological defenses (as noted earlier) of splitting and projective identification among them and a paranoid organizational mind driven by a collective fight–flight mentality.

The use of war and battle metaphors, for example, signifies fight–flight basic assumptions and, hence, deeper feelings of being under attack and in search of leadership to command the troops (hospital management and staff) in targeting the enemy (Lewin and Maggiano) to fight against or flee from. Psychological forces of splitting and projective identification have polarized the organization vertically and rendered effective leadership implausible.

For example, speaking of the lack of policy and leadership from above, one manager says, "We need a game plan. We need to know if we are supposed to support primary care in order to figure out how to do it. We are so fragmented and specialized. . . . We don't know where we are going. My peers in other hospitals have already made commitments to a direction. The troops are all over the place and we haven't figured out where the war is."

Hospital management and staff mistrust and disrespect the second consulting firm. SPC and the executive leadership (Maggiano and Lewin) have merged and seem to mirror each other in practice and in the minds of hospital workers. They are identified as one and the same. Similar to Maggiano and Lewin, SPC says one thing and does another. Or as one interviewee put it, "The behavior you see is not congruent with the talk." Speaking of the consultants, one interviewee said, "Outsiders turn off people, especially SPC." Consider the "inside–outside" split and paranoia represented in this employee's comments.

The persecuted (psychological and cultural) interior of General Hospital, as represented by hospital management and staff holds onto whatever remains of good it can muster and externalizes and identifies the bad object world with SPC, Maggiano, and Lewin. Outsiders are feared and deeply mistrusted based on recent experience. Nevertheless, infiltration continues and SPC tries to manage the change effort in a fashion mirroring the leadership style of Maggiano and Lewin. The consultants seem uninformed of the transferential nature of their twinship merger with the two executives.

Evidence of mirroring may be observed in this interviewee's comments about SPC: "We are placing our hope for survival in the hands of the consultants, which makes me a little nervous. They seem to be thinking for us. They write minutes of our meetings and say things in them I can't recall saying. The consultants are doing the whole thing instead of us taking over the work. People recognize SPC is driving the organization rather than the organization driving SPC." The client here seems to know more about effective consulting than SPC. The same employee continues, "Ideas that are surfaced that the consultants don't approve of are nicely discounted or diffused or redirected. They have a plan and are following it." No wonder people are paranoid. It sounds as if the plan itself is undiscussable. Moreover, the process directed by SPC does not seem to encourage open feedback and advocacy. It is a top-down, unilateral, imposed change rather than a change based on collaborative problem solving and team building. The leadership of General Hospital and their consultants have colluded in a deceptive and contradictory process of institutional change which will erode the assumed legitimacy of their mutual authority.

Insufficient Attention to Systemic Learning and Group Dynamics   There is little to no evidence of executive openness to feedback or a willingness to engage in double-loop organizational learning at General Hospital. Maggiano and Lewin do not seem to question their own assumptions and attributions about themselves, others, and the management of change. Furthermore, there is no evidence that they genuinely encourage constructive advocacy for the sake of inquiry among their management teams and staff. There has been no apparent willingness to tap the expertise of their own organization, nor promote a good dialectic. That is, they have not taken advantage of the practical and experiential reflective knowledge of the employees. Doing so might suggest they test their own assumptions (and those of the consultants) about the best route to effective change at General Hospital.

Moreover, there is no evidence of serious group process facilitation among the committees with assigned tasks. No consultants or facilitators are engaged with the groups in helping to produce openness and genuine dialogue that is then shared with the executives in feedback sessions. Contrary to what the executives appear to assume, hospital management and staff participants are attentive and thoughtful. They view these groups as ineffective and ingenuine efforts on the part of the executives to promote participation. This further aggravates mistrust and disrespect between the executives and the hospital employees. One interviewee observes,

There are a lot of committees that don't seem to be coordinated. Each person has his or her own agenda to work. There doesn't seem to be much progress. The people organizing meetings don't seem to know the direction that they should be headed in. There is a lack of focus on issues that need to be worked. In one committee there were a number of good ideas put on the table but the ideas were lost when the physicians on the committee did not want to set policy for their colleagues. Many physicians said they were too busy to participate.

This group needed serious process consultation and did not get it. Committees lack effective facilitation and clear direction in the form of clearly stated goals, tasks, and explicit time frames for completion.

While the new consultants have produced working committees to examine hospital operations, no changes or tangible outputs have resulted from their efforts. In fact, many hospital workers are quite skeptical of the work groups. Some workers question the rationale for selection of committee members that excludes "essential" people. Others observe that group members avoid addressing difficult issues and are afraid to speak out, fearing retribution or termination of their jobs.

Job security remains an issue in the hearts and minds of hospital employees. As one interviewee stated, "They fear that their jobs are in jeopardy. . . . Everyone is feeling a bit paranoid." The expression of persecutory and paranoid anxieties among hospital workers is striking. General Hospital is a system incapable of learning, particularly when it challenges the authority and "superiority" of Maggiano and Lewin.

Breaking the Psychological Contract   Individual self-esteem is predicated on the degree to which one's self-image moves toward meeting the typically unreachable expectation of the ego ideal, or how one views oneself at one's future best. The degree to which narcissism influences one's personality will also affect the grandiosity or self-effacing quality of the individual ego ideal. At work, individuals make a psychological contract with their employers. This contract is oftentimes unconscious. However, it is a primary motivating factor within the self, predicated on the opportunity to acquire the goal of the ego ideal—the mind's acquisition of one's idealized self.

At General Hospital, the employees' ego ideals are under attack and, in some instances, they are damaged as a result of the employer's violation of the psychological contract. That is, employees are feeling betrayed. Job security has been taken away. Career advancement seems all but eliminated. Acknowledgment of high-quality work and reinforcement of workers' talents and skills, which is central to self-esteem, are missing. Employees who have survived the downsizing experience guilt and shame: guilt over why they were not fired and others were, and shame about their remaining affiliation with General Hospital. General Hospital has become the bad, rejecting parental object. It is difficult to work for a "health" service organization that destroys rather than repairs people's lives.

Concluding Remarks: Intervention

The following thoughts are preliminary and reflect General Hospital at eight or nine months after the initial interviews and the onset of the downsizing effort. The leadership (Maggiano, Lewin, and Dohrman) of General Hospital must be removed. The hospital and medical center can no longer operate effectively with the current executives in role. A planned change effort to effectively downsize General Hospital must genuinely involve hospital managers in a collaborative, problem-solving process. Despite what the executives think, hospital employees acknowledge the necessity for change.

General Hospital needs consultants who can direct a planned change effort based on genuine participation of managers and staff. This effort must be driven by valid information (interviews, observations, policies, and facts) gathered from a process of organizational assessment, diagnosis, and feedback sessions designed to confirm or reject findings. In other words, the strategy for intervention must be consistent with the findings of an unbiased organizational assessment that would be intended to identify barriers to change. In this case, barriers to change means any impediments to developing a more resilient organization that is capable of responding effectively to managed care. Hence, if the employees of General Hospital understand the demands for change triggered by healthcare reforms, then the best response to such conditions—one that will ensure the continued integrity of the institution—must be the result of a collaborative strategy owned by hospital management and staff. Finally, this effort must be directed by independent consultants who are sufficiently reflective and can thereby avoid the inclination to overidentify with any one individual (executive) or group (of executives) and lose perspective and focus on the total system change.

INTERPRETATION BY HOWARD STEIN

> The baby is a belly joined on to a chest and has loose limbs and a
> particularly loose head: all these parts are gathered by a mother
> who is holding the child and in her hands they add up to one.
> —Donald W. Winnicott. Quoted in
> M. Davis and D. Wallbridge, 1983, p. 110.

[Stated matter of factly, without emotion:] We have some money left over from the recent RIF process to hire graduate students. We'll pay them a thousand dollars a month without benefits. We don't have to worry about medical insurance and other benefits. Straight wage, no strings attached. We'll use the $15,000 saved by the RIF process. Look at that as an investment to bring in more money through external funding.
—Clinical chairman to his medical department faculty
at an American medical university, late 1994.

Introduction

I did not look forward to this third and final set of interviews. I dreaded the moment I would open the package in the mail—so my counter-transference, my subjective response, was present even before reality showed up from the postal service. Though I could not know, I expected the worst. Here, the anticipatory quality of my anxiety, and of my management of my anxiety, is obvious. I could at least translate my own dread into a protoknowledge that was not merely or entirely projection. Or so I told myself. Having read and emotionally incorporated the two previous interviews, I could feel prepared and, in a way, buffered. I could prepare for the unpreparable. I trusted my inner world as a cue, if an imperfect cue, to the emotional outer world of General Hospital. I was, in short, already imagining myself once more into the inner world of those at General Hospital, where what is, isn't and what isn't, is.

Receiving the transcript of the third set of interviews in early October 1994 (i.e., not quite four weeks before Halloween), I had already formed an image of General Hospital as the "Hospital from Hell." Who needs the torments of *Walpurgisnacht* (eve of May Day), or the sadistic revelry of Witches' Sabbath, or the Medieval depictions on canvas of Hell? Who needs to await the next world after death? Hell was here for all to see, and it was anesthetically and euphemistically called "downsizing," "reengineering," and "restructuring"—and unmerciful waiting. I already had a history with the hospital, even if only a history on paper and via the interviewer; which is to say, through my countertransference (my emotional response). General Hospital, Dr. Allcorn, his interviewees, their supervisors and supervisees, had all become objects in my fantasy world. I dreaded the next stage.

The modern Moloch is a hungry god; its name is "the marketplace." Images of the Nazi Holocaust, of the living near-skeletons in the death camps, kept recurring to me as I read. I struggled to separate, to differentiate, that family and ethnic past from the present while trusting the image as a vital link as well. No blood had been spilled at General Hospital; no corpses littered this battlefield. It was all business as usual, or maybe business in extremis; mutilating, degrading, Pine Sol–scented business, but just business. (*The Godfather* movie series comes to mind.)

As I read and reread the interview transcripts, I kept stumbling over many questions: How could Dr. Allcorn tolerate sitting across from these people who were going through so much? How could he bear (literally carry upon and within himself) so much pain; so much chronic suffering? And how, at interview's end, could he walk out of the room and say, in essence, "I'll see you in three months"? Maybe part of the answer lay in the division of labor he and his three interpreters had agreed to: He would interview, collect the data; the rest of us would tell him what the data meant and felt like.

I did not envy him, and yet I also envied him. I wished to be closer to the data, yet I cherished my distance. This, in turn, directed my attention to the division of labor Dr. Allcorn and his three interpreters had agreed to. Dr. Allcorn did not have the luxury of geographic distance from General Hospital that we three interpreters did. Yet his chosen role of data gatherer gave him a greater emotional distance within the interview and within the larger General Hospital milieu. What struck me as most distinctive in this set of interviews is that my own viewpoint had changed. I was now paying greater attention to— and identifying with—Dr. Allcorn and his role, and not looking primarily, if not exclusively, at what his interviewees were saying. He was not merely a medium through which the interview data were collected; he was a crucial presence in the data.

"What was it like," I now began asking myself, "to be the consultant in Hell?" That was a different question from asking about the experience of the interviewees. In short, this interview set pressed me to think more methodologically as well as substantively. Dr. Allcorn had humorously said to me several times on the telephone that he was "only" the data collector; that it was the task of Baum, Diamond, and Stein to figure out what all this meant and what all the feelings were going on and what a consultant should or could do. Maybe that was the only way he could be in there, at least at that point. Perhaps inadvertently, he was suggesting a team mode of consulting in an emotionally consuming situation.

Themes

Once again I remind the reader of my own ground rules—which the reader will in turn test and not take on my authority. I have inferred a number of thematic categories from the first and second set of interviews; in the second set, I added supplementary themes as well as offered data in support of the continuity of prior themes. As before, I urge the reader to take on this task for himself or herself in this third set.

Main and Subsidiary Themes   If the second set of interviews is dominated by an oppressive waiting like an emotional smog that never lifts, this third set is heavier yet. Maggiano and Lewin are invisible and isolated. Yet Lewin sits in on meetings as if every day were the Day of Judgment. Nothing is happening. The expected transition from downsizing to restructuring has not happened. There is an eerie twist, however; for with the organizational stagnation there is frenetic activity, from the consulting company (SPC) to the many committees. For many, the mood of dread has shifted to a forced indifference and to action: to leaving General Hospital altogether.

The subordinate theme of leadership, past and present, gains new, harrowing poignancy. There is the further weight of a new past; of new losses. Joseph Greene explicitly states the triad of change, loss, and grief. Wirth's name does not now appear at all. Instead, there are the losses of an idealized Matt Towner, a demonized Jacob Dohrman, and of many physicians, nurses, and other staff. There is the expected departure of Stan Pittman. There is the open expectation and anticipation of further, future losses, including of oneself, of the hospital's hierarchical structure (though with Lewin retaining final control even with the flattening of upper administration), and perhaps the very destruction and disappearance of General Hospital.

There is also the new presences of the Hospital Director and Assistant Provost. If many physicians are leaving, at least a few have joined. If for some, SPC is an intrusive Lewin-hatchet, for others, SPC is an unseen presence, a sword of Damocles that might strike at any time, but—to change metaphors—a kind of Stealth bomber that strikes undetected and is virtually undetectable.

American organizations pride themselves on running on rationality, objectivity, and affectless function. If anger, sorrow, depression, and sexuality (in a hierarchy of increasingly greater taboos) are not psychologically repressed, they are certainly suppressed. Yet now at General Hospital there is open anger and open grief. There is unbridled profanity, and often words as symbols for oral and excremental violence and other scarcely disguised, aggressively discharged bodily functions. Here, for the first time in all three sets of interviews, there appears with one interviewee (Julie Nugent) a hint of the theme of sexuality and of sexual excitement, in the person of the Assistant Provost and Dr. Lewin's preference for young, good-looking, petite, and bright women executives. Where this rare hint of sexuality is, can magical organizational procreation, gestation, and hoped-for rebirth—and dreaded annihilation—be far behind? Dr. Lewin is the nearly omnipotent father; the mother is the good-looking Assistant Provost or the Hospital Director, Penny Hill, who is described as "liaison" (whose role connotations could be many) between hospital and ambulatory (or hospital and ambulatory and Lewin).

Metaphors In this section, as in my previous chapters, I present some of the key metaphoric words, phrases, and sentences as if they were the core of the interviewees' narrative. By taking them out of one context, the individual interview, and by placing them together in their own context, one obtains insight into unconscious dimensions of an organizational group's narrative with fewer distractions of the transcript's grammatical structure and the inevitable wordiness of even focused interviews.

Respect life.

Human dignity.

Big Brother paternalism (no caring) versus self-management.

Top management versus self-management.

More and more police-type people.

Mergers.

The new consulting company does not know my area.

They [the consulting company] have to look good and deliver.

Divide and conquer.

No vision.

Reabsorbed.

Eliminated in the redesign.

Angry with the loss of our autonomy.

They are clever and bright and are just not using the word "layoff."

Long and drawn out [vs.] getting it over quick.

Do we have a fundamental change or new nomenclature to justify another fiefdom?

Dr. Lewin is trying to impose his philosophy on the rest of the organization. We don't know where we are going.

SPC is driving the organization rather than the organization driving SPC.

The troops are all over the place and we haven't figured out where the war is.

Meetings are killing me and everyone else.

Everyone is getting good at CYA (cover your ass).

There are three players; Dohrman, Lewin, and Maggiano. Dohrman doesn't move out of fear of making waves. Lewin is busy talking TQM but doesn't talk to the department heads. Maggiano is insulated from what is going on by Lewin's position.

The cash cow [the hospital] can no longer subsidize the [university] campus.

We are all experiencing the same thing.

People are leaving and other good ones are looking to leave. It seems clear no one really cares.

Lots of mickey mousing around. TQM is a bunch of crap. It slows decision making down.

Dr. Lewin sits in lots of meetings which makes everyone anxious. No one knows why he is there. It seems like he is evaluating people.

No one asked, they just assumed the hospital was bad.

The faculty are in a state of panic.

Expecting too much from us.

Low raises.

I thought it sucked.

Outstanding evaluations. These folks needed to be rewarded but the across-the-board low raises didn't permit it. It made me look like an idiot. People are pissed. Morale is at an all-time low.

Everyone wants everything.

Lost two of their colleagues.

Overworked.

Lots of people have already left. If you have good people, they are the first to leave. We lost a good person in Matt Towner. They ran him out by working him to death. He didn't see any future here.

More like a shell game.

I trust Dr. Lewin. I have faith in him. He has great goals.

There has to be a lot of paradigm busting here.

When it stops being fun, I'll leave.

A lot of people are just waiting.

No one is taking any initiative. Everyone below Jacob is afraid to make a decision.

I need empowerment to get going. I have ideas and without support I get frustrated.

Managers and supervisors.

Normally the supervisors supervise staff and the managers coordinate programs and projects. If flattening occurs the managers may be cut and the supervisors will have to do the whole thing.

Chaotic.

Supervisors are not trained to manage.

More and more responsibility and work. People expect us to be able to just take over something. No appreciation.

Reshuffling of responsibilities and jockeying for more responsibility to avoid being laid off.

I don't have passion for my work anymore. I'm looking for a new job. I'm disappointed with the organization. Normally I'm a change agent. I have no empowerment and lost any I had. There is a lot of micromanagement going on from the top and a lack of collaboration among the departments. Everyone is talking the talk. I'm disappointed.

I have also had periods of illness and getting really sick. I'm not pleased with my performance and lack of passion.

The door is closed to listening to problems from below.

Crisis management. TQM is not solving problems either; it's too slow.

Vomiting and my back has hurt.

Stress.

Heart attack.

Disappointed.

I wake up in the morning anxious. I fear losing my job, which I can't afford to do, or that I will make a mistake.

Information overload. It is often published first and then we talk to our people. The process is backwards.

Out of control.

We had to keep all the changes hush hush [referring to the reductions] at my level.

I was afraid to say much at the beginning [of the interviews]. By the second interview I was pissed off and frustrated and more open. Now I'm so pissed off I don't care and I'm really open.

I don't see Jacob [Dohrman] staying here much longer.

Attrition. People are choosing to leave.

SPC's process is not believable. It's like mental masturbation; busywork. There is lots of talk and no action. Nothing has changed in the last six months.

The committees are too big to do work; forty people many times. They are called together to bless the work of the consultants and decisions made by top management. Just like rubber stamps. I feel manipulated. Soon the talk will be over and people will be cut.

A total waste of time [the changes].

I know what is getting communicated because I'm on the communications committee.

Dr. Maggiano and Dr. Lewin don't know what they're doing.

I wouldn't have hired SPC.

I also function sort of as the conscience of the organization to point out wrong. I would have sent a clear message to everyone's employment status, a message of commitment to people. Morale would be different.

Last year the layoffs were a wake-up call that we could survive, but the last nine months of doing nothing have been a big mistake.

We waited too long. Good ideas have been put on hold. We needed to let the remaining people know that they are very valuable to us. This didn't happen and the disempowerment is also a problem.

Who could have seen the disempowerment and arrogance.

Rumors.

Satellite-type approach.

Eliminate my role.

No one seems ready to say it.

Dr. Lewin may be awaiting for the new director.

A weak person.

Reduced responsibility.

Everything is in transition.

I'm beyond feeling angry, I just don't care. They are losing someone who is very loyal. They don't deserve my loyalty.

No challenge.

I'm still busy but there is no desire or plan to do anything.

Buy out.

Fake.

A person from ambulatory [versus hospital] was selected to chair a committee I should have, mainly because these are Lewin's people. I feel betrayed by Antonio.

Betrayed.

Angry.

Upset.

We built everything and it is now all being torn down. It was like your child. I am being nice to others and not angry. Every day is difficult.

Antonio has no feelings.

Victory.

Total defeat.

If they can do this to me after so many years, they can do it to them.

Antidepressant.

Insomnia and I wake up throughout the night. I'm anxious.

Jacob was not promoted after fifteen years. General Hospital has always been a family.

Some of the top docs have left.

The word is out. We're not giving the right image.

Looking for destruction. People are starting to wonder what the goal is. Is the goal to destroy this place by running it into the ground and then sell it off?

I absolutely don't know [about changes relative to the position].

My direct reports feel overwhelmed.

Fragmentation. There is no coordination or focus.

After the cuts last October, we have been expected to wait which is frustrating. We waited for the new consultants and we are now waiting for the new process.

It seems like an unspoken expectation to wait. We were then asked by Jacob Dohrman why we were waiting.

We have learned to live with what we've got. We know more is to come but nothing has happened.

Most managers are not participating in the new consulting company's phases of work. No one knows what is going on. There is apathy and fear.

I never see Dr. Lewin. Jacob is anxious; he has a new boss.

Neither Dr. Lewin, Jacob, or the manager of ambulatory show their feelings. This tends to block the discussion of feelings in the hospital, but the ambulatory manager holds open meetings where people can and do express their feelings. I think Jacob's management style is inconsistent with where they want to go.

We knew we should do some work on grieving for those who remained and we didn't do anything.

I wish we could get things over . . . and move ahead. We keep waiting for direction.

Our ethical foundation is eroding. People who speak out are told to be quiet. Those who seem to be responding positively are those who are quiet and passive. They are doing and saying what they are told. Speaking out for me is becoming a disservice to me. Independent thoughts are dangerous. You don't question the establishment.

Be quiet or else. I'm not intimidated, but I'm getting very angry about it. I'll do my best even if no one appreciates it.

Very scary [the changes to be made].

Recently I lost all of my supervisors.

Penny Hill just started. She will bring some freshness and hopefully create a bridge between Dr. Lewin, who is still oriented toward ambulatory, and the hospital. She'll serve as a liaison.

I never felt so unable to control most minor things. Every requisition for even a two-day temporary has to be approved by Dr. Lewin. It's so hypocritical. He says he wants to push decision making down into the organization. I feel good about myself. . . . It might sound a little cocky, but I feel very confident I know what I'm doing.

Anxious, depressed, frustrated, disempowered, distrustful and all in all pretty rotten [how I think those who report to me are feeling].

Jacob feels better now. He didn't get the job and life goes on. He seems relieved.

I just realized I've lost three weeks of vacation. I hadn't taken any vacation for the past eighteen months. I went last week. I reached my maximum accumulation almost a year ago. I worry about everything else except me. Maybe that's a female thing to do, or maybe I'm just stupid. I'm still crabby. Yesterday my husband confronted me about taking my attitude out on him.

Stress-related headaches and backaches which have gotten worse. I used to have them occasionally, now it's every day. I didn't realize how all of this has affected me until I took a week's vacation recently.

I feel very supported by Jacob, but not by my colleagues.

Growth experience.

I have no confidence it will end up better the way I had hoped. I thought that we could be efficient; provide patients better quality and user-friendly care. I thought the employees would settle in but that is not happening.

Some good will come of it, perhaps in several years when you look back.

The Executive I role may be diminished relative to the Director's role because her role is diminished because of the way it was defined by Dr. Lewin. This may lead to the Executive I role being redefined or eliminated. [Here, Jacob Dohrman, the Executive I, is speaking in the third person about himself].

Eliminate . . . expanded duties.

[Direct reports] might feel that although those leading the organization claim to foster empowerment, they feel just the opposite is happening. They feel disenfranchised.

[Upper administrators] are doing more in isolation. They are inadvertently isolating themselves from information and others.

Great frustration at all levels of the organization.

In the absence of a hospital Director, I initiated and directed the initial cost restructuring, which was successful. I have not been at all involved in planning and implementing the next phase.

Based on past performance and recognition from others other than Dr. Maggiano and Dr. Lewin; that I am prepared, ready, and willing to leave and I have, in fact, accepted a senior-level management role in another hospital. I am feeling very good about myself, self-confident.

[In Dorhman's view, those who report to him have] lost a significant amount of their influence in guiding the organization. They feel very much separated from Dr. Maggiano and Dr. Lewin and ambulatory care administration.

Dr. Maggiano and Dr. Lewin feel good about what they are doing. They believe that now that they are in the driver's seat they will be able to more than surpass past successes and overcome their past inertia.

Maintain my close relationships, but I have been discussing the organization and my personal frustrations more frequently.

I believe everyone is very anxious and frustrated and concerned about their roles and the new management philosophy relative to their roles and the philosophy of Dr. Maggiano and Dr. Lewin.

I have been provided a lot of latitude regarding operating the hospital, which would seem like I am being supported, but at the same time, Dr. Lewin has not expressed any interest in the hospital and what I do.

I would have relied more on individuals, myself, and the senior management team to support the next phase of change [restructuring].

We knew morale would be adversely affected.

Impatience about moving on.

Trepidation.

We are doing more with less and we have lost some of our effectiveness. The quality of care that we deliver varies with the volume.

Lip service to a patient/customer focus. Implementation is incomplete.

Overwhelmed and they wonder if they will have a job.

As staff have left and not been replaced, those remaining have had to pick up additional responsibilities. More consolidation may lead to some being laid off. They also feel left out at times and wonder about why they haven't been appointed to certain committees.

For some it has been schizophrenic. Some are acting out now, which didn't occur before. Some are able to manage the extra work and stress and others are having problems with it.

We are progressing in a logical and methodical manner that permits a lot of involvement and participation. There has been a real effort to listen. The group-process people have helped. There is a lot of skepticism about decision making. Some feel that their participation is just playing along with decisions that have already been made. I don't think so though.

The new hospital Director will probably redefine many roles. People in key positions have left or are leaving and the remaining positions in senior management are overloaded.

Reorganization of patient care to develop a patient focus which is supposed to drive down decision making to the lowest levels.

More empowerment.

Cross-train people. The lower-skilled people are feeling more vulnerable than those with technical skills.

Roles might be eliminated or end up with less responsibility.

I have a lot of vacant positions.

The doctors are leaving.

The doctors have low morale, which has impacted on the staff and I think quality has suffered. Recruiting is also tough.

A lot of stressed-out people.

Everyone has a work overload. We got used to the lower volume and now it is back up.

Afraid for their job.

No choice, we had to survive.

Too much talk and no action. It's all group process.

The process is moving along too slowly.

They replaced the hospital Director. Now it seems that they don't need all the remaining layers. There is no place for Jacob.

The committees get a large cross-section of people on them which generates some ideas but nothing much has happened. They are skeptical that they are not being told everything. People want to know where the beef is. There is communication but no one trusts they are being told everything. Sometimes it seems like overkill.

I'm afraid to answer the phone or open my mail for fear of getting another deadline or assignment.

The work is unmanageable.

Dealing with Jacob is difficult. Jacob is a micromanager but not a decision maker. He's intimidating in his approach and can be rude. He lacks an appreciation for what others can contribute. He has no sensitivity to what is going on.

I see a lot of stressed-out people and very low morale. People are very unhappy and frustrated.

Overcommunication.

Control over filling positions. We are wasting a lot of time by not responding faster.

Requests go to a committee that always approves the request, then to Jacob and eventually to Dr. Lewin. Why do it at all? If we agree on the numbers of staff, why wait?

Control over filling positions wasn't foreseen. Those making the decisions are disconnected from operations. The 2.5 percent raise was devastating. Morale is in the subbasement. Some people are very angry and absenteeism is up.

I'm looking for a new job, maybe out of healthcare.

His [Stan Pittman?] days are numbered. His leadership style might have been the problem. He is very formal, militaristic in a way, paternalistic at times, but he is also sensitive and caring but only those close to him really know it and him. He is an introvert who hires a lot of extroverts to work with him.

Everyone is very loyal to him that works with him. He hasn't thrown anyone to the wolves in twenty years. He turned the department around when he came. Others don't think he cares about them and some fear him. This is inconsistent with the warm fuzzy environment Dr. Lewin wants, but he was also a person who hired very strong people and then delegated to them considerable responsibility and autonomy. He did try to hold them accountable though.

He is known to be fair and honest.

SPC has not interacted with us either. Perhaps they are waiting for the new Assistant Provost who will start to work next week. She is young and attractive. There is the belief that Dr. Lewin likes to hire sweet, petite, attractive, and young women who are bright. She commented on this when I had a chance to talk to her. She knows she is young and attractive and now she has to prove she is smart too. Dr. Lewin is a charming, intelligent, and warm person, but I don't know him very well. I think he knows what he is talking about, but many doctors are leaving, which is new.

I'm concerned about us surviving. Everyone is wondering when they will go into the other schools and ambulatory. We will have a blueberry pancake that Tom Peters talks about. We are told that Dr. Lewin, the head of ambulatory, the new Assistant Provost, and the new hospital Director will all be coequal and that the organization will be flat as a pancake. This doesn't ring true. They all work for Dr. Lewin so there is no coequality. I've also heard about problems in ambulatory with their team approach. It is horrendous over there.

I'm fifty years old. If they get rid of me, what will I do? What do I want to do is the question. I'm concerned about the future. I try to keep from feeling fearful, but it is getting to me. For some here, their job is their whole life.

Some are very upset. Some are terrified that they will lose their job. It threatens their basic needs.

People ask why this is going on.

I'd get people involved right from the start rather than use all of this top-down process. I wouldn't drag out the change for so long either. No one feels that they know what is going on.

The famous committees are making people anxious. There are those who are selected to participate in them and others who end up being excluded. There is competition to get on them because they believe that if they are selected, they will keep their job. But once they are on the committee they don't make waves to stay on the committee. Being on the committee is sort of like being anointed by Dr. Lewin that you are okay. They are heavily staffed with ambulatory people and in some instances by people from the hospital that are not seen as the best or strongest representatives of their area.

Uncertain about the future and whether they will be laid off. They feel that their expertise doesn't count.

Everybody wants to get this over with. It's hard to do your job when you are wondering if you will still be here in a month.

People who have had to put their lives on hold.

[Matt Towner left to take a position at another hospital.]

I'm preparing my department for decentralization and self-direction in the belief that my position may be eliminated. More staff may be cut. The census has been in the low 60-percent range for a number of months. It may go back up in the fall. There has been a shift to ambulatory, same-day surgery, and same-day admissions.

The staff may be cut.

We are moving toward self-managing teams.

We continue to develop innovative programs, but we don't get any recognition for our work. I think our program is still good for the hospital.

I feel anxious about the center and that it has lost ground.

All the changes have been losses and everyone is grieving. We lost Wirth, Dohrman, Pittman, and several Manager IIIs. It is sad.

Confused. I don't know if they will be here. They aren't saying much, but I think that they [those to whom the interviewee reports] are running scared. They are also overwhelmed with work.

There has been lots of communication, but it's all just words.

We had a good team here that made the place what it was and I think that they would have been willing to reexamine their process. Now we have three people from the outside, Dr. Lewin and the new Assistant Provost and the hospital Director, calling all of the shots, or perhaps more accurate just Dr. Lewin.

All I have seen is tearing everything apart.

We are losing patients and doctors and we don't have any new affiliations.

My position might be eliminated. I might be assigned more work or have another department merged with mine. There is a loss of sense of control over what will happen, but I can accept it. Even getting fired is an opportunity.

Cut costs and improve our service.

If you look at the broad picture, we are making progress. We are getting used to working together even outside of the lab, in teams.

It [work] is what I make of it. It depends on me. I'm still interested in my
work. There are days that I don't like it but that is because there is something else I would prefer to be doing.

[The interviewee thinks the person to whom she reports (Ted Olsen) is feel-
ing] dismal. He is feeling pain. It's difficult for him. He's stressed-out.

Job security issues.

I would have tried to avoid alienating the doctors. They don't trust Dr.
Maggiano and Dr. Lewin but they are still acting honorably and trying to
help us out.

People want us to be successful and they want to be a part of those who are
concerned about success even if there is a funk now from treading water.

We are moving toward product lines and there promises, although I'm not
sure how it will affect my role. I'm not concerned anymore. There isn't
much I can do about it.

Cutting down barriers to horizontal communication will cut down on the
amount of communication that has to flow up to senior levels of management, which will mean that they have less to deal with.

Jacob has left [Antonio Lozano was one of the last to be interviewed]. I frankly
feel better now because he could be controlling and not always respectful
of me, which seemed to get worse with time.

We aren't waiting to be told what to do now and we have some input. I am less
afraid of change because I am part of it, although this may be a naïve attitude.

My continued assumption, as in the first and second interviews, is
that metaphors alone can reveal conscious and unconscious feelings,
fantasies, and anxieties in organizations. They are unfettered by the
real-world business being discussed; they are, in a way, the most real,
ultimate, "business" and "work" of the organization. The emotional
impact of reading these metaphors in this third set of interviews is
even more overwhelming than the second set. I could not imagine
how it could be worse—now I know. The sheer length of this section
attests, I believe, to the unconscious coming more easily and more
urgently to the surface. Although in one sence the preceding sequence
repeats everything in Dr. Allcorn's third interview transcription, I hope
that what the isolation and association of symbols provides the kind
of condensation typical of dreams and of such psychoanalytic prin-
ciples as the Pleasure Principle, the compulsion to repeat, and the
quest for mastery over passivity.

Control versus Out of Control   As I look at this category from the
vantage point of the third set of interviews, I realize how far from the
original group ideal and expectation the General Hospital interviewees
have moved. Everything now feels out of control, including out of personal control. Irrespective of how well one does one's job or performs

one's (increasingly ambiguous and expanding) role, one is still not in control and does not feel in control of one's situation or destiny. There is no known or knowable route to such control. There is no connection between one's behavior (what one does, one's task performance) and one's fate. And there is no way to determine what the parameters are. Conversely, interviewees feel increasingly, if not totally, controlled by others above them; some known, others utterly invisible. As Shakespeare's Prince Hamlet says, "The time is out of joint," and no one has an inkling about how to set it right.

Except, that is, Maggiano and Lewin, whose sanction for this economically phrased scorched-earth policy comes (presumably) officially from above; and more tacitly from below and from the wider embedded cultural ethos in which real and symbolic violence are not only permitted, but are adopted as problem-solving strategies. Personal control, self-control, control over one's future, and "internal locus of control," all core American values and expectations, are at General Hospital entirely negated. Virtually un-American attitudes of helplessness, fatalism, resignation, and futility prevail. It does not require a Freudian imagination or concepts such as "regression" to hear in the interviewees' accounts the experience of accomplished adult administrators who are suddenly thrown back into the helplessness and vulnerability of infancy—and this within a rather crazy medical family of unreliable elders as well.

Expected versus Unexpected Story Line   Nothing has turned out as expected or as hoped. "This is not the way it was supposed to happen," and "This is not the way we were told things were going to happen," are recurrent themes in the interviews. Everything is at a standstill, rather than restructured, productive, and with high morale. Even occasionally improved "productivity" and "efficiency" does not help people to feel better about working at General Hospital, about the structure, and about the future. What has happened was not supposed to happen. Stagnation and dread reign instead of progress; and no end is in sight. Most interviewees, with sadness, bitterness, or open anger, say they have no idea what to expect. Penny Hill as "liaison" and the other cute, smart, new Assistant Provost are expected to be a ray of sunlight in the dismal corporate fog, but hopes are not high.

"Us" versus "Them"   There are several heightened polarizations: Maggiano and Lewin versus everyone beneath them; the mysterious SPC consulting company who execute the will of Maggiano and Lewin (as the executioners, so to speak) in behalf of the judges; and these all over and against the waiting and condemned workforce at General Hospital; supervisors (who supervise staff) versus managers (who co-

ordinate programs and projects); the hospital versus ambulatory; and the hospital as once-fat "cash cow" that was expected to feed "the campus," the entire university, but can no longer do so. A new facet of the us versus them between the hospital and ambulatory is the distinction between styles and atmospheres of the meetings that occur in each: For example, "Neither Dr. Lewin, Jacob, or the manager of ambulatory show their feelings. This tends to block the discussion of feelings in the hospital, but the ambulatory manager holds open meetings where people can and do express their feelings."

A more subtle us versus them takes the form of two religious fantasies: that of the excluded, ignored, but religiously oriented good respectfulness, human dignity, and humanitarian ideals versus that of the bad committees which are called upon to "bless" what Lewin and Maggiano decree.

With the departure of Jacob Dohrman for a different hospital, one of the much vilified "them" is now gone. But the anticipation of his leaving and the poignancy of his interview tell us how complicated even this is. "There is no place for Jacob," said one interviewee of this most loyal henchman to his superiors. Dorhman, who had long been regarded as one of the brutal, if not evil, "them" by most of those beneath him, now turns out to be one of "us," in fate if not in function. Even Jacob was not safe from being fired or forced out. Dorhman's fate might give many at General Hospital pause to wonder whether "us" might all be "them" and vice versa. No one is safe, perhaps not even Lewin or Maggiano; not even the hospital or the university.

I think of the final scene of Wagner's opera *Die Gotterdämmerung* (*The Twilight of the Gods*), from his tetralogy, *The Ring of the Niebelungs*. Here, the mighty castle of the gods, Valhalla, is aflame and collapses from the weight of its own fate. From their own greed and arrogance, the gods destroy themselves. In his introduction to this third set of interviews, Dr. Allcorn reminds the reader that although one hospital program lost physicians, media coverage made it sound as if the hospital had lost the entire program; in fact, it did not. But there is a grain of truth in "the media's" overdoing. If one blames the media for exaggeration (hyperbole, especially in the area of cultural violence, is one of its central tasks), one should equally blame the inflamed fantasy life of the interviewees. The attitude, *Après nous, le déluge* (After us, [let there be] the flood) abounds; the virtually undisguised wish for total, wanton destruction (at the same time as it is feared).

Communication   Too much communication vies with not enough communication from the right people. These in turn contend with the belief that all communication from above is now a sham; is totally untrustworthy. At worst, communication itself has become the problem; murderous "overkill."

The third set of interviews is replete with double messages, in which (as in classic double binds) the contradiction (itself expressing the ambivalence) is not supposed to be noticed or acknowledged: There is the pressure from above for greater decentralization, self-direction, self-management, and more horizontal team building across disciplines; and greater official organizational "flattening" (the ostensible decrease in distance between top and bottom); but all this is somehow supposed to be achieved amid the total control of major and minor decisions by Lewin, who speaks for the even more invisible Maggiano. General Hospital executives, physicians, and staff are simultaneously expected to act as if they have additional authority and responsibility and as if all authority comes from the top two (no longer top three) administrators.

Without belaboring the obvious, any discussion of communication must include those metaphors that convey the feeling of what it is like to be in General Hospital: police, fiefdom, family, war, troops, mental masturbation, beef, and so on. Those metaphors fester at the core of the frustration, the outrage, the despair, and the disappointment; all part of daily "communication."

Boundary Uncertainty   Nothing is solid anymore; there are no clear identity demarcations. Virtually every boundary is unclear or rapidly changing: from personal work role, to reporting structure (who to whom), to work-group constitution, to both hierarchical and horizontal directions, to hospital and ambulatory, to the medical center and the university. The loss of actual persons and their historic role relationships with those who remain at General Hospital, together with their replacement in upper administration (including their style; e.g., the way Lewin is present, the way Maggiano is absent, the way Dohrman detonates, the way the consulting company acts in their behalf), is the most obvious boundary issue. It is only the most conscious of boundary issues. The statement, "There is no place for Jacob," is a stark example of a group boundary issue, not only a personal one. It is also the most vivid illustration of where personality, social structure, and change intersect. There is little that cannot be understood as a vital boundary issue.

A more elusive boundary issue is the very process of change: the official way it is supposed to occur and be experienced, and the way people at General Hospital actually experience the change. Throughout the interviews there is much stylized jargon about the process of change (restructuring, redesign, reengineering, self-managed teams, cross-training, changing the reporting structure). At the same time, these technical, managerial terms have the quality of euphemism when compared with the emotions that are unleashed with the dissolution of all reliable (not emotionally equivalent to "predictable") boundaries (overwhelmed, overworked, scary, waiting, hard to trust, paranoid, overworked beyond control, frazzled, anxious, frustrating, no vision, at their limits, people are leaving, no one really cares, ambivalent and very angry, very unhappy, betrayed, apathy). Uncertain boundaries about time (What and who will be in the future?) parallel uncertain boundaries in space and relationship.

Metaphors offer some guide as to the type of boundaries wished for, expected, dreaded, and so forth. The image of General Hospital as a good family, as having built something worthwhile and enduring, contrasts with the image of devastation, destruction, and troops looking for where the war is. Families and armies are composed of people; whole people. Their boundaries are collapsing, expanding, and being invaded. Even this image, however, might be too solid to hold all the profound perceptual and emotional ambiguity being described: I keep thinking of persons, units, and the medical complex as a liquid; unable to be contained by anything or anyone. Tidal waves, flooding rivers, stormy oceans, and boiling cauldrons seem like images that evoke deep levels of interviewees' experiences.

The events and experiences described at General Hospital force me to rethink the very nature of human boundaries: What happens to the boundary between inside and outside, between subjective, intersubjective, and objective, when reality actualizes fantasy and when fantasy actualizes reality? If the rule of loyalty and job retention is "be quiet or leave," when any boundary violation is condemned and punished as disloyalty, the gravest sin, what is the possibility for reality testing and organizational resilience?

Functioning versus Feeling   The split is wider than before. For instance, Jacob Dohrman, the just-resigned hit man for Lewin and Maggiano, described the split he experienced: "I have been provided a lot of latitude regarding operating the hospital, which would seem like I am being supported, but at the same time, Dr. Lewin has not expressed any interest in the hospital and what I do." Moreover, Jacob Dohrman not only describes a split, but early in the interview he eerily personifies it in his choice of voice. He speaks in the third person about himself and his role, as though the speaker were standing outside himself, watching and reporting on an altogether different person. He said, "The Executive I role may be diminished relative to the Director's role; her role may be diminished as a result of the way it was defined by Dr. Lewin. This may lead to the Executive I role being redefined or eliminated." I nearly gagged and gasped as I read this. He was speaking of his own imminent symbolic death as if it were happening to another person who was but a thing.

More widely, there seems to be a split between the almost mechanical, impersonal functioning at (increasing) tasks and the feelings interviewees express about what it was like to work at General Hospital these past three or so months; that is, between people's roles and how they feel within these (rapidly changing) roles.

The Experience of Change   Past change has already been overwhelming, and interviewees are in a kind of suspended animation waiting for and expecting even more ruthless change. They feel helpless, and often even hopeless. At the more surface level, there is a lot of busywork; at a deeper level, nothing is happening yet. Many are waiting for someone else to do something to them; others are taking matters into their own hands and leaving or planning to leave.

Keeping an Upbeat Attitude   Trying to keep an upbeat attitude, to think positively, to remain optimistic, while the overall mood is of resignation and dread is still an issue: There is some upbeatness and almost forced optimism, but much less than in the prior interviews. Now, indifference and cynicism prevail: "No one really cares," at the same time as people are working "at their limits." In addition to the prevailing mood of resignation and dread is unabashed rage and even open grief.

The Relation between Empathy within the Workplace and outside the Workplace   Val Kasman says, "I'm still crabby. Yesterday my husband confronted me about taking my attitude out on him." This example (displacement?) reverses what I had taken to be a minipattern in the second interview set (greater empathy at home, less at work).

Increase in Illnesses, or at Least in the Reporting of Illnesses   Reports abound in mental, physical, even marital symptoms; absenteeism; diseases; and cultural code words (stress, stressed-out, and burnout). If ever a case could be made for workplace-induced pathology, it is at General Hospital, where the workplace itself is a toxin.

Significance

What do all these themes mean—what meanings and themes have endured and what others have changed over the nine months between the initial and final interviews? And who determines this significance, this meaning—only consultant–interpreters such as myself?

In large measure, the interviewees are telling Dr. Allcorn the significance of their own data through their language, symbolism, metaphors, and emotion. This is different from saying that consultant and client (person or organizational group) each have a version of history, a sense of meaning, about what is taking place. More radically, I am arguing that in large measure they are articulating the unconscious and are increasingly aware of doing so. If we as consultants have insights and wisdom to contribute to them via our further interpretations, they as interviewees are already contributing to our joint work (and working alliance). If the interviewees are not speaking in the professional languages of psychoanalysis, organizational theory, sociology, and anthropology, they are telling Dr. Allcorn about now-chronic trauma, narcissistic injury, ego regression, and the upsurge of primitive anxiety and defenses against it (e.g., intrapsychic defenses such as splitting, projective identification and externalization, and denial; interpersonal defenses such as brutalization, indifference, withdrawal, and leaving).

My hypotheses and recommendations build upon what I have learned from listening to Dr. Allcorn and the interviewees. In the remainder of my comments, I ask the reader to keep uppermost in mind the fact that each interviewee has an individuality of response (because of an individuality of biography), and commonalities of response due to, among other things, sharing the human condition, being American, and being part of the culture of General Hospital—a culture that has been incorporated into the self and is "more than just a job."

Hypotheses

More so than before, in these final interviews there is abundant evidence for group regression to early developmental conflicts, fantasies, and feelings. The Freudian triad of orality, anality, and genitality are virtually worn on the surface of consciousness. Pre-Oedipal annihilation and separation anxiety and Oedipal castration anxiety are all but stated outright. Modes of thinking and feeling we usually associate with hospitalized backward schizophrenics are here common utterances of culturally normal, high-placed managers. The extent of the primitiveness of the group regression can be seen by examining the metaphors people use to describe their experiences. Consider Maria Meyers' statements that, "I expect my job to be reabsorbed or eliminated in the redesign," and "[Those who report to me will feel] terribly. They will be angry with the loss of our autonomy." Beneath the obvious reality aspects of this statement is the very earliest dreads humans can have about their existence being annihilated by a literal reabsorption into the mother's body and self. Threatened elimination and loss of selfhood are not abstract, symbolic fears to be taken lightly; they take us to the essence of our existence as separate biological organisms.

I read the final days and resignation of Jacob Dohrman as an organizational sacrifice by a General Hospital group, top and bottom alike, who had viewed him as henchman and brute, and he himself was consumed by his own institutional revolution (not unlike national revolutions, from German National Socialism to the Russian Revolution). In Brenda Early's interview, powerful associations occur: "There is no place for Jacob. . . . People want to know where the beef is [allusion to the 1980s television commercial about the absence of real beef in hamburgers]. . . . It seems like overkill [of communication, but no trust]." Symbolically, I would read her as saying that Jacob Dohrman is the sacrificial cow (beef) who is killed (sacrificed, driven to leave) for the sake of the organization's survival. Even if I am reading too much into Brenda Early's statement (wild analysis), it is indirectly corroborated throughout the interviews. Dohrman, who was expected to control, abuse, and betray those beneath him, is betrayed by those whom he served. Others at General Hospital place him with Maggiano and Lewin; he himself feels keenly separated and isolated from them. If Dohrman betrayed others by his style, he is now betrayed by his isolation. I find my earlier contempt for him muted by sadness and a sense of epic tragedy. Jacob Dohrman was not simply acting out an inner mean son-of-a-bitch character compulsion. There was a fateful match between Dohrman's character and the uses (abuses) to which he was goaded by his station; between uppermost administrators and everyone beneath him. His was not a soliloquy, a monologue; and if it was, it occurred on a crowded stage and before a large, demanding audience. The butcher of General Hospital will be missed no less than the beloved Mr. Wirth—though, of course, their psychological burdens differ.

The usual moral universe (in corporations and hospitals, as in ethnic groups and nations) divides the human world into "we," the good people, and "they," the bad people. Increasingly, I hear General Hospital interviewees feel overwhelmed by the feeling that little but badness remains inside its walls. Many good people are either leaving or have left. Ambulatory holds more open, expressive meetings. Whatever else describes General Hospital, it is in a crisis of its very identity and the worthwhileness and future of its members' ideals.

Religious overtones are present. The good fathers are (all?) gone. Presumably, the departed leader Wirth represented an earlier embodiment of this dependency wish and, to a degree, fulfillment. One interviewee as much as said that now General Hospital practiced a bad religion, one of abandonment and sacrifice, for the committees "blessed" (rubber stamped) the wishes of Lewin and Maggiano.

At one level, there is clearly a regression from secular reality testing to the wish for rescue by prayer, by ecclesiastical authority, by some good father or mother, or even by magical thinking. Splitting abounds between sacred and profane, even between a kind of Mass of Grace and a Black Mass. At another level, though, it is too easy to pathologize the interviewees entirely and write off Wirth as an idealized dependency leader, one all the more adhered to in memory because of the contrast with bad internal objects.

I have no doubt that this inner world of good and bad objects is part of the story; but it is not the entire story. The interviewees are also raging and deeply grieving over the sense of inner and organizational worthwhileness at the levels of psychology and task alike that the Wirth era represented. Part of the rage and part of the regression is over the replacement of organizational authenticity with sham. It is the loss of the sense of worthwhileness of work itself. And this is no small, entirely fantasized loss.

The fantasy, the near conviction, is that there are no good parents anywhere. It is a world entirely bereft of love. One can no longer even be a good (managerial, supervisory) parent. If one cannot be saved by parents from above for certain, one cannot save any of one's organizational dependents for certain, or even oneself. One feels helpless in the face of one's own aggressiveness or death wish, and equally helpless to love or to repair one's angry wishes or deeds.

A third interviewee asserts that Maggiano and Lewin are "letting SPC run over the organization. I feel that our ethical foundation is eroding. People who speak out are told to be quiet." It is as if two kinds of ethics are being described: one a more personal, benevolent, internal guidance, perhaps operating more in accordance with a Kleinian "depressive position" or a Bion basic assumption of dependency (such as on Wirth); and the other a kind of Irving Janisian "groupthink" (Janis, 1982), an externalized superego working in the Bion fight–flight mode.

If the idealized, bygone days were those of Bion-type dependency group, the current ones are a fight–flight group within Bion's framework, with much of the aggression directed inwardly within the hospital, symbolically killing some of the hospital's very own offspring for the sake of the others and for the sake of the "bad" fathers who expose them to greater vulnerability. General Hospital, once a good mother, once a good family, and once ethical, now consumes and discards her own. General Hospital as religious icon, not only as workplace, is now bad rather than good.

Let me take the image even a step further. As I read and reread the last two sets of interviews, I keep having an awful physical feeling that takes the form of a recurrent fantasy: General Hospital is a pregnant mother and the baby (the future General Hospital) is long overdue; stuck in the birth canal. That is part of what the interminable waiting means and feels like. They wonder whether the delivery will be a live birth or a stillbirth. What kind of fathers will Maggiano and Lewin be? What kind of mothers will Penny Hill and the new attractive Assistant Provost be? Is there any hope for rebirth—or is General Hospital already a dead baby inside a dead mother? In a single horrific condensation, General Hospital is evil; General Hospital, once Heaven, is Hell.

One compulsory reality principle is the iron law of the economic marketplace: A lowered inpatient rate requires a drastic reduction in the hospital workforce, not only at General Hospital, but across America, where outpatient ambulatory care is the wave of the future. According to the obligatory cultural doctrine, itself an unexamined fantasy, there is nothing more basic than the bottom line, one of Americans' most gripping and unchallengeable metaphors. Yet another principle that presses its claim as reality is the wish for rebirth amid the death of the once familiar and flourishing General Hospital. If the mother must die in order for herself be reborn, what happens during childbirth? Will the children now be born without a mother to care for them? Will mother, father, and children—the entire hospital "family" and "team"—all perish together of their own murderousness?

As I read the interviews, I consciously looked for gender-based differences in interview content and style. I did not find what I had expected. On the surface, there was, among male and female interviewees, much obviously "hard" language, characteristic of male-dominated organizational style. Anger prevailed over the softer, more vulnerable sadness or depression. One does not succeed as upper management in an American organization if one is not "aggressive" or "macho" in demeanor if not in motive. (Of course, women must live the contradictions of being more diminutively feminine and not bitchy while still being unflinchingly aggressive and product rather than person oriented.) Organizations are not supposed to run on affect but on productivity. Whatever affect seeps in is supposed to be can-do male. (I owe these insights to a telephone conversation with Dr. Seth Allcorn on November 7, 1994.)

But it feels trite to note the obvious. Viewed from a Freudian approach to psychosexual fantasy, developmental phases, and wish, what more can these final interviews tell us? While I did not conduct a computer-based content analysis, multiple readings of the interviews persuade me that, indeed, male interviewees tended to use more military or war and sports images, while female interviewees tended to use more intimately relational, even domestic, images. But not entirely. There was some crossover. I am more impressed by the fact that the scourge of destructiveness and of endless waiting for later destruction (and the regression that this shared experience induced) led to far more commonality of symbols that I had expected.

If anything, in gender symbolism (specifically, the reification of General Hospital into a human organism) the image evoked is of the passive feminization (and its fear) of the entire personnel of General Hospital beneath Maggiano, Lewin, and Dohrman. Past, present, and future feel like a violent "primal scene" of parental intercourse, with most of the managers and employees feeling "screwed," assaulted, raped, and annihilated by upper administration. Castration at the hands of vicious Oedipal fathers; children or dependents witnessing and being themselves victims of sexual "primal scenes"; and (at the most emotionally primitive levels) body mutilation, abandonment, wanton destruction, and unending annihilation of the physical body and of self-worth now condense together into a perverse psychosexual picture of General Hospital in this third set of interviews. The brief Dr. Lewin-Penny Hill fantasy was the closest to a whole-person fantasy of sexuality and rebirth.

Organizational regression to catastrophic anxiety, fantasy, and defenses against these not only colored any developmentally higher psychosexual levels, but subordinated them to the more primitive experience and organization of the world. The result is a homecoming to an American hospital of all the fantasies and feelings associated scarcely a decade and a half ago with imminently expected nuclear war and nuclear winter. Sexual fantasies and gender experience, like everything else, are organized around the terrifying experience of looking every day into a shattered and further shattering window of disappearance.

The story of General Hospital is not especially about a hospital, or even about a hospital and an ambulatory care center within a university. For all its detail about biomedicine, the story of General Hospital is about the corporate downsizing of modern America. The story of General Hospital is the story of a cultural compulsion in the rationalized guise of economic necessity. It is about hierarchy-induced mystification and self-mystification as an organization's own holding environment. The interviews persuade me that anger in the workplace (Allcorn, 1994), identity in the workplace (Diamond, 1993), and psychological invisibility in the bureaucracy (Baum, 1987) can often be understood to be derivative of total personal degradation and demoralization in the workplace.

The larger cultural story that General Hospital encapsulates is about killing our own; not with bombs or bullets, but with paper trails, spread sheets, bottom lines, profit margins, productivity quotas, and indifference. It is about the setting up of economically and technologically armed camps of organizational alliances and the waging of symbolic wars between them. It is about increased rhetoric about self-management and interdisciplinarity, and increased authoritarian domination, micromanagement, and central control from above.

Symbolically, Americans believe we "defeated" the Soviet Union in the late 1980s and early 1990s—the resignation of Gorbachev and the breakup of the USSR into nation-states supposedly represents a triumph of democracy over communism. We have become the very enemy we once detested, with which we proudly contrasted ourselves, and with which we were willing to wage nuclear war and bring upon the planet nuclear winter. "They" are now "us." We are now free to hate (Hockenos, 1993); we are now free to annihilate one another in endless volleys of RIFs, downsizings, delayerings, restructurings, and other euphemisms of induced suffering for the sake of sacrifice. We are executioner and condemned, at once or in sequence. Who can be clearly (I almost wrote "cleanly") bounded conceptually as oppressor and who as oppressed, who as victimizer and who as victim, in a system in which brutality and escalating brutalization are normalized, routinized, and rationalized? Where does this paranoid process even geographically end (Meissner, 1978)? When destructiveness and the multiple motives behind it are so firmly disguised by millions, not only intrapsychically but intersubjectively, what shall we say is "cause" and what "effect"?

Downsizings are part of our American internal war against "internal" enemies; and everyone is as much a potential enemy now as he or she was a potential ally yesterday. In this war, on these battlefields, there are no assured survivors, even as economic and corporate survival is stated as the paramount goal. If their ostensible goal of this war (economic, corporate, or medical) is to survive, if not to win, the deeper goal is to destroy—first to avert one's own death; later to bring it about. Total downsizing is ultimately total self-annihilation.

With the fall of the Berlin Wall, the resignation of Soviet President Mikhail Gorbachev, and the disappearance of the Soviet Union as a historically reliable repository for all our (in the democratic West) disavowed "bad" parts, emotions, and fantasies, there has occurred not only the return of the repressed, but the even more violent return of the projected. They haunt even our hospitals. We—our own "badness" on the home front—are the enemy we endlessly try to identify, to distinguish from ourselves, and then to torture, maim, and kill. The study of the downsizing of General Hospital is a local study of this self-destructive war.

There are no essential workers (or essential managers); there is no CEO Oscar Schindler (hero of director Steven Spielberg's 1993 movie) to befriend, shelter, and protect us. There is now security in neither commitment, productivity, or longevity. Nor is there a corporation- and monopoly-busting President Theodore Roosevelt in sight. There is only the fantasied corporate collective to be worked, and if necessary, for which to sacrifice others and oneself. In many ways, Americans have become many of the disturbing unconscious fantasies and wishes the Soviet Union once represented to us. Further, General Hospital is America and America is General Hospital; and not in some mysterious parallel process, analogy, or exaggerated poet's license. They are our world of relentless, thankless work, of unrelenting hate, of unspeakable grief, and of banished love. Officially (at least), at General Hospital there were to be functions and products, not people. It is Melanie Klein's (1946) "paranoid–schizoid" position become both public and public policy.

American courtrooms, family therapy consulting rooms, television programs, and newspaper articles are filled with stories of real and alleged "ritual abuse" and "missing children." Whatever the official psychiatric epidemiology of these pathological forms, they are enchanting, if disturbing, distractions from those less noticed forms of "normal" ritualized cultural abuse that go by the names of RIFing, downsizing, restructuring, and reengineering; forms that make potentially abandoned, missing (adult) children of us all. Here, social reality enacts fantasy, mirrors fantasy, and induces fantasy. At this moment in American history, the nation that most adulates personal autonomy, in fact most prizes corporate totalitarianism. The social process of RIFing—at General Hospital and elsewhere—resembles nothing more than it does the perversions elevated to social policy.

From Erik Erikson's (1968) writing on American and German adolescents, we learned that when individuals and whole groups cannot hope for an increasing sense of "wholeness" they fall prey to ideologies and identities of "totalism." All-or-nothing closed systems of thought and feeling fill in where the synthetic function of the ego no longer feels possible. Erikson also described those negative conversions wherein people who cannot hope to achieve their ego ideals renounce them and embrace the negative identity, the emotionally polar opposite of what once was most precious. In the language of the American dream, the once hoped-for inclusive land of opportunity becomes the exclusive land of psychopathic opportunism (Stein and Hill, 1977). In the mid-1990s, we still live in the long, grief-filled shadow of the 1960s assassinations of John and Robert Kennedy and Rev. Martin Luther King, Jr., ambivalently beloved symbols of the fruition of that dream.

To borrow a metaphor from corporate consulting psychologist Tim Murphy (personal communication, November 9, 1994), we are organizationally and nationally like patients with anorexia nervosa: We consume our own projected distorted organizational body, now filled almost entirely with bad objects; a condensation of outer and inner tormentors (self- and object-representations). No matter how much "fat" we cut out, we still fill bloated, obese, evil, and inefficient. If we cannot hope to achieve, restore, or mourn our ideal (e.g., the "good," "familial" General Hospital during the Wirth era), we destroy all vestiges of even its memory. Perhaps an "anorexic" institution's unconscious mission is to starve itself to death—as have many individual anorexics in real life. Perhaps only death is redemptive enough for the good finally to rise again from the ashes of the bad objects.

These interviews raise a question for me that has reverberations both for social theory and for any consultant's would-be interventions: What does the recent history of General Hospital tell us about the boundaries between individual personality, institution, the larger American society, this moment in world history, and human nature? Simply put, where does all the aggression come from? And where do we intervene? I do not believe that we can either comprehend anything about the hospital or consult genuinely with individuals or with "the group" if we do not attempt to hold all these levels or viewpoints in our consciousness simultaneously. Which is also to say that if the consultant cannot hope to help the entire hospital system (not to mention the entire national system) to achieve a change of heart, even the consultant's smallest contribution, anywhere in the system, constitutes an intervention. Culturally popular short-term "outcome measures" are at best spurious; we rarely truly know our effect upon others.

This study, then, is of the interior of institutional totalitarianism in the process of formation (what anthropologist Erving Goffman [1961] called "total institutions"); the creation first of acute terror, then chronic terror, inducing regression to dependency, primitive rage, and the search for social control from that regressed position. Now, as psychoanalytic organizational writers have observed since the 1950s, it is of the very nature of bureaucracies to create interpersonal voids we fill with our (psychotic) anxieties and defenses against them. Where information and intimacy fails, we fill in with fantasy and unconscious affect. But that is during "ordinary" times. During times of massive change, the anxiety heightens and the regression deepens. The General Hospital style of change made both worse. For if the top-down style of decision making and information giving was not deliberate terrorism, it was, in the least, sufficiently callous to induce the most primitive catastrophic feelings and defenses against them. And it was conducted in a national, even international, group psychology that gave greater and greater free reign to such indulgence in brutality (see Freud, 1921, 1930).

In many respects, in the third set of transcripts I hear the same visceral, somatic level of feeling I have long read about in countless psychiatric accounts of therapy with patients who survived the Nazi concentration camps (e.g., Krystal, 1968, 1984). There is a virtual regression (partial, not total ego) to a predifferentiated psychosomatic state, where bodily tensions, buildups, and discharges are literally one's feelings. Theirs is a largely preverbal world, one in which people live trapped in bodies that have become internal battlefields from chronic degradation. The tormented are now the self-tormentors (and often tormenters of the next generations, family or occupational, all fueled by identification with aggressor and the now-sanctioned direct expression of sadistic impulses), cut off from their own feelings and fantasies as a result of so deep a regression.

I wish to raise one final theoretical issue, but one interwoven with practicality. There is no such thing as a "group psyche," a "group unconscious," or an "organizational mind." All these reifications are, in fact, widely shared fantasy–wishes about groups to which people hunger to belong, in part to undo separation from mother–child fusions. Part of the reality of General Hospital and its massive change is its role as transference object and the inner significance of threats to the continuity of that very object. Each interviewee is a person who brings an entire life history, childhood, and unique defensive and adaptive patterns to General Hospital; to the process of training as a manager or staff member; to previously stable role performance; and now to the major changes the hospital is undergoing. How do we assess the relative weight to personal, developmental factors, to situational, traumatic factors, and to their interaction; for, at one level, there is virtually no such thing as a trauma unmediated by personal factors? This is not only an issue for clinical and organizational theory and practice, but one laden with ethical issues as well.

Since the liberation of the Nazi death camps at the end of World War II and the deliberations over reparations to survivors of the Holocaust, debate has raged among psychiatrists, psychoanalysts, and jurists, among others, as to how much of the suffering in the concentration camps (and the "relocation" itself) was due to the actual severity of the trauma of living in them, and how much they activated and lived out earlier, predisposing conditions (e.g., Luel and Marcus, 1984). Some writers elevate the concept of "survivor syndrome" to an all-encompassing explanatory principle; at the opposite extreme, others altogether individualize each case of suffering based on life history and not entirely on the Holocaust atrocities.

That debate (see Luel and Marcus, 1984) has bearing on our understanding of suffering and decision making at General Hospital. As is clear from the interviewees, not everyone responded identically to the mass layoffs, the waiting, and the imminent restructuring. No culture, even organizational culture, is homogeneous in experience, affect, fantasy, and so on; especially at the deepest characterological levels. Still, there is clearly a sense of assault on meaning; a sense of personal degradation, widespread anger, and even open grief. Paralleling the conclusion of many health and legal professionals after the Nazi Holocaust, I would argue that the fact of the individuality of response is separate from acknowledging the collectivity of assault on all persons in General Hospital. It is at once an ethical issue (as if the "predisposing conditions" argument of childhood overdeterminism and conflict could diminish or erase the horror of the degradation; more abstractly, it is a confusion of logical types, as Alfred North Whitehead and Bertrand Russell described and an issue of group psychology (the brutalization and terrorization of an entire workplace and workforce).

In sum, any account of the mass layoffs and of subsequent workplace life at General Hospital must acknowledge both individual uniqueness of experience and the group nature of the trauma (not as some mystical "group mind," but in terms of group culture and identity as the interviewees have repeatedly and poignantly described). All in all, the image I have is of a deeply depressed organization, one overwhelmed with symbolic deaths, many of which have already occurred and many others of which are awaited. (Here I do not indulge in reification but in an interpretation of shared emotion, fantasy, and identity.) There is a wish to be able to be resilient, at least to mobilize for fight or flight, but I fear that the punitive, bitter, masochistically tinged depressiveness will prevail. The result, sadly, will be a demoralized group of "survivors" who are more exploitable than ever before. I would guess that, despite their wish to be devoted to patient care (which, I even need to remind myself as I read these battle-weary stories, is what the hospital is ostensibly for), they will be less rather than more productive in any humane sense of caring, although their hospital statistics (fewer persons caring for more patients) might look good.

Before turning to my recommendations, to what I would do as consultant to General Hospital, I want to say a few words about how these interviews have forced me to think and rethink psychoanalytic and cultural theory. (And theory is never academic, for behind one's recommendations are assumptions, stated and unstated, about the nature of the subject matter for which one is making recommendations.)

General Hospital consists of an organizational world constructed largely by the externalization of so much of the desolate, hate-ridden, inner world, and its reinternalization. Under such now-chronic emergency circumstances and ego operations, one psychoanalytic ideal of the gradual replacement of object relations by internal mental structure becomes virtually impossible. In such a persecutory, schizoid world, introspection and mourning (to take only two processes vital to organizational resilience [Diamond, 1993]) which would in fact help the organization to heal, rarely occur. To make matters worse, this description of one hospital could equally apply to modern America. To put it colloquially, what does personal responsibility mean under such circumstances?

What is the nature of human aggressiveness under circumstances such as at General Hospital, and where in turn do these "circumstances" come from? Perhaps no single model or theory of aggression accounts for the myriad of expressions at General Hospital. We are far from a Newtonian, mechanistic rendition of the Freudian universe. Some aggression at General Hospital is patent sadism, rationalized and intellectualized by institutional role and by the need to make deep cuts via downsizing. No doubt the same unconscious defenses will be used during the restructuring. Economics will be the obligatory "Big Lie," the current Orwellian Newspeak, or the smokescreen for bribing the superego to do the unconscionable with impunity (i.e., "Economic exigency requires it").

For others, the release of aggression from civilization's repression (see Freud, 1930) will occur via identification, "suggestion," or "contagion," especially as such expression of destructiveness is sanctioned by authorities from above (see Freud, 1921). Through identification and adaptation, further girded by projection, one need not take responsibility for acting out one's own unconscious rages, wishes, and vendettas. External authority replaces inner ego ideals (which echoes my first point). What one unconsciously wishes to do uncannily turns out to be none other than company policy.

Yet another source for aggressiveness at General Hospital is projective identification; people are provoked into acting out brutality at others' behest, yet are singled out as characterologically evil (Jacob Dohrman is the clearest example of this). Stated differently, people are goaded into embodying and acting out (for their own internal motives as well) others' "bad" parts. So, as we observe this, exactly whose id or punitive superego are we talking about? Dohrman's alone, or do we not need to say Maggiano's and Lewin's as projected into Dohrman? And, sado-masochistically, a similar projection up the vertical hierarchy into Dohrman, so that all his victims are innocent? Finally, under emergency conditions, the ego cannot tolerate the additional vulnerability and helplessness required for grieving to occur. Instead then of mourning's sadness, fury and chronic group depressiveness show their heads. The only hope is for Lewin, the presumed alpha male (the dominant male primate who has access to all females; the ruler of the Oedipal horde), and Penny Hill or the new Assistant Provost to pair sexually and regenerate General Hospital. Except for this brief mention of sexuality (taboo in the workplace), aggression in its many guises and motivations consumes General Hospital. If the expression of aggression often airs an unconscious wish, it at least as often serves as a massive defense against exposing the vulnerable, besieged self. In short, how primary is aggression as a drive, and how much is it secondary to feelings of lovelessness, worthlessness, and loss? Such a question takes us beyond the boundary of General Hospital to the experience of being an American in the 1990s—specifically, to the mental function of the rampant violence everywhere.

It also takes us to the very boundary of being a cultural animal, American or otherwise: for no institution, however good, and no ethnic or national culture, however flourishing, is immune to change or immortal. Change does not have to be inflicted so ruthlessly as at General Hospital to be felt keenly as a loss—a loss of one's outer skin, a loss of identity, a loss of meaning, or a symbolic death. And we humans define our very selves by our affiliations with these organizational and other cultures—symbolic and institutional successors to our mothers, fathers, and wider families.

As much through our workplaces as through our churches and ethnicities, we seek to purchase immortality, to fend off death, and to reverse painful separations. And however much we protest the fact of our death through our proud cultural monuments and restructurings, we must fail. Without love, there is only death. In order to love, we must also grieve our lost cultures and our dashed hopes (or atone for our failure to grieve) or we will kill again and again so as not to feel our deeper hurt. And there is so much to grieve: not only the losses of people and of organizational identity, but one's protective envy and hatreds, one's paranoid anxiety that made upper management even more monstrous than they were, and even one's sense of betrayal by "the organization"—including the guilt and shame of not being able to avert that very betrayal.

If General Hospital could have been a better holding environment in which people performed their work tasks, it still could not be a perfect one for the ending of an era. If change had been more gradual and more humane, if General Hospital employees at all levels had been more actively included in the process of their own fate, there would still have been imperfect "parenting" by the leaders. Anxieties over separation, castration, and annihilation are inevitably evoked by such situations and directed toward (transferred onto) leaders and toward the reified institution. There is no way the hospital could be a "good" (ideal) mother, even when the hospital is not a "bad" (murderous, abandoning) mother either. General Hospital, like all workplaces, churches, ethnic groups, and nations, is an object of dependency and of all other unconscious wishes; a projective container for them. When the container is threatened, so are those who feel held together by its shape. In short, if General Hospital could have been less than Hell, it also could never be Heaven. There is never a perfect fit (in stable times or during massive change) between institutional structure and personal desire.

In saying this, I do not in any way intent to diminish the real loss and feelings of profound suffering at General Hospital, but rather to situate them within the human condition. The downsizing of General Hospital belongs, I believe, to the class of human revolutions in which erstwhile group ideals, and the loss of persons themselves, are not grieved, but are instead redefined and discarded as if they were garbage or excrement; and where this discarding is enforced from above by the organizational, religious, ethnic, or national hierarchy. Where the sense of assault is too great, where the sense of vulnerability would be too great were loss acknowledged, and where previously repressed aggression now senses an opportunity to unleash itself, the aggression will be directed toward the unattainable, former institutional ideal and toward those who have the audacity to insist that something valuable was lost and that there is indeed something to mourn. Alas, the inability to mourn and the refusal to mourn are nonetheless monuments to the sense of loss by the vehemence of their denial and by the reversal of affect they display. Part of the lesson of General Hospital is how the inability to mourn can be enforced from above and (via identification with the aggressor) from within. Where mourning is prohibited, there can only be deeper and deeper "cuts."

What I Would Do as Consultant

I prefaced my interpretation with a quotation from Donald W. Winnicott, who wrote about the baby's earliest experience of being a collection of parts and about the crucial healing role of the mother holding the baby in her hands. That holding helps the baby to add up to one experience. I am uncertain whether Dr. Allcorn would define his interviews as an act of consulting, since the official role he had negotiated with the General Hospital hierarchy was simply that of researcher and interviewer. He would gather data, period. But the action, the experience of the interviews, was unmistakably clinical, even if that was not either of the participants' intentions. Certainly neither an individual interviewee nor General Hospital as an organization is a baby, but individual and collective part-regression to harrowing experiences of alienation and fragmentation make Winnicott's quotation more than allegorical to the interview process.

In fact, Dr. Allcorn helped his interviewees transmute an embattled collection of parts back into one experience. As consultant, I would try to continue this process, in one-to-one meetings and in group meetings alike. I would continue to inquire into their experiences and their changing sense of history and selfhood. I would continue to explore the relationship between outer task and inner (and intersubjective) meaning and feeling.

As imaginary consultant to General Hospital, I hope I could help my client organization to grieve their enormous losses, to fully feel the entire range of emotions (and unconscious affects) they have, to free themselves from the compulsion to repeat the traumatic past, to liberate themselves from the guilt of having somehow survived the mass firings, and to become once again a resilient, alive-feeling group; all these in the service of the tasks of running a hospital and taking good humane as well as technical care of ill people. That is quite a tall, self-imposed, ambitious therapeutic order. However, whatever else a consultant might do or aspire to do, he or she must also perform the safety-giving holding and containing that is the ultimate foundation of every consultation (in fact, the foundation of all human authenticity in both relationship and task). The holding is not in the words alone but is in the sense that another human being is fully present to take in even the most horrible feelings and thoughts one can have, that this human being will not retaliate, and that this human being will do the utmost to make one to feel understood (which is to say, safely held). As the interviewees said repeatedly in response to Dr. Allcorn's final question about the experience of the interviewer and the interviewing process, Dr. Allcorn did precisely that.

Much of what I would do, and much of the way I work as a consultant within organizations, Dr. Allcorn already did (see also Stein, 1994b). I would allow open-ended interviews, supplemented by "hanging out" in the organization, so to speak, doing observation and participant observation (if permitted) among those interviewed. Such independent observation would allow me to compare an individual's self-perception or self-report with actual behavior (and inferences I would make about the motivation for that behavior). That is, it would allow me to compare meanings and feelings expressed by interviewees with those I might infer or deduce from actual organizational behavior (such as meetings or formal and informal conversations).

In addition to asking my own questions, I would ask interviewees what questions they were pondering about the organization and about their lives; their replies would in turn shape questions I would never have thought to ask. Still, within the context of our American society that relies so much upon question-and-brief-answer approaches to everything, I would not place primacy on question-asking itself. Rather, I would place primacy upon relationships in which questions, musings, and feelings would naturally arise—in short, a relationship in which a face-to-face visit or a conversation over lunch or during a walk down the hall would be conducive to psychoanalytic data.

Further, given the enormity of the scale of General Hospital as an institution and of the emotional demands of the interviewing and consulting process, I would now prefer to work with Drs. Allcorn, Diamond, and Baum as a consulting team rather than try to take on General Hospital alone. In order to serve this vital containing and holding function, and in order to serve developmentally later functions such as interpretation and task recommendations, those consultants who serve as "containers" also need—for their own good and for the welfare of the consultation—to be "contained." By working as a team, we could frequently gather, not only to compare notes about those different facets of General Hospital we covered and to develop further strategy, but in order to be able to express our own "crazy" feelings evoked by the consultation.

Dr. Allcorn's interviews have taught me additional respect for structured, even protocol-like, interviews that repeated the identical format with each participant (as long as the interviewer is ready to accept the curve balls interviewees throw). They do not replace unstructured fieldwork and the unexpected data one learns from participant observation or from classical psychoanalysis. But they are not anathema to anthropological or even depth psychological organizational inquiry. If "the couch" is the psychoanalytic gold standard, it is equally true that there is no form of inquiry that cannot reveal the unconscious at least in part. Antonio Lozano said that Dr. Allcorn was "a good listener, patient, and willing to let the conversation go off on tangents. You were respectful." Are these not the heart of free association? The open-endedness came from what Dr. Allcorn and interviewee did with the question; with what Dr. Allcorn allowed the interviewees to do. I am thinking specifically of the "mental function," so to speak, of such formal organization: During times of such massive uncertainty, anxiety, lack of structure, and sudden authoritarian spasms of structure, it must have been comforting for the interviewees to have interpersonal, emotional, as well as cognitive constancy. I refer to something more profound than obsessive "predictability" (psychoanalysts clumsily call it "libidinal object constancy"). I do not know whether Dr. Allcorn designed his list of questions with this purpose or goal in mind, but this is how the interviewees used the questions. In a world without boundaries, or in a nearly liquid world where there is stagnation and then top-down tidal waves, Dr. Allcorn provided benign, safe boundaries in which some reconstruction and repair of the self was possible.

I will even admit to initial misgivings as to whether such a small list of tautly stated questions could ever evoke the depth and breadth of the experience of change at General Hospital. Could these questions really conjure psychoanalytically valid data? My answer is a resolute "Yes." Of course, the questions do not exist apart from the relationship Dr. Allcorn had with his interviewees and with others who had given him permission to conduct the survey in the first place. In the word associations and in the replies to the questions, the interviewees offered plenty of data from the unconscious. In sum, the emotionally organizing structure of the questions and of the interviews served as a countervailing force to the emotionally disorganizing structure of recent history at General Hospital. When a consultant is considering any intervention, including the very preliminary act of data collection and assessment, he or she needs to ask the crucial countertransference-type questions: For whose good am I asking this question, or asking it in this way? What does the interviewee or client need at this moment in the consultation?

In such an asphyxiating, emotionally numbing world as characterizes General Hospital, one can only be grateful that Dr. Allcorn was perceived by the medical center's uppermost administration to be non-threatening enough to enough men and women of high rank that the interviews were possible at all. Under the circumstances of what existentialists such as Karl Jaspers and Martin Heidegger half a century ago called "extreme situations," the degree of differentiation and integration the interviews nourished was little short of miraculous. Much as I might wish to have done more, I am mindful of what was achieved under the guise of rigorous, controlled data collection. The interviewees were Dr. Allcorn's clients in the absence of a formal consultant–client relationship or contract. The therapy, the healing, is in the living, not in the label. If it cannot be measured in immediate, numerical "outcomes" or in quarterly reports, its flesh nonetheless throbs on the typed page. To offer another person his or her own voice—even once every three months—is no small intervention, though by our conventional outcome measures it probably does not even count.

"What would I do as consultant?" is also constrained by what I would be allowed to do and by whom. The most obvious and most immediate questions are "Who hired me?" and "For what?" That is, his or her or their conscious objectives and unconscious transference tasks to the consultant. If General Hospital hired me, I would obviously need to remember that it was this same hospital hierarchy that hired SPC as the delegates (castrating henchmen, axe blade with which to hew separations and mutilations) of their agenda, including the acting out of a brutal, dehumanizing style of change. It is also the same hospital hierarchy that, via projective identification, found in Jacob Dohrman an internal henchman (to embody and induce dreads ranging from castration anxiety to separation anxiety to catastrophic annihilation anxiety), only eventually to isolate him and offer him up as sacrifice to their own self-consuming destructiveness and grandeur. So, in such a destructive, self-destructive, anxiety-fomenting, and unself-reflective setting, who would hire a psychoanalytically oriented consultant; and if so, under what guise? What would be his or her or their motivation and perception of the situation and of the task in need of being done? Reparative, destructive, sham or the shoring up of splitting between caring functions (persons) and destructive functions (other persons or persons as part objects)?

A separate issue is what the individual could accomplish informally within whatever the formal role is. If the consultant made an organizational diagnosis, could it be communicated, and to whom? Other similar questions arise, related at once to ethics, to technique or method, and to theory: Should the consultant try to help people to stay or to leave? To help them to adapt to an unquestioned and unquestionable situation? To help them to acquiesce to "reality"? To help them to explore individual and group resistances to feeling and comprehending the full magnitude of their plight? Where does "autonomy" (one of the sacred tenets of psychoanalytic therapy) end and confrontation of group delusion (that protects people from feeling and seeing the full brunt of what is taking place) begin?

In any event, one key task I would try to initiate would be to help the organization to identify core unconscious conflicts, fantasies, wishes, defenses, and the like; and to explore with them the forms they take (for instance, symptoms and official "problems"). If I could not formally do this, perhaps informally I could—and then the question arises as to how I or anyone in the organization could openly use what is learned in any setting at General Hospital.

The biggest question about General Hospital's recent history that remains unanswered for me—and which is a guide to further information about the organization and to my imagined role as consultant—is where Maggiano is in all these monumental events. To me, Maggiano has, throughout these interviews, been the most imaginary, elusive person of all. He is most vulnerable, then, to unconscious elaboration. To whom, for instance, does he report? I presume that he reports to the university President and the President in turn reports to some statewide or regional board of regents for education. But in the interviewees' story line, the world of General Hospital begins and ends with Dr. Maggiano. The interviewees depict him as if he were an Aristotelian *causa causans* (a cause of all later causes; a prime mover; a first cause, himself unconstrained, similar to the most severe images of God and the ultimate fantasy of self-creation). The fantasy of Maggiano is of an absolute sovereign, aloof and isolated from those utterly dependent on him for their careers, wages, roles, and futures. A more infantalized bureaucratic circumstance is difficult to imagine. I would wish to do my own reality testing, to ground my own fantasizing, by speaking with him and by observing him at work, such as in a decision-making group.

Were I consulting with General Hospital I would want to know more, both structurally and informally, about the relationship between Maggiano and the rest of the university. I would try to interview him (as well as Lewin, for that matter), and also to interview the university President to gain their viewpoints—much as a geographer and geologist often work as surveyors, looking at the same site from multiple angles and vantages. I would ask several questions, or if not ask them directly, try to discover answers through conversation: Is the President now so preoccupied with other matters of university governance (and, specifically, why these now) that he leaves Maggiano to usurp the power and authority left in the vacuum of benign neglect? How much of this is innocent ignorance; how much is denial; how much is a projective identification of the President's own aggressive impulses with those of Maggiano; and how much is tacit collusion with the institutional terrorism by turning a blind eye and a deaf ear to his own medical campus? How much is real geographic separation (especially in the era of telecommunication everywhere on earth), and how much is emotional geography?

For instance, at my own institution, the University of Oklahoma, the medical campus (Health Sciences Center, in Oklahoma City) is separated by about thirty miles from the rest of the university campus, called "the main campus" or "the Norman campus," in Norman, Oklahoma. "Sibling rivalry" and mutual institutional recrimination between campuses ("The other campus is always being favored," "The President is on the Norman campus, so the Health Sciences Center is the stepchild.") have characterized my eighteen years there. If, like the god Zeus, Maggiano is a mystery to those beneath him, the very nature and source of his authority, power, and dread are also a mystery to me. Were I consultant with General Hospital, I would want to break the glass bubble that further shrouds Maggiano in such awesome mystery. I would want to try to talk with him. I would want, in short, to try to test reality for myself.

What is the proper demeanor and approach of an organizational consultant who is swimming in all these changes, meanings, and feelings? Above all, to trust one's own feelings and fantasies as the most crucial data. Beneath the ocean of words uttered in the interviews, to recognize, and then to relinquish, the immense therapeutic ambition (to do something dramatic and major) induced by the overwhelming suffering of the situation as well as by one's narcissism; to distinguish between the greater potential for healing and resilience in organizational groups driven by depressive as opposed to fight–flight positions (and General Hospital is, for the most part, decidedly functioning in the latter mode at this time); and to be able to shift attention constantly between the individual interviewee and the hierarchical and horizontal situation in flux at General Hospital, and the "open systems" relationship between the layoffs, uncertainty, and reorganization at one hospital in relationship to the larger national and international picture. None of this is easy: least of all for the consultant to be an emotional holding environment for so much, and all at once. The central methodological lesson I have learned from examining and interpreting the three sets of General Hospital interviews is that all a consultant's other skills and concepts are experientially secondary to the emotional strength and durability of the holding environment.

During World War I, the British poet Wilfred Owen (1964) said, "All a poet can do today is to warn." Sometimes, that is the best a psychoanalytic interpreter or consultant can do as well. I do not mean "even" a consultant with psychoanalytic insight, but especially one with psychoanalytic insight—because one must know the difference between acting out based on anxiety, guilt, and shame and action that is based on what the client truly needs and "where the client is." Sometimes the warning comes less from what we say and infer than from what we hear, attend to, and allow to be heard—even formed into words, feelings, and narrative structures (story lines) as people talk and feel in our presence. The latter is what Dr. Allcorn did long before the three outside consultants received the transcripts of his interviews to make sense of.

What Dr. Allcorn did, despite his resolve to be neutral and do nothing but collect interview data, vindicates such notions as "containing function" and "holding environment." His interviews were an intervention even though he was no one's consultant. To create room for intimacy, for even a reprieve in which to become a whole person again in those circumstances, is an act of grace for all participants. What Dr. Allcorn did has profound implications for consulting far beyond the boundaries of General Hospital and the current downsizing of hospitals. It sets the tone and mood for what I would aspire to do as a consultant anywhere.

OVERVIEW OF INTERPRETATIONS

A great sadness has befallen the managers of General Hospital. The consultants consistently identify a depressive, paranoid, persecuted, and anxious group of managers who have, it seems, in many ways moved beyond fear or dread of what they fantasize will happen (which has not happened) and a totally dependent and helpless state, to one of resignation, withdrawal, retreat, and alienation from oneself, others, and the organization. Feelings are not discussed. There is a flatter effect and a death-like calm. Feelings of doing anything, including flight or fighting back, are deeply suppressed. There is less self-awareness, while at the same time remaining awareness seems to be almost entirely focused on oneself and survival. Also noted is that the boundary between self and experience is being obliterated as anxiety-ridden experience floods into those interviewed, often leading to psychosomatic symptoms associated with chronic fight–flight mobilization. Survivor's guilt seems to be omnipresent, as well as a paranoia-filled lack of trust. Indeed, the consultants say things are much worse and possibly very hard to repair in what has become a living hell on earth for those experiencing it, including the interviewer.

A primal scene such as this, with its accompanying anxiety, promotes regression and the use of primitive psychological defenses such as splitting and projection and projective identification. It is particularly noteworthy that Jacob Dohrman may be understood to have become a projective vessel for both Maggiano and Lewin as well as for his staff. Jacob may have absorbed many of the projections associated with the negative aspects of control. Maggiano and Lewin may have projected their needs to control onto him, and his identification with these projections may have accentuated his preexisting tendency to be controlling, perhaps leading to greater irritability on his part. At the same time, staff may have projected their controlling tendencies onto him to free them of any sense of being able to control what was happening, which then permits them to feel helpless and persecuted by controlling Jacob. Certainly, psychodynamics like this must be considered.

Once again, a film-related image comes to mind—the journey into darkness depicted in *Apocalypse Now*. Reality becomes surreal and hard to believe as experience continues to unfold at General Hospital. In this movie, Marlon Brando's character at one point exclaims, "The horror, the horror." The experience at General Hospital is understood by the consultants to promote primitive self, other, and organizational experiences accompanied by equally primitive psychological defenses. In some ways it seems as though Dr. Stein, in his lengthy listing of the metaphors, is trying to assure himself and the reader that yes, this is occurring. This assurance by repetition is not unlike the Holocaust museum's wall-sized list of hundreds of Jewish towns that were eliminated for all time. The experience and learning is in the list and its incessant repetition that pries into one's mind.

Yet, another image involves staff being selected as not having the "right" leadership "stuff." They learn that they are not right (some have left or are being excluding from committees) and must be eliminated, not unlike a wave of European ethnic cleansing.

Little more need be said about the events at General Hospital. The consultants have captured its essence. However, in saying this, a new concern is introduced—that of how those interviewed are living through their experience. The consultants provide a number of psychodynamically informed analyses of their experience.

In particular, the inescapable anxiety has resulted in a regression on the part of many of those interviewed. This has occurred to such an extent that it can be understood as a collective or group regression to an earlier state of development—in particular, to the classical anal stage of development where issues of external expectations of control of self arise. The consultants offer a number of descriptions and points of view about regression. In particular, the image of the staff at General Hospital being passively processed toward elimination (much like food in the colon) is striking. The case seems, in many ways, to validate the applicability of developmental perspectives to understanding regression in organizations.

At the same time, the consultants struggle with another profound split in experience. The dominant mode of action is male—control oriented and destructive. Maggiano and Lewin emerge as a dominate and controlling force that castrates all before them. Their paternalism casts everyone else in a role of helpless and even morbid dependency. In contrast, there is also a female voice, often heard on the part of some of the females interviewed. These women speak of family, children, and nurturing (regeneration versus destruction), which are understood to be antithetical to the warlike scorched-earth policy of Maggiano and Lewin (although they often espouse them). This voice is, however, hard to hear and seems, at times, to puzzle the consultants.

Closely related to the above split is the emergence of the first sense of sexuality or male–female pairing at the top of the organization (Lewin with one or both of the new, young, and attractive executives). Penny Hill is, in fact, understood to serve a role of liaison between the paternalistic, homosexual father-pair, Lewin and Maggiano, and the helpless and degraded children, the staff. The role of liaison carries with it the sense of a caretaking female or mother figure who will now try to take care of the staff (her children) by sheltering them from the rage of the father (Lewin in particular and Maggiano by extension). Perhaps the pairing of Maggiano and Lewin to give birth to a new organization has resulted in an insemination and gestation but no birth, which must possibly be left to females to accomplish. It is also noteworthy that the female nature of the liaison role had been fulfilled by Frank Wirth in the past.

A theoretical perspective provided by Karen Horney (1950) also sheds light on General Hospital. The perspective describes three types of responses to the experience of excessive anxiety. The first is an appeal to mastery, which amounts to an effort to get control by any means available. Mastery is associated with perfectionism, arrogance and vindictiveness, and narcissism (you will be as I wish). The second is an appeal to love, which amounts to doing whatever is necessary to be taken care of by powerful others, including self-effacing morbid dependency (I will be as you wish). The third is the appeal to freedom, which arises when neither of the above two appeals works or when they are not available to individuals to act out because of psychic conflict. The result is resignation from active participation, which involves withdrawal from self, others, and organizational life (just leave me alone). Using these three perspectives to understand events at General Hospital is helpful. The masters (Maggiano and Lewin) have, by the time of the second set of interviews, made the staff feel worthless, morbidly dependent and abused, and in need of caretaking (the appeal to love). The third set reveals that the staff may have moved toward the appeal to freedom after finding the unrelenting stress and stripping of self-esteem too great to bear. There are many signs of withdrawal and alienation from oneself (including one's feelings), others, and the hospital in the third set of interviews.

The notion of intervention is also difficult for the consultants to focus upon, in part because Maggiano and Lewin were not interviewed and data are missing, but also because the scope and magnitude of events seem to transcend any notion of exactly how to make things better (other than stopping the damage by, figuratively speaking, terminating the terminators). In fact, the scene resembles a cartoon, once seen by the author, of a little soldier in the foreground whose uniform is tattered saying, "I think we won," when in the background there is only devastation. It is also worth noting that the actual apocalypse is yet to befall the management and is described in the epilogue that follows; which, it turns out, is more extraordinary than any the managers might have imagined.

A last point worth noting is that Dr. Stein once again reminds us of the larger social and even national significance of the events taking place at General Hospital. He asks the question of whether it is possible that Americans have located a new post–Cold War enemy and the enemy is us.

Part V

Looking Back: General Hospital in Retrospect

Thus far, the events at General Hospital, which have included completion of a downsizing (Phase 1) and preparation for the much anticipated restructuring or flattening of the management hierarchy (Phase 2), have been the dominant themes of the interviews. Phase 3, which will involve reengineering or, more specifically, working to find ways to conserve the use of clinical resources, is but a distant concern, although some efforts have been undertaken to locate cost savings from operations. The consultants to the case have offered many insightful interpretations as to how these events have affected the employees of the hospital. It is perhaps an understatement to say that the top-down handling of the restructuring process has left all levels of management feeling vulnerable, disrespected, worthless, ineffective, and unwanted. It is also noteworthy that the experience at General Hospital is not unique and, in fact, has been played out in many organizations throughout the United States. In this regard, it is likely that the case is familiar to many readers, as it was to the three consultants. This familiarity to the consultants and the accompanying unconscious resistance to reexperiencing these types of distressing experiences become part of the conclusion to this book.

Chapter 9 provides an update on events at General Hospital. The interviews ended just before the announcement of the restructuring which, as will be found in the epilogue, was more devastating than anyone might have imagined. Chapter 10 concludes the book with reflections of the three case consultants about the case, each other's work, and their work processes. The consultants met with the first author for a two-day meeting to discuss the work before completing their concluding remarks. Prior to the meeting, they had the opportunity to read each other's work. Chapter 10 concludes with a final overview prepared by the first author.

Chapter 9

Epilogue to the
General Hospital Case

This chapter is provided as an update on events at General Hospital. In particular, the time of the third set of interviews was, it turned out, just before the restructuring was announced. The nature of the restructuring is an important part of more fully understanding the case.

THE RESTRUCTURING

Shortly after the final interviews were conducted in September, Dr. Lewin announced the long-awaited management restructuring in mid-October 1994. The essence of the restructuring was that every management position in the hospital was eliminated and an entirely new management structure provided. The number of staff affected was never published, but a good guess is that 175 to 200 management positions were eliminated. The restructuring reduced the number of management layers from eleven to seven.

The restructuring involved two steps. The first step eliminated all of the senior-level management positions in the hospital. It was announced that twenty new positions had been created and that anyone interested in them could apply. Job descriptions were published. The restructuring recast the reporting lines for the departments of the hospital to a number of positions. The Manager III positions to which they had reported were eliminated. Some of the positions were entirely new, such as a number of service-line management positions. General Hospital did not have formal service lines.

Staff had three days to apply for one or more of the positions and anyone could apply. Dr. Lewin, the new Hospital Director, the new Assistant Provost (both started in July) and the manager of ambulatory then selected from the pool of applicants who would receive one of the twenty positions. It is important to appreciate that not only were all positions eliminated and entirely new positions created (for which staff often had no experience in performing), but a product-line approach was implemented with its accompanying needs to create horizontal integration. In sum, it is hard to imagine a more profound change process for any organization to experience.

Those selected for the twenty positions learned of their selection in two weeks, by the end of October. Many selected were not from the senior ranks of management. Many senior-level executives who had been with the hospital for many years (and some since it opened) were simply informed by a Friday phone call from the personnel department that they were not selected. Friday became their last day at work. They were provided outplacement services and severance packages. They were not provided receptions to celebrate their departure, as had been the tradition. A general observation of the selections offered by many staff was that those selected were "team players," people who were not outspoken or opinionated and who openly endorsed Dr. Lewin's management philosophy.

Starting early in November, an additional ninety-five mid-level management positions were announced. Staff were once again provided a few days to apply and selections were announced in two weeks, by mid-November. It is worth noting that the managers recently selected for the twenty senior-level positions were obliged to select their staff within two weeks of their appointment. This precluded their knowing their area, the positions, or many of the people who applied for the positions. The selection process used was described as each applicant being announced and discussed by the group as to whether they were "our kind of people." Those not selected once again received the Friday phone call and the outplacement services, as well as severance packages. This very fast-paced process tended to support the belief by many that all or many of the staffing decisions had been made by Dr. Lewin well in advance of the process, possibly as a by-product of his interviewing staff in the hospital and sitting in on meetings as an observer.

In sum, during a thirty-day period, General Hospital received an entirely new management structure and new management "team." All positions were filled from within; and since many of the positions were entirely new or, at the minimum, reorganized reporting responsibilities, it must be noted that every manager appointed had no prior work experience (at the best very limited) in his or her new area of responsibility. And, like a game of musical chairs, those managers not selected were terminated. Information is not available as to who and how many lost their positions. Nothing was published. Of those selected for interviews, 40 percent are no longer employed by the hospital.

Many of the managers who were terminated were senior employees who, as a result, were also older and received high salaries. In general, those selected for the new positions were younger, less-experienced individuals. These senior employees, who were often highly respected and carried institutional history with them, were occasionally seen on Friday with smiles on their faces as they headed toward an exit with a box of their office possessions under one arm and a fist full of strings to helium-filled balloons in their free hand. Estimates are that between sixty and one hundred executives and managers lost their jobs.

STAFF REACTIONS TO THE RESTRUCTURING

During November, there were several instances where the feelings of some staff were expressed by the posting in common areas of information that represented their point of view. Two examples of these responses are Figures 9.1 and 9.2. Other than these reactions, the changes and departures were accepted with silent resignation by the staff of the hospital. Figure 9.3 is provided to update the reader on who stayed (60%) and who left (40%).

SUBSEQUENT EVENTS

During December, to everyone's surprise, Dr. Maggiano announced his resignation and his appointment to a new position at another institution. He was to stay in his position six months as a lame duck before leaving. It was also generally believed that Dr. Maggiano's departure signaled a time for Dr. Lewin and perhaps others on Dr. Maggiano's immediate staff to seek out new career opportunities. The phrase, "Those who live by the sword, die by the sword," came to mind. However, if everyone was surprised about the first announcement, everyone was astonished when, in February, Dr. Maggiano announced that he would be staying (after announcements at the other institution of his appointment there). No meaningful explanation was provided.

During the first quarter of 1995, it was discovered that the restructuring required creating entirely new budgeting and information systems, something not easily achieved in the short run. Six months after the changes, senior management is still working hard to come to grips with the effects of the convulsive change while contending with SPC's implementation of Phase 3.

This summary of additional events concludes the epilogue to the case. The reappointment of Dr. Maggiano, it is felt by many, now firmly establishes him in absolute control of the medical center and by extension his immediate staff. SPC is now to proceed to perform its work of downsizing the schools, starting with the medical school.

Figure 9.1
Feel on the Verge of Extinction?

Here Are Ten Ways to Survive the Health Reform Age

1. HIRE AN INEXPERIENCED BOOB AS CEO
2. REDUCE OCCUPANCY RATE OF HOSPITAL TO 50%
3. SHUN HMO CONTRACTS
4. ACQUIRE A SECOND RATE COMMUNITY HOSPITAL IN A BAD NEIGHBORHOOD
5. PISS ON YOU AFFILIATE HOSPITALS
6. THREAT YOUR ATTENDING PHYSICIANS LIKE SHIT
7. LAYOFF NURSES, SECRETARIES, AND ANCILLARY STAFF
8. MAKE MIDDLE MANAGEMENT TAKE THE FALL FOR BAD DECISIONS MADE BY UPPER MANAGEMENT
9. HIRE HIGH PRICED CONSULTANTS TO COME IN AND TELL YOU THE OBVIOUS
10. BE ARROGANT

Figure 9.2
Open Letter to All Employees

ARE WE ALL SHEEP, OR WHAT?
WHEN ARE WE AS A GROUP GOING TO UNITE?!

GOD KNOWS, IF WE CAN'T WIN, WE SHOULD AT LEAST GIVE
THE BOARD OF TRUSTEES AND THEIR HENCHMEN CAUSE TO
PAUSE AND CONSIDER THE CONSEQUENCES OF THEIR
ACTIONS -- BECAUSE AFTER MANAGEMENT IS PURGED ...

YOU'RE NEXT!

NOT ONLY ARE YOU GOING TO BE FORCED TO TAKE ON MUCH
MORE WORK IN THE FUTURE (IN SECTIONS THAT ARE
ALREADY UNDERSTAFFED), YOU'RE GOING TO RECEIVE LESS
PAY FOR YOU LABORS!

YES, THAT'S WHAT'S NEXT -- PAY REDUCTIONS AND LAYOFFS
IN EARLY '95. ITS A FACT, JACK!

CONSIDER THIS:

FOR YEARS AND YEARS, THE UNIVERSITY BLED THE MEDICAL
CENTER OF ITS PROFITABLE ASSETS -- DISTRIBUTING OUR
PROFITS THROUGHOUT THE UNIVERSITY SYSTEM. WE'VE
NEVER BEEN ABLE TO CONTROL THE FLOW OF THOSE CASH
ASSETS.

WE WERE THE PROVERBIAL GOOSE THAT LAID THE
GOLDEN EGG

NOW THAT WE'RE EXPERIENCING FINANCIAL DIFFICULTY --
WHAT IS THE UNIVERSITY'S RESPONSE?

WHY, KILL THE GOOSE THAT LAID
THE GOLDEN EGG!

YOU'VE BEEN PRIMED FOR THIS FOR SOME TIME NOW. WE'VE
ALL SUFFERED THROUGH THE MAGGIANO-LEWIN VAUDEVILLE
ACTS -- OUR FINANCIAL WOES HAVE BEEN EXPLAINED AD
NAUSEUM -- AND WE'VE ALL DUTIFULLY TRIED OUR BEST TO
CUT CORNERS AND WATCH EXPENSES.

SURELY, WE ALL KNOW THAT THE HEALTH-CARE INDUSTRY IS
SUFFERING THROUGHOUT THE COUNTRY. WE'VE ALSO BEEN
TOLD THAT SIMILAR MEASURES ARE BEING INTRODUCED IN
ALL HEALTH CARE SETTINGS ... BUT SINCE WHEN HAS "WHAT
OTHER PEOPLE ARE DOING" BEEN A MANDATE FOR US?

Figure 9.2 (*continued*)

WHY ARE WE FOLLOWING AND NOT LEADING? WHY AREN'T
WE PROVIDING INNOVATIVE RESPONSES?

WE SHOULD BE A CREATIVE
INDUSTRY LEADER

WE SHOULD BE AT THE
CUTTING EDGE OF CHANGE

INSTEAD, PIECE BY PIECE, THE BOARD OF TRUSTEES HAS
DECIDED TO FEED THE GOOSE TO THE SHARKS. INSTEAD OF
WORKING WITH US TO TURN THIS PLACE AROUND, THEY HAVE
IDENTIFIED US AS THE REASON WE ARE IN FINANCIAL
TROUBLE AND HAVE BROUGHT IN HIRED GUNS TO DO THEIR
DIRTY WORK.

QUESTIONS TO CONSIDER:

1. WHO THE HELL IS SPC AND WHAT DO THEY REALLY KNOW
ABOUT US AND OUR CORPORATE CULTURE?

2. WHO THE HELL ARE THESE NEW VICE PROVOSTS
(OBVIOUSLY NOTHING MORE THAN RECENTLY HIRED
HENCHMEN TO DELIVER THE "SPC CURE" TO THE MEDICAL
CENTER).

3. LET'S CALL A SPACE A SPACE: THIS IS NOT A
RESTRUCTURING -- THIS IS A SHAM USED TO JUSTIFY A GROSS
REDUCTION IN WORK FORCE -- ONE THAT WILL SERIOUSLY
JEOPARDIZE THE ENTIRE OPERATION OF THE MEDICAL
CENTER (DESPITE OLD MAGGIANO'S ASSERTION THAT "THINGS
ARE JUST FINE" FROM HIS PERSPECTIVE.) SHAMS SUCH AS
THIS SHOULD BE ILLEGAL (AND IN A CLASS ACTION SUITE
THEY MIGH BE!)

4. WHY ARE WE CUTTING OUT JOB CATEGORIES & FORCING
OUR BEST, MOST EXPERIENCED, PEOPLE OUT THE DOOR,
ESPECIALLY IF WE'RE READY TO SPREAD OURSELVES OUT
INTO THE BURBS AND BEYOND? WOULDN'T IT BE WISER TO
"WAIT AND SEE" HOW THOSE EFFORTS GO BEFORE WE
CASTRATE THE WORK FORCE?

5. WHY HAVE WE NEVER UNIONIZED?

ISN'T IT HIGH TIME?

THE VICE PROVOSTS AND SPC CAN GO TO HELL -- WE NEED
THE AFL/CIO!

238

Figure 9.3
Where Have All the Managers Gone?

The following individuals either left voluntarily or were terminated.

Jacob Dohrman	Left to take a position at another hospital.
Tom Frey	Left to take a position at another hospital but returned to take one of the new positions.
Joseph Greene	Terminated.
Judy Harris	Terminated.
Peggy Lubin	Left without locating a new position.
Stan Pittman	Left without locating a new position.
Chris Regan	Terminated.
Rosetta Shelton	Did not apply for a position. Diagnosed with cancer and on leave of absence.
Matt Towner	Left to take a position at another hospital.
Cynthia Winston	Terminated.

The following individuals were appointed to one of the new management positions.

Brenda Early	
Chris Forbes	
Jeri Glover	
Mary James	
Val Kasman	
Doug Lofgren	
Antonio Lozano	
Maria Meyers	
Ed Mills	
Julie Nugent	
Ted Olsen	Continues to look for new employement.
Mike Payne	
Bob Ryder	

Chapter 10

The Case in Perspective

HOWELL BAUM'S FINAL ANALYSIS

Questions of Method

This project was an experiment in method. Would it be possible to understand an episode in organizational restructuring by interpreting notes from three sets of interviews with twenty-three middle managers? In particular, would responses to twenty-five questions in interviews usually lasting an hour or less provide data on which meaningful psychoanalytically sensitive interpretations could be based?

When I started this project, I was sensitive to its methodological weaknesses. The questions did not ask about people's personal histories; it would be difficult to speculate about how their personalities affected their reactions to organizational change. Because I would not do the interviews, I could not directly know how the interview situation might affect what they would say. For example, if people came to have mixed feelings about restructuring, they might select Allcorn as the audience for their angry feelings while telling him little about any ways they supported restructuring.

Because I was not interviewing the managers, I could not ask follow-up questions to encourage them to say more about anything that puzzled them or me. I could not get the tacit sense of these other persons that an interview relationship allows. Not being on the scene at all, I would be unable to know about the situation from information that was "around."

Moreover, since the interviews would not be taped, Allcorn's notes would be his distillations of what people said. In my work, I have recorded hundreds of interviews in handwritten notes. Over the years,

I have come to recognize how hard it is to write as quickly as people speak; to listen, think, and write simultaneously; and to avoid occasionally paraphrasing others' words in one's own. I try to evaluate the accuracy of my notes in my own work, but, while trusting Allcorn's competence and integrity, I could not assess what he would write up.

There was a risk that, while the notes might provide rich information, it would be difficult to draw accurate inferences from what Allcorn reported people saying to him to what these people thought and felt and how they acted. For example, I would not have the chance to hear them talk among themselves or see them at work. All these limitations would encourage me to project my own thoughts and feelings onto these people and this situation to a degree that made me uneasy.

I am again acutely sensitive to these methodological limitations now that the case is over. Indeed, a crucial characteristic of the case brings these issues to the center. Not only were Maggiano and Lewin unavailable for interviewing, but they consistently withheld information from nearly everyone in the hospital. Consequently, the managers interviewed were themselves forced to speculate and fantasize about top managers' intentions and activities. The case invited projection from everyone, not least the interviewer and interpreters. Although that fact is important information about the restructuring process, the case is still incomplete without information from and about Maggiano and Lewin.

How would Maggiano and Lewin present this case? Would their account seem as crazy as the version shared by the middle managers? Would they provide information about improvements in revenue flow or patient care that would provide a positive context for the middle managers' experiences?

As much as we need to know what the answers are, we do not. We are forced to speculate on the basis of our own thoughts, feelings, and experiences. And yet, having acknowledged this, I was surprised to note how firmly I returned to these methodological questions at the end of the study. They are all valid concerns. Yet none of these questions kept me from interpreting the interview notes earlier. None of these problems led me to doubt the notes described deep personal and organizational pain.

I think the explanation is that such methodological questions can serve as an unconscious defense against recognizing this suffering. These are not coal miners, with whom we might sympathize but not identify. These are workers like ourselves: professionals, people with advanced college degrees. Many of us who became professionals, managers, or academics assumed that, because we were neither the blue-collar workers nor the small entrepreneurs that our parents were, we were safe from economic vicissitudes. Yet many of us have already been buffeted around by "restructurings." We are no more secure than the workers at General Hospital.

After the detachment and the black humor of the first set of interviews, I found the unmediated pain of the second and third sets often overwhelming. I have no question about its reality, nor does Allcorn, Diamond, or Stein. One way I might shield myself from recognizing it, empathizing with it, identifying with it, and feeling helpless before it, especially as I was simply forced to watch and could do nothing about it, is to raise methodological questions in the unconscious hope that, perhaps, this did not really happen.

I urge the reader to think critically about the research method and ways of improving it. The reader may or may not believe a great deal that psychoanalysts say about unconscious desires and anxieties. However, the reader should not let doubts on either score become a shield against recognizing the dire human consequences of restructuring, in this hospital and elsewhere. The case forces us to think about other ways of managing organizations.

Understanding an Organization Psychoanalytically

This project was an experiment in understanding an organization psychoanalytically. In general, the psychoanalytic approach focuses attention on how people think and act, unconsciously as well as consciously. In addition to our conscious intentions, we have unconscious desires and anxieties that lead us to make unconscious plans as well. We may succeed at our unconscious aims even as we seem to fail at our overt intentions. In short, we bring some of our troubles on ourselves.

One implication of this approach for the study was methodological. Allcorn, in asking questions and recording answers, should reflect on how his own conscious or unconscious thoughts or feelings might influence what he recorded, just as Diamond, Stein, and I should consider how such biases could influence how we interpreted the case. Might we be too willing to side with subordinates against their bosses, or vice versa? Might our own experiences with restructuring lead us to make this case a case against top managers?

Beyond individual efforts at self-reflection, the study's structure helped to limit unconscious influences on interpretation. Stein, Diamond, and I each engaged in the task of analyzing the interview notes without communicating with one another. In this way, we would have three independent views of hospital events. Strikingly, although the interpretations differ in emphasis, they are complementary. This consistency suggests unconscious individual biases played a small role in the analysis.

When we all met after interpreting the three sets of interviews, we challenged one another's analyses for possible unconscious influences. In the course of these conversations, we discovered ways we had resisted and coped with recognizing the suffering of downsizing. It was as a result of these discussions, for example, that I concluded my methodological questions were partly an unconscious defense against that pain. These collective consultations enabled us all to write more clearly about events.

Substantively, the question of the psychoanalytic approach was whether it could shed light on aspects of organizational change that would otherwise avoid notice. Did restructuring have unconscious motives or consequences that distorted its aims or increased its costs in ways that rational managers would not recognize?

In fact, when I began reading the interview notes, I felt no special psychoanalytic understanding was necessary to see the organizational and personal damage caused by restructuring. Those interviewed spoke well for themselves. They were realistically anxious and angry. Neither a reader nor a top manager at the hospital could miss the problems reengineering was creating.

In looking more deeply at this situation, Diamond, Stein, and I brought our psychoanalytic perspectives to bear on three questions. One, to which I gave considerable attention, was how restructuring affected staff members' abilities to continue working and recreate a caring institution. I explored how deeply people seemed wounded—how seemingly simple references to losing hope, vision, or loyalty referred to feelings of infantilization, impotence, and death.

Frankly, I was surprised at how devastated people seemed. Though chronological adults, many spoke in the primitive emotional terms of children and infants. They saw themselves as small and helpless, facing forces that were powerful, ubiquitous, continually fragmenting and unpredictably re-forming, and malevolent. Mature behavior is unlikely under these conditions. I want to emphasize what this means. Some of us are accustomed to saying that organizational change can be harsh, but is necessary and that workers can "take it": They will suffer, but they can adjust and go on. Some of us who go through organizational upheaval try to reassure ourselves with such words.

The evidence here is that people are not perfectly resilient. They can take only so much, and then they are traumatized. They may recover but will not do so immediately. And, to put it more simply, they may be too angry about how they have been treated to go on.

Still, having seen what led me to these conclusions, I had difficulty imagining the likely consequence for the hospital: The institution would be unable to continue functioning as an entity whose employees collaborated in caring for patients. It is hard to believe a large organization can simply die.

In reality, social units, from families to corporations, often continue even when they no longer function well. We maintain them out of habit and desire. They rewarded us emotionally, socially, or financially in the past, and we want to believe they will do so in the future. Those at the hospital show us common attachments to workplaces: They identified themselves with the organization and identified it with their personal ideals. They wanted to think of it as perfect, powerful, competent, and loving in the ways they wanted to be (see Schwartz, 1990). In reality, being part of it allowed them to be good in some ways; in fantasy, being part of it let them think of themselves as very good in many ways. Intellectually and emotionally, they could not imagine the hospital's death. Perhaps such faith supported the top managers in their dark moments.

A second question that Stein and Diamond particularly addressed was how unconscious relations between top managers and subordinate staff contributed to problems in restructuring and hindered their resolution. Stein and Diamond considered how each group could unconsciously split the organization morally into two parts, identifying themselves with goodness and the others with evil. They examined how the two groups could have distorted beyond recognition real differences in interest and perspective, closing out possibilities for reconciliation and driving out Jacob Dohrman, who was caught in the middle.

I have no doubt many people engaged in such splitting. However, listening only to the subordinates, I was inclined to take the essence of their version more or less at face value. Being at such a distance from the hospital, I felt in a poor position to distinguish excessive vilification from what was deserved.

The third question, on which Stein wrote at length, is what the top managers thought they were doing. I don't know. They were not interviewed. Whether they engaged in Manichaean splitting I cannot say. Whether whatever sadistic satisfactions they may have derived from restructuring were their primary motivation, that I cannot say either.

How Could This Have Happened? And What Happened?

But the pain and damage inflicted by reengineering on an institution supposed to care for people have forced all of us to struggle with two questions. The first is whether the events at General Hospital are not one local manifestation of a societal phenomenon. The second is to what degree the hospital restructuring reflects Maggiano and Lewin's personalities and to what degree institutional cultures or incentives.

General Hospital in a Societal Context

Reengineering is a national movement, and yet, as Allcorn's literature review shows, its results consistently fail to meet its promise. In other words, managers could not be choosing it because of any evident widespread success. If they know of disappointing results elsewhere, they may imagine their organization will be an exception. Or else, perhaps unconsciously, they may value restructuring for meanings and effects aside from profitability.

Reengineering commonly proceeds from the top down, and one normal premise is that subordinates are to blame for the organization's poor performance and should be downsized out. In reality, the question of causes for organizational problems is an empirical one, and responsibility might rest complexly in many places, including top management. Yet, in practice, restructuring offers top managers a reassuring fantasy: It blames others and justifies punishing them.

Stein associates enthusiasm for downsizing with the end of the Cold War, recognition that America still suffers many social and economic problems, and a collective emotional need to unleash aggression against defined villains. The political and psychological dynamics, he suggests, are not unlike those that led to support for Nazism in post–World War I Germany. There are similarities in the dynamics, though the torments of restructuring do not compare with the deliberate mass exterminations of the Holocaust. At the same time, there are other powerful societal influences on the hospital.

America has a capitalist economy. Owners normally have different interests from employees. In this context, the General Hospital restructuring is little different from the Robber Barons's practices for maximizing profits and keeping the labor force under control. Union organizing was built on a history of both emotional and physical brutalization of workers.

General Hospital's managers are responding to the constraints of capitalist medicine. The hospital is a private institution that must at least break even in delivering services. It cannot appeal for public subsidy. Nor can it expect patients to pay with national health insurance. Whatever the managers' competence or personalities, they are trying to act rationally in the context of a capitalist economy. Consistently, they concentrate on the "bottom line," rather than patient care or staff morale. The pain of the hospital's restructuring tells a story about capitalism.

Still, modern capitalism differs from entrepreneurial capitalism: Not only do firms have specialized managers who are not necessarily major owners, but these managers also consider and explain their actions distinctively. Reengineering is an effort to apply rationality and objectivity to human relations in organizations. These terms express a faith in scientific knowledge—the belief that one or a few experts can discover the best way to do anything. Moreover, they suggest that reason alone, without emotion (thinking without feeling, the head without the heart) is the only means to discovering the best way. Feelings are the bases and products of relations with other persons. Allowing emotions into consideration, this view has it, inappropriately admits concerns about others' well-being that would divert calculations from the best, "objective," most profitable solutions to problems.

In our culture, medicine offers the prototypical example of this faith in scientific expertise, where the doctor knows what the patient needs. In fact, General Hospital's difficulties reflect challenges to that assumption. Moreover, as some patients say, they may not know medicine, but they do know how the particulars of their lives affect their habits, needs, and abilities to comply with treatments. Healing, they would clarify, is more than the one-directional administration of medicine; it has to be the collaboration of partners with different, but equally valid, knowledge. Calling their needs and desires "irrational" might reassure doctors who are uncomfortable dealing with them, but the aim of medicine, they would say, should be to enable them to live as well as possible with their needs and desires.

All this could be said about organizational management. Bureaucratic ideology that equates hierarchic authority with intellectual authority reinforces the tendency toward autonomous-expert decision making. Physicians who become administrators may be particularly vulnerable to believing they know all they need to know; to assuming those who can cut patients to heal them in surgery can also cut organizations to heal them. Many who are trained specifically for management also end up believing much the same. If anything, beginning with abstract knowledge and working in large bureaucracies without prior experience with flesh and blood patients, they may have little sense of the limited range within which humans respond to intervention.

Thus, General Hospital's restructuring is also a story about the modern culture of scientism that confuses single-faceted rationality with sophisticated examination of complex institutional conditions. This culture reinforces the political interests of managers concerned with maximizing profit. Psychologically, it shields top managers from troubling self-scrutiny, as well as confusion and uncertainty. Nevertheless, as the literature review suggests, the culture does not automatically serve economic interests.

It should be clear, as well, that General Hospital is a story about power. Those at the top of large bureaucratic organizations do not have to consult or collaborate with their subordinates. When they are physicians, professional authority reinforces their formal authority to enable them to do a great deal without short-term internal checks. Even if, as in this case, subordinates regard top managers as misguided, insensitive, or simply wrong, subordinates can do little to get the managers' attention, let alone influence them.

Personality and Social Structure

Were Maggiano and Lewin sadists who enjoyed controlling and tormenting hundreds of staff members? Because Maggiano and Lewin were not interviewed, any answer must be especially speculative. Perhaps they did have relatively few inhibitions against acting sadistically, and perhaps they did enjoy their control over others. But there is no reason to see downsizing as simply something they did for their pleasure.

Regardless of what else one might say about Maggiano and Lewin, their actions show us how difficult it is to understand and manage a complex organization. They show us the results of pressures on top managers to look as if they can do everything on their own and to implement simple and quick remedies. They show us how the rational language of management can lead and enable managers to inflict pain on subordinates. And they show us how easy it is for managers to ignore this pain while responding anxiously to these pressures.

Not everyone could do what Maggiano and Lewin did. This is not a statement about their intelligence. It is an observation about their ability to take the top managerial roles in this institution at this time. On reading the case material, one would wish for more imaginative, courageous managers, and yet Maggiano and Lewin are not deviants in capitalist medical institutions. Broad social structures shape roles. Although managers always have discretion in interpreting roles, Maggiano and Lewin apparently have personalities that especially suit them for conventional enactments of roles like these.

Thus, General Hospital's reengineering is a story about the psychological implications of social institutions and the fit of personalities with social structures. Although the psychological dynamics found here are not an inevitable concomitant of efforts to change the structures of organizations like hospitals, the fit between managerial personalities and the larger social structures makes them especially likely.

A Concluding Question

Unfortunately, the story of General Hospital and the pain of restructuring is commonplace. What would it take to proceed alternatively by involving all an organization's stakeholders—including staff, clients, and community members—in creating a viable institution that cares for staff and patients? That would be a problem worth trying to solve.

MICHAEL DIAMOND'S FINAL ANALYSIS

Any claim that we proffer a psychoanalytic perspective on downsizing an organization would demand a sincere examination of countertransference. In this instance, the so-called consultants (who are not actually consultants but interpreters of a text) did not interact with the interviewees. Nor did we have a contract with the hospital to assess its operations, and there was no agreement with any client on what we were trying to accomplish. Moreover, it can be argued that we do not really know, psychoanalytically or clinically, the organizational participants. We did agree to interpret and analyze the three sets of interviews administered by Allcorn. And we implicitly agreed that there was something of value in analyzing the text as presented by Allcorn. Despite never having met the interviewees and having no direct interview data on Maggiano and Lewin (only that which came from the interviewees), I believe we have learned something of value about the human and institutional costs of downsizing and reengineering. In this conclusion, I first address countertransference so that the reader can appreciate how my intersubjective world imposed upon and aided my interpretations of the interview data. Then, I plan to discuss what I believe we learned from this unusual research project.

Countertransference and the Interpretation of Organizational Identity

It was late in the evening that Allcorn took the three of us to visit the hospital we (coauthors/consultants) had been analyzing from afar for the past year. As we drove into the parking lot of the medical center complex, we jointly commented on how ordinary it appeared in comparison with other medical centers. As we walked in through the hospital lobby and toward the executive suite of offices, I was struck by the clean and orderly feel of it. But that feeling didn't last. After all, I was looking at the surface appearance of General Hospital. I knew there was something terrible that had occurred behind that facade. As we stopped by the Provost's (David Maggiano) office, I looked through the locked glass door into the reception area with its soft, cheerful colors and I thought to myself, "Where's the blood?" On the lower right-hand side of the glass door was a poster that read, "Penny for your thoughts." There was some program being promoted, in which for every $100 saved by an employee with an idea, he or she would receive one cent. Was it serious? If so, how would it affect employee self-worth? And how did it reflect upon Maggiano and Lewin's genuine or artificial commitment to employee participation?

My experience told me that a serious crime had been committed. I imagined the blood spilled in the executive office suite. As I walked through the hospital, I felt a strange sense of connectedness and familiarity with hospital employees. I knew what they knew but worked to hide. The actual (real) organization resided behind the organizational camouflage of artifacts: white coats, sanitary walls and floors, modern medical technology, memos, and the like. I was an observer of the scene of a crime I wished I could have been there to stop.

In contemporary psychoanalytic practice, countertransference is viewed as a tool for empathy and introspection with the patient and as a conscious monitor of the unconscious feelings and actions of the therapist. As an experienced psychoanalytic consultant to organizations, I make an intentional effort to examine my feelings about and experiences of clients and their organizational culture by exploring these dynamics within myself, the consulting team, and its members, since often the team becomes a container for and mirror of clients' feelings about the workplace. In other words, it is crucial to examine the impact of the organizational case and the participants' experiences upon one's self and one's assessment and diagnosis of the organizational paradox. The General Hospital consultants appeared to ignore and deny the personal and intrasubjective impact of the case material. Since the rules of this engagement prohibited the coauthors from examining up-close (what Kohut [1977, 1984] described as the "experience-near" in contrast to the "experience-distant" analytic position) the psychic reality of General Hospital and its members, I had to settle for the more cerebral task of interpreting the text as presented in the interview data and as presented in Allcorn's descriptive updates.

Despite feeling handicapped by not doing the interviews myself and not directly observing (in the form of participant observation) the client system on site, I was able to guess what the collective staff of General Hospital might be experiencing. In retrospect, however, I defended myself from and resisted the unconscious material presented in the interviews of hospital employees (the physical distance between General Hospital and myself making it possible). Similar to my colleagues in this project, I have personally experienced an organizational cutback—not as a consultant, but as head of a program faced with defending itself in a hostile academic environment. In fact, it was such a painful and fairly recent experience for me that I unconsciously defended myself from more fully digesting the material in the three sets of interviews. I had not completely worked through my own feelings in relation to my organization and the emotional injuries it imposed upon me.

What did this mean? It meant that my three earlier responses to the material, while valid as psychodynamic interpretations of interview data, did not adequately explore the heart of the General Hospital experience as portrayed by the interviewees. My own responses mirrored the depressive and persecutory nature of interviewees' responses. It also meant that, until now, the individual staff members never really came alive in my imagination. Since my trip to the hospital site, I believe I have located them (the interviewees) as internal and external human objects (what Kohut called self-objects). That is, the interview data now have an emotional quality for me that they lacked prior to my visit to the hospital and my subsequent ability to reflect on their personal meaning.

If Harry Stack Sullivan (1953), a pioneer in American psychiatry and originator of the "Interpersonal Theory of Psychiatry," was correct in his observation that ultimately (to paraphrase) we humans have more in common than otherwise, then I believe there is validity in psychoanalyzing the downsizing and reengineering of a hospital by reading and interpreting the interviews of workers undergoing the procedure.

Final Analysis of General Hospital

In the case of General Hospital, the procedure of reengineering and downsizing triggered similar images of the Holocaust in the minds of coauthors Baum, Stein, and myself (three Jews) independent of each other. There was one interviewee's reference to the Holocaust and then the spectacle of "efficiently" terminating large numbers of people simultaneously in the hospital auditorium, triggering the often overdone and misplaced Holocaust analogy. My intent in using this comparison is to illuminate the psychological and cultural dynamics at work at General Hospital. None of the employees in the case died or were murdered; there were no ovens and no concentration camps. Yet there is a troubling psychological parallel that cannot be ignored.

As a psychoanalytic political psychologist, I was driven to study bureaucracy and organizational totalitarianism in part out of a fear of Fascism, authoritarianism, racism, and anti-Semitism. Many scholarly books on these subjects have influenced me. Most notably, Robert Jay Lifton's (1986) *The Nazi Doctors* is helpful in more deeply imagining the horrible events at General Hospital without overstating the likeness to the Holocaust. Lifton referred to the psychological phenomenon of doubling in trying to explain the Nazi physicians' proclivity to split the world into good and evil. By day, the Nazi physician stood on the platforms of incoming trains, identifying those doomed for the incinerators and those condemned to the labor camps. Life and death decisions were made by ordinary physicians with extraordinary, godlike authority. These omnipotent Nazi decision makers would then go home at night to what we might imagine to be the center of a loving and intimate family.

How is it possible? For Lifton, they engaged in doubling or psychological splitting that enabled them to cleanly delineate the evil (Jews, Gypsies, and others) they fought during the daytime and the good they embraced at night. Obviously, the correlation between downsizing at General Hospital and the Holocaust can be taken too far. Nevertheless, there is a comparable psychological phenomenon operating in both instances—a deeply primitive, regressive, psychotic, narcissistic rage. In fact, the human capacity to authorize massive job terminations may stand or fall upon the underlying proclivity to engage in what Lifton called doubling and what I would describe as a schizoid withdrawal into a homogenized subculture (Diamond, 1993).

At General Hospital, Maggiano, Lewin, and Dohrman appeared to engage in what Guntrip (1969) called the schizoid problem. Out of their desire for a magic solution (e.g., downsizing and reengineering) to cope with managed care and a declining hospital census, Maggiano and Lewin took flight from this perceived hostile and persecutory healthcare environment and unconsciously established their own homogenized subculture. This executive group subculture (viewed unconsciously as "good") operated somewhat separately from the larger culture of General Hospital (unconsciously seen by the executives as "evil"). Consequently, the executives could scapegoat the hospital for the terrible situation and, thus, justify termination and downsizing. What Bion (1959) called the fight–flight basic assumption of work groups emerged as a driving force of the executive team, forcing them to psychologically split the hospital into enemies and allies. In the context of a rapidly changing, threatening, and volatile healthcare environment, and under the influence of annihilation anxiety, the executive pair (Maggiano and Lewin) retreated from the everyday work world of the hospital and its staff and psychologically constructed a defensive bunker for themselves and their consultants (the homogenized subculture) against the rest of the hospital organization.

The primary unacknowledged task of the homogenized work-group culture is individual and group survival (Diamond, 1993). Consequently, the executives authorized the consultants, who they viewed as split-off aggressive parts of themselves, to direct the downsizing initiative. The consultants, in turn, were unconsciously colluding with the withdrawn and depersonalized executives. Hence, this enabled the consultants to apply methods of termination and reduction-in-force akin to those used to incinerate large numbers of targeted scapegoats in Nazi Germany. Despite (and possibly due to) feelings of persecution, Maggiano, Lewin, Dohrman, and the consultants became the persecutors of others (outsiders) and perpetuated an unconscious repetition compulsion. That is, those who feel persecuted and victimized often become persecutors and victimizers.

As psychoanalytic consultants, we use our imagination (that potential space between reality and fantasy) to locate cultural experience (Winnicott, 1971). In the psychodynamic process of analyzing the text of the case, our imaginations generate assumptions, hypotheses, and theories for testing. We decode the responses of interviewees, not only through the lens of countertransference, but from the actual evidence presented in the case material.

At the conclusion of the project, Allcorn provided some additional artifacts of the General Hospital culture that offer further evidence of a demoralized and persecuted organization in which the executive members (Provost Maggiano, Assistant Provost Lewin, Executive I Dohrman) and hospital employees (mid-managers, nurses, physicians, and other hospital staff) are split and divided.

Memos as Artifacts of the Hospital Culture   Cultural artifacts signify organizational membership. At General Hospital and Medical Center, several artifacts in the form of memos are noteworthy.

Figure 9.1, printed on university medical center stationery accompanied by a cartoon of a dinosaur, read, "Feel on the Verge of Extinction? Here Are 10 Ways to Survive the Health Reform Age." The list included the following:

1. Hire an inexperienced boob as CEO
2. Reduce the hospital occupancy rate to 50%
3. Shun HMO contracts
4. Acquire a second rate community hospital in a bad neighborhood
5. Piss on your affiliated hospitals
6. Treat your attending physicians like shit
7. Layoff nurses, secretaries, and ancillary staff
8. Make middle management take the fall for bad decisions made by upper management
9. Hire high priced consultants to come in and tell you the obvious
10. Be arrogant

An open letter to all university medical center employees (see Figure 9.2) included the following statements:

Are we all sheep, or what? When are we as a group going to unite?! God knows, if we can't win, we should at least give the Board of Trustees and their henchmen cause to pause and consider the consequences of their actions—because after management is purged . . . you're next! Not only are you going to be forced to take on much more work in the future (in sections that are already understaffed), you're going to receive less pay for you [*sic*] labors. . . . We should be a creative industry leader. We should be at the cutting edge of change. Instead, piece by piece, the Board of Trustees has decided to feed the goose to the sharks. Instead of working with us to turn this place around, they have identified us as the reason [General Hospital] is in financial trouble and have brought in hired guns to do their dirty work.

Interpretation of the Meaning of the Memos   The organizational image of the monster–dinosaur as extinct and vicious is rather apparent. The dinosaur (as organizational symbol), with its deadly jaw and terrifying teeth, is capable of orally consuming and devouring its prey (hospital employees), human and otherwise. The dinosaur represents the omnipotent, all-incorporating, bad mother organization, capable of infanticide by means of engulfment. It also signifies, in the form of a memo, the collective projected aggression of hospital staff onto the organization which has disappointed, emotionally wounded, and narcissistically injured them. The unconscious assault by the executive group and their consultants stripped many employees of their dignity and self-esteem; hospital staff then express their narcissistic rage at the depriving and sadistic mother organization. Organizational identity at General Hospital is comprised of projected aggression in the form of collective feelings of disappointment, betrayal, and anger.

In addition, the references to the CEO (Provost) as an inexperienced boob and middle management taking the fall for bad decisions by upper management signify the deep disrespect, mistrust, and lack of confidence in the leadership of General Hospital—leaders who deny responsibility for their actions and displace that responsibility on weaker, more vulnerable middle managers.

The final comment on arrogance in the memo refers to the perception among hospital employees of top leaders as expansive, narcissistic, arrogant, and vindictive. Not surprisingly, many interviewees noted with irony the appointment of a new layer of executives at General Hospital. To assure narcissistic power and omnipotence at the top, Maggiano and Lewin required, and thus appointed, loyal and admiring subordinates at the next hierarchic layer of authority; loyalists who would not only reinforce narcissistic leadership, but reinforce the character of the homogenized executive subculture at the top. The angry and persecuted tone of the second memo reflects the current emotional climate of General Hospital and the level of hostility aimed at the executive group. The perpetuation of uncertainty and job insecurity will continue to produce high levels of turnover, absenteeism, and demoralization. The quality of healthcare at General Hospital will continue to erode.

Conclusion

If asked to help General Hospital as a consultant at this time, I would make the following recommendations based upon my one-year study of the hospital and its staff. First, hire new leaders genuinely committed to repairing a deeply damaged organization. Second, organize numerous retreats in which the agenda would center on the opportunity of employees to share their thoughts and feelings about General Hospital past, present, and future. In psychodynamic terms, these sessions would be structured as a holding environment where employees could on the one hand mourn the destruction and devastation at General Hospital, and on the other hand plan for their future. Moreover, the university President would have to endorse the process and publicly admit to serious errors in judgment and a further commitment to a new era of employee participation and empowerment. Third, with the aid of the consulting team, General Hospital would need to construct a strategic plan; the process would involve employees at all levels. Thus, the hospital and medical center's mission statement and vision would be rewritten based upon the demands of managed care and an identification of the hospital's niche in its host metropolitan healthcare environment. Fourth, with the assistance of a psychologically informed consulting team, General Hospital would reorganize and reconfigure itself in a manner that responded directly to the strategic plan. Fifth, the hospital and medical center would develop a formal structure (a committee comprised of physicians, managers, staff, and other professionals from within and outside) to monitor implementation of the strategic plan and, then, to propose changes as necessary. Realistically, both General Hospital and the Medical Center could reorganize and retool in a relatively short time. However, cultural and psychological change will take much longer. It is therefore critical to combine structural and strategic change with a coinciding effort to repair the human damage and attempt to rebuild mutual trust, respect, and worker self-esteem. Thus, General Hospital should be treated therapeutically; it has been traumatized and violated. Any change effort that avoids confronting the abuse committed within this hospital will fail.

Finally, my role as (off-site) organizational researcher and interpreter of the case differs significantly from that of a psychodynamic organizational consultant to General Hospital. If I were the consultant, my thoughts on countertransference and the Holocaust analogy would be shared only with my consulting team, not with the clients. It might have the effect of accelerating the clients' defenses as a result of their feeling outrageously and unfairly judged. Nevertheless, I would acknowledge and explore these lamentable images with my consulting team in an appropriate context, and then analyze how these images might affect the consulting work itself. Why? Because these powerful images help consultants to better empathize with their clients, and that deeper understanding reinforces a therapeutic alliance between consultants and clients. I would, however, talk to the executives about the consequences of their managerial methods and the counterproductive alliance (or collusion) with the consulting team hired by the hospital. I would address the central paradox of the leadership as producers of organizational culture, which in this case would require a transition of leadership at the top to promote change and reparation in the hospital.

In contrast to the role of organizational consultant, as organizational researcher and interpreter I have, ironically, found more freedom to associate and theorize. In this role I am uncensored by the practical requirements of formulating productive feedback to my client and the organization. In fact, I am limited only by my proclivity to defend myself against the deeper subjective meaning of the downsizing experience of employees at General Hospital, as told to Allcorn in the structured interviews.

HOWARD STEIN'S FINAL ANALYSIS

The sets of interviews are completed. Each interpreter has fulfilled his task with each set of interviews. Dr. Allcorn has mailed us the nearly finished book manuscript. Now, for the first time, we can read what the others have written and thought; compare what we saw and heard and felt with what our colleagues on the "team" did—and feel alternately pleased and ashamed, and wonder through the eyes of "sibling rivalry" how we each compared in the eyes of "father" or "elder sibling" Allcorn. A month and a half later, we met for a two-day research meeting to grapple together with what we think we have learned, then to go back and write our final thoughts. Events at General Hospital continue to unfold. The punctuation of beginnings and endings to consultation and research is necessarily arbitrary. The most difficult part remains: the summing up, the leave-taking, and the regrets. Walking away will be hardest, even from an organization I know only from and on paper. Reading the interpretations by Drs. Diamond and Baum and the introductions and summaries by Dr. Allcorn helped fill in my blind spots and confirmed—reality tested—my speculations. These affirmed my belief that General Hospital was a socially created nightmare; that atrocities were being committed. In their company—imagined symbolically on paper and later realized in person—I felt less "crazy," less overwhelmed by my own self-doubt over whether it was real. From a methodological viewpoint, I am impressed—and surprised—that psychoanalytically valid data can be generated through ostensibly empirical research. It is a world there for all to see and to enter into for themselves—though the very magnitude of the destructiveness may make us wish not to see it.

This study has been written in, and for the most part for and about, the United States of America in the 1990s. True, it is about the universal unconscious as it manifests itself in Western, hierarchical, mixed-capitalist organizations, to which our description, findings, and recommendations should be extrapolatable and applicable. But General Hospital, and downsizing as a genre or cultural form of decision making, are vintage American. Likewise are the expectations and wishes both a writer and reader in America bring to any "Conclusions and Recommendations" section of a book. We expect problems to be mastered. We insist that no problem is insurmountable. And it is in the final chapter that the summit will finally be conquered. It is a matter of finding the right expert, the right tool, the right team, the right combination, to get us there. Above all, action is required. "Prairie optimism"—and even the psychoanalytic ego psychology that stresses ego autonomy, mastery, and adaptation—has served America well. But taken for the entire picture, it is a dangerous delusion that everything can be "fixed." It has long served as a cultural antidepressant that makes depression and despair virtually un-American. One does not dare pause in frozen horror at the history of General Hospital that one has just witnessed.

Of course, this expectation of a dramatic, even redemptive, finale or denouement, is far from only American. To say only the obvious, it pervades the great European symphonic tradition. Think only of Beethoven's Third, Fifth, and Ninth; of Brahms's First and Second; of Sibelius's Second and Fifth; or of Tchaikovsky's Fourth and Fifth. But Tchaikovsky threw us a curve we can still scarcely forgive. The tragic, despairing Adagio that ends his Sixth ("Pathétique") Symphony was at first so startling an anomaly, so great an affront to its early listeners and interpreters sensibilities (and underlying emotional needs), that one conductor reversed the composer's order of the third and fourth movements. He insisted on ending with the ferocious, presumably upbeat, march. So much for the triumph of the reality principle. Triumphs, even comedies, are preferable and emotionally easier than tragedies.

For myself, as I initially leafed through the pages of the hefty manuscript and sat at my computer to compose my own finale, I put on Gustav Mahler's Ninth Symphony—and yes, it ends with a sad, resigned Adagio rather than a triumphant Rondo Allegro. With this music, I prepared myself emotionally for my task ahead. The music provides the prescription. Whatever else I might do as consultant to General Hospital, I would try to help those with whom I have consulted and with whom I might consult in the future to face and to emotionally hold on to the enormous tragedy and sorrow present. Reality testing and reality acceptance, my own included, comes first. What Diamond (1993) calls the "resilient organization" can only become genuinely renewing (in contrast to manic spasms of doctrinal boosterism and ferocious "productivity" in flight from feeling) if its members have the courage to face their history: the irreversible, irrevocable course of events; their own helplessness, if not complicity, with them; and the emotional tidal waves that both produced that history and were churned up in its wake.

Much of the work that remains to be done in the hospital, in ambulatory, and in the wider university consists of coming to terms with the recent history of the institution ("working through"). And there is

no guarantee that it will be easy or that it even will be done institutionally at all. The inability to mourn has characterized Germany's flight from
its own history since the 1940s (Nedelmann, 1986). Yet in workplace institutions as much as in nations and religions, it is only from grief
following fear and loss that regenerative resilience—joy and love in
work tasks and in relationships—rather than repetition is possible.

If a psychoanalytically oriented consultant or team is invited to work
in the General Hospital setting, a number of issues come to mind that
must be anticipated. Who or what is the unit of care or of consultation? Who is, or who wishes to be, the client? To whom should the
consultant be loyal? If the consultant fosters sufficient individuation
(differentiation), integration, and sheer courage in an employee or
manager that the person elects to leave the hospital or ambulatory rather
than further "adapt," is that success or failure? And in whose eyes
(and superego)? Reality testing and a fostering of the true self (in contrast with the conformistic false self) are, to my thinking, two measures of any kind of helping. Surely they apply to a consultant's task at
General Hospital.

The psychoanalytically oriented consultant to General Hospital, and
to any organization undergoing massive change such as large-scale
layoffs, must be prepared to endure, not merely tolerate, an enormous
amount of confusion, ambivalence, dependency, and sheer hate as well
as occasional gratitude and relief. We are, after all, trying to help individuals and groups hold onto, examine, and feel what most people
wish to be rid of through action; often violent action. As Bion said so
beautifully of fight–flight groups, "The fight/flight group expresses a
sense of incapacity for understanding and the love without which
understanding cannot exist" (1959). A lynch mob does not want understanding; it wants a lynching—many lynchings. (See Walter Van
Tilburg Clark's [1940] classic novel of the American West, *The Ox-Bow
Incident*, for an example of this. How do psychoanalytically oriented
consultants work in such an environment? Understanding, whether
individual or group, rests on an affective foundation—love, the feeling of being loved, and of being symbolically held. And without that
libidinal tie, that therapeutic alliance or contract between client and
consultant, understanding cannot occur. It may, of course, occur informally with the least expectable people and in unanticipatable moments
of insight: with a member of housekeeping or nursing rather than the
CEO, or serendipitously with the CEO upon the death of the CEO's
parent or spouse.

But any consultant should first accept the fact that employment under
conditions such as General Hospital's downsizing and restructuring
occurs under extraordinary emotional circumstances. Such consultation takes place in the wake of the destruction of the previous long-

lived "average expectable environment" of the workplace. The consultant needs to be aware of his or her own magical, transferential, and rescue fantasies that may interfere with this unwelcome realization. The consultant likewise must impress the client organization of the need for more, rather than less, time to foster organizational healing— a quantity that is likely to be emotionally as well as monetarily in short supply during a time when virtually everyone is redefining the cultural "reality principle" in terms of the bottom line and when they want instant results that will not interfere with the scorched-earth policy. Precisely what is emotionally needed to help those at General Hospital deal with the long-term effects and meanings of the downsizing is what is now regarded as virtually un-American. "Cut your losses and run" ("From what?" we do not ask) is more our national style.

The consultant or consulting team to General Hospital must ask certain questions in preparation for consulting: Who came before us? Who were hired as consultants, and what tasks were they asked to accomplish? Any psychoanalytically oriented consultant who works with General Hospital must also work with the legacy of the clients (or the clients' predecessors) who had hired a consulting firm like SPC to do their hatcheting or to be puppeteered behind the wall of secrecy. The psychoanalytically attuned consultant must wonder about what upper management (or whoever sought this style of consultation) expects or wishes from this radically different type of consultant and consulting (e.g., What do they think they are getting, and how does it differ from what they thought they were getting from SPC?), for military-like operations and campaigns (SWAT teams, Special Forces, surprise attacks) are far more commonplace than are in-depth consultations (see Stein, 1995).

Indeed, companies, hospitals, universities, industries, and governments are increasingly hiring military retirees to lead and staff the downsizing and RIFing of their organizations (Seth Allcorn, personal communication, December 1994). At the national level, the Republican Party's "Contract with America," victorious on the Bloody Tuesday of the November 1994 election, bears considerable resemblance to the organizational psychology in which brutalization and victimization are normative. If part of an organization's tacit unconscious contract among its members is to consume or to sacrifice its own—to destroy morale and make the workforce abjectly dependent—where, how, and with whom does the consultant work? And under such circumstances, how can empathy be sustained—let alone become a foundation for conflict identification and resolution? I remind myself that all this is occurring in a clinical setting where the "therapeutic alliance," caring, is supposedly foundational for all tasks. Throughout the downsizing and reorganization at General Hospital, "cost" and "cost containment" or "cost cutting" is the central theme and clarion call.

Patient care is mostly a marginal topic. Many upper-level executives (and not only at General Hospital) assume and expect—magically—that patient care will continue uninterrupted, as if nothing happened.

As an anthropologist, I situate the events and the response (ongoing) to the events (also ongoing and imminent) at General Hospital in the broader cross-cultural and cross-historical context of disasters or catastrophes, natural and social; from earthquakes and floods to the Stalin purges in the Soviet Union of the mid-1930s (e.g., Ablon, 1973; Devereux, 1955; La Barre, 1954, 1972; Erikson, 1976; Rangell, 1976; Niederland, 1968; Luel and Marcus, 1984). The study of General Hospital must be situated as part of the larger, ongoing study of adaptation to catastrophe, the creation of catastrophe, and the constellation of meanings, feelings, fantasies, and defenses brought to the experience of trauma. In the General Hospital situation, overlapping and even competing models of what happened tax the participants and the consultants alike: For instance, socioeconomic necessity, traumatization, and adaptation to events and adaptive modes brought from childhood to events are modes that influence the experience and shape the course of subsequent events. If anything, this longitudinal study shows how projective identification infuses and contaminates the reality principle. For psychic reality is part of the outer reality to which people must adjust.

Since the 1950s or so, many anthropologists have come to realize the ubiquity of change in all culture; that permanence is a cherished illusion, often born of the nostalgia that massive social rupture unleashes. Permanence of circumstance—changelessness—is every nativist's dream–wish and no society's reality. This, though, is different from the induced terror of downsizing such as occurred at General Hospital—a symbolic, bloodless, equivalent of the Stalin purges. In RIFing, downsizing, rightsizing, reengineering, and restructuring we are dealing with a very specific style of change and language, where euphemism is not far above the surface of sadism, annihilation, separation, and castration anxieties, to name but a few to which the very words of euphemism allude.

If much of the catastrophe at General Hospital is induced (that is to say, the profound, shared regression and defenses against primitive, persecutory anxiety), how can we radically separate inner from outer? Worse, a *Modern Healthcare* survey published on January 16, 1995, proposes that some 40 percent of American hospitals will soon be undergoing a similar course of massive layoffs (Bell, 1995), ostensibly for the sake of institutional survival, productivity, and profitability. Reality is surely analyzable here, and not only the responses to that reality. This analytic conundrum is, ironically, the source of my own hope for the consulting process. For, if schizophrenic-like, deeply regressive, catastrophic reactions are internal and intrapsychic, they are also deeply intersubjective.

People can literally drive others crazy, try to do so, and succeed; people can actually make others sick, try to do so, and do. This study is grim testimony to precisely that. Even the mechanisms of destruction and of self-destruction have been made clearer by Allcorn, Diamond, Baum, and myself. Do we as organizations and as whole nations still have the courage and the ability to love? Can we allow ourselves the vulnerability of a change of heart, and of atonement for the hurts we have afflicted in the sacred names of profit and production? The consultant's gamble is that the "depressive" as well as the "paranoid–schizoid" parts of us all can still be unlocked and tapped during the consulting process. The question, "How do people adapt to catastrophe?" (see Parin, 1988) becomes inseparable from the descriptive, interpretive, and ethical question of "To what circumstances should people not be required to adapt (induced regression)?" That is the preventive side of how consultants can help in increasingly widespread situations, such as at General Hospital.

As of this writing, Dr. Maggiano has resigned but then decided to stay (surely effecting organizational "object constancy"). Dohrman has left. Considerable experience and knowledge have disappeared from the collective cupboard; not only are people bereft, but skills and roles must be reinvented anew. What is emotionally "solid" (libidinal object constancy) in organizations during such times? My own reply, from organizational consultation with similar institutions, is that often the inside or outside consultant comes to be experienced as more reliable, more emotionally present and constant over time, than those who are more formally a part of the institution's hierarchy. As Dr. Allcorn said in our research meeting at the conclusion of the project, "I'm the only one who was willing to listen [to them] nonjudgmentally"—itself a profound judgment on the entire, inherently judgmental downsizing process.

Shakespeare's Lady Macbeth sleepwalked, obsessed with purging herself of the blood, the guilt, on her hands and soul from the murder of King Duncan (CEO of Scotland). At the conclusion of this project, when I toured General Hospital and its huge campus, when I walked by the offices of Maggiano, Lewin, and Dohrman, everything looked tidy, in its place, and in order. Office windows were squeaky clean; no fingerprints. The walls and the carpets were all delicately appointed "Santa Fe" pastel. I looked for blood—even symbolic blood—as did others among the authors. The scene looked surreal, macabre, to me. Of course, I should not have expected to walk among ruins even as I knew I was. I saw no Lady Macbeth (or cowardly Macbeth himself) with the grace to be haunted by the devastation. I saw no blood. But I knew there had been blood—and that to see blood was forbidden.

After the downsizing, rightsizing had been expected by those who remained; after sacrificial death, rebirth was expected, perhaps now even permitted. But at General Hospital, the fantasy went wrong. It was unclear as to who were the more fortunate: those who were fired or those who remained. The hoped-for revival, rebirth, and redemption from all this violence did not take place. The cleansed are still unclean.

Group sanitizing (from nationalist ethnic cleansing to corporate fat trimming) is more than a mask of ruthlessness; it is a gambit, a wager against the terror turning back upon oneself. It is the creation of still one more step of remove from the deed and from expected retribution. An executive, having scapegoated others to save himself and his institution, says to me in terror, "I have cut and chopped. There is blood on my hands. Please don't cut me." The next line of defense is to deny that there even is, or ever was, any blood on anyone's hands; then comes the rationalization that "It's just sound business." In turn, the psychological violence becomes so commonplace, so culturally acceptable ("ego- and culture-syntonic"), that, via identification, it would seem unusual not to solve business problems this way. The damage done to individual lives, to families, to institutions, and to communities is diminished from awe inspiring to trivial.

What is happening, we come to believe, does not happen to people but to spreadsheets. And, should we be startled into realizing that this happens to real people, we rationalize away the deed by ingeniously contriving ways to discount those who became our organizational waste products. The erstwhile personal ego ideal and organizational ideal which we once strived to live up to, we now disavow and take out with the morning garbage.

The exercise of this project has humbled me and laid to rest any Lone Ranger rescue fantasies I had earlier ("What I couldda done if I'd been there"). Just as the consultant must serve as a holding environment and container for General Hospital (as a group, and each individual at a time) in order to help them, so likewise the consultant must have a holding environment and container in order to continue to work productively at both the emotional or developmental and task levels. The consulting team can serve this need.

Over the many months of writing my portions of this book, my often long phone calls to Seth Allcorn helped me not only to keep on task with respect to realistic issues such as length, manuscript format, narrative style, and other technical issues, but also to reassure me that I was not going utterly crazy with the feelings the interviews were stirring up in me. Our conversations helped me to endure the sense of worlds ending, of inner fragmentation, of my own unrepressed insatiable brutality, and of my own sense of despair and total helplessness (Does the savage rage come from identifying with victims' helplessness, from the oppressors' indulgences, or both?) and to then translate these wild countertransference feelings into productive work. Being heard, truly listened to, and understood rekindles the nearly extinguished capacity to love and to hear again.

The more regressed the organization, the more the consulting team needs to make time and space for dealing with their own inevitable regressions. This is why the meeting of the four of us at the conclusion of this project was vital—not only for the good of the book, but for ourselves and the book in turn. Had we been working together literally as a consulting team, it is likely that we would have had to deal on an ongoing basis with our own inner and interpersonal (intrateam) conflicts that played out, via identifications, the dynamics of General Hospital. What, for instance, would become of the internalized bad objects within and between us as members of a consulting team? At issue is not whether such primitive fantasies, anxieties, and wishes will be conjured, but what we will do with them.

I shudder to think how SPC must have dealt with them by maintaining an ironclad, lockstep, "fight–flight" or "groupthink" attitude in order to continue functioning as the executive (executioner) extension of Lewin's or Maggiano's will. If I imagine SPC to have been their "SWAT team," or worse, their "SS" or *Einsatzgruppen* (special forces), their bad object under the iron law of unconscious delegation via projective identification, how would we—Allcorn, Diamond, Baum, and Stein— avoid a similar seduction? How, to safeguard our paycheck and our emotional dependencies, would we avoid becoming like them? I do not trust my current answer.

I wish to conclude on a comparative note, for this book contributes simultaneously to the already considerable literature on human catastrophe and to the more specific study of response to organizational downsizing. Researcher and consultant alike cannot help but be struck by the ubiquity, if not the universality, of death imagery and feelings experienced by people going through downsizing. A consultant colleague told me, for instance, of his recent experience at a national research and development laboratory. The widely shared image of the RIFing within the corporation was "sudden death." The supervisors who did the actual firing were called "angels of sudden death." Those who were to be laid off were given absolutely no preparation (except, of course, rumor). Security guards escorted the RIFed persons to their cars in the parking lot after they had cleaned out their offices and desks the same day as they were notified of the fact that they were being fired. Out of upper management's fear that computers and other vital equipment would be sabotaged or stolen, none of those fired were let back into the building after the security guards had led them out.

At my own place of employment, the University of Oklahoma Health Sciences Center, I learned in late January 1995 that in the university hospitals some 300 people would soon be fired and 300 additional unfilled positions would be eliminated. The rehabilitation hospital is to be closed and position transfers to other hospitals will not be permitted. The campus learned of this decision and of its imminence through the local newspaper in mid-January 1995. I have been asked to work with the department of human relations of the university hospitals to assist a task force in helping the campus through this process. My role is now called "continuous consultant to the crisis."

During an initial two-hour meeting in late January, members of a planning committee said many things that echo and resonate with what was said and felt at General Hospital. The comparative study of accounts of organizational disaster will help consultants and theorists alike to identify and distinguish between local and universal themes, and to learn how to be helpful. Among my notes from the meeting appear the following:

I'm planning a funeral for somebody who's going to die but doesn't know they're going to die. . . . I as a manager feel it's like World War II. The Nazis have come in and tell us "Point out all the Jewish people so we can get rid of them. Then tell us the Gypsies, then the Poles." . . . That's what it feels like. . . . We're asked to plan a funeral and we don't know who's going to be attending. . . . This is my home [the health sciences center; spoken with tears in her eyes]. . . . Nursing is nurturing and it's difficult to let people go. So how does a nurse tell another nurse she's fired? I'm a manager. How do I work with a shorter staff [and still be nurturing]? If I survive this time around, how do I know I'll be here the next cutback? . . . I have vast concerns that I will not be employed here long, and I'm one of the people in charge of the program for the people who are being fired now.

Around the same time, the CEO of another multihospital system said the following of his need to preside over downsizing the hospital at which he had trained and now practiced for thirty years:

This is the most difficult thing I've been through in thirty years here. It's beyond the direct control of us [i.e., upper management, the "Restructuring Task Force"]. It's like the collapse of Union Bank here fifteen years ago. People believed, "This is the University Hospital, and nothing will happen with it. It can't happen to us." We need to acknowledge we've really struggled with the decision. . . . There's a lot of compassionate people in this profession. Nurses and schedulers are now asked to be managers and to carry out a difficult task of deciding who should be laid off. They've never had to do this. A University Hospital job just isn't as secure as the federal government. . . . There just was no final solution [pause]—a poor choice of words! But [hospital] leaders need to help in decisions where there are no simple answers, no final solutions. Americans have this belief in infinity, that there's a Big Totalizator Board out there that makes the decisions. (from notes, January 1995)

Even these brief quotations from other institutions are rich in imagery and in the middle and upper management's ambivalence. The ghost of the Nazi "Final Solution" to the "Jewish Problem" hovers in the language, even as the CEO dislikes his own thought. There lurks the wish for a decisive, definitive "final solution" where decision makers would not have to feel guilt, shame, remorse, anxiety, and responsibility. There are clear allusions to who are the Jews ("It can't happen to us") and who are the Nazis (upper management who regretfully make their decisions). Upper management are symbolized as Nazis who come in and demand to be handed over Jews, Poles, Gypsies, and the ever-next group to be eliminated.

And middle management? They became the complicit collaborators (German, Jewish, Polish, etc.) with the Nazis, though they see themselves more as twice victims: first, for having been placed (and for allowing themselves to be placed) in the position as executioner; and second, as potential casualties of future layoffs.

For me, the "Big Totalizator Board" conjures images of totalitarianism and the impersonal, technological violence of Arnold Schwarzenegger's *Terminator* movies and other current moves of this genre. Ultimately, no one is secure from damage in this consuming process. No one is truly exempt, and everyone in some way becomes complicit. Boundaries are unclear: Everyone is a potential Jew, and everyone is a potential Nazi.

Certainly, whatever happened at General Hospital was not the World War II Holocaust designed to eliminate every Jew on earth. But much of its systematic degradation and dehumanization of non-"Aryans" commends analogizing, precisely because at the unconscious logical, if not the behavioral, level, the two had similar objectives. But there is still another level that cannot be impugned, what one might characterize as the phenomenological level, the way people at General Hospital and elsewhere experience the event and process of downsizing and of being downsized. To live through downsizing, to witness it firsthand, is so horrible, so devastating, that the only consistent image that can do it justice is the Holocaust. The first question is, "Was it real?" or "Did this really happen at General Hospital?" To answer in the affirmative—whether one is interviewer, outside interpreter, or hospital employee—is to be able to experience intolerable guilt, shame, and anxiety; even terror, rage, and remorse so as to overcome the inevitable denial. The next question is, "What images sustain those feelings, wishes, fantasies, and defenses against being overwhelmed by them?" Those who insist on analogy with the Nazi Holocaust have much to teach us about removing the shroud of euphemism and unreality from the face of downsizing. The metaphor is misplaced only if we are expected to take it literally.

I leave this study of General Hospital with questions not only about interpretation and consultation in an individual, intensive case, but about what we can learn about conducting additional, comparative, "applied" studies of a subject that occupies the core of American fact and fantasy. I also leave this study with the sorrow and regret that our four-person study team must come to an end with the completion of the project—though, in reality, our friendships will remain, feelings that complement and intensify the haunting feeling that there was nothing we could do to halt or reverse the circumstances at General Hospital. I must leave. I must draw a boundary in time and say that the project is over, it is finished—though I wish to do neither. The project is as much about the four of us, about how General Hospital touched and troubled our lives, as it is about General Hospital. The publication of a book only partially salves both kinds of losses.

My final consideration concerns less organizational consultation per se than the question of long-term recovery from the ravages of downsizing. There are at least two levels or units we must somehow face. We need to recover, and to foster recovery, not only from the individual organizational mass layoffs of particular hospitals, corporations, universities, and government agencies; but also from the national arrogance, callousness, and short-sightedness that has led us to believe since the 1980s that survival, if not magical rebirth, could only be achieved by dramatic, ruthless sacrifices that go by the name of downsizing. General Hospital is, in this view, but one theater in which our internal, domestic war has been waged.

We will somehow have to ask and face the question, "What have we done to our own; our own whom we have made into the enemy, into discountable, discardable refuse?" Not only, "What have we done to them?" but "What have we done to ourselves as well? What have we all become?" Beneath the bottom line's rationalized necessity (cost, its containment, and its endless cutting) is the tragedy begotten by arrogance, by greed, by sadism, by indifference to suffering, and by the partly conscious, partly unconscious, wager that one can postpone or entirely avert suffering by making others suffer instead. The story of General Hospital's downsizing is an account of one medical campus and of its nation. Emotional recovery from it will require no smaller a scale.

CONCLUDING OVERVIEW

The work is now complete. The longitudinal case study has been written and interpreted and the work of the case consultants has been analyzed during a two-day retreat. The three case consultants have provided many insights as to what happened at General Hospital and they have shared what they have learned from this work. There remains only leave-taking from General Hospital, but this is not easily done without many furtive backward glances. Leave-taking is, in fact, filled with many hard to accept feelings: anxiety, dread, shame, guilt, helplessness, vulnerability, anger, and many other emotions that threaten to turn anyone looking back upon General Hospital into a biblical pillar of salt.

The work on this case began without any idea of what would happen as the hospital commenced its change process. The goals of the book were to better understand organizational change and the insights that psychoanalytically informed case consultants could develop from reading the case from afar. My colleagues, while skeptical that this would be a productive effort, nonetheless agreed to try. All of this seems like a long time ago and it sounds naïve and dispassionate. In retrospect, whatever preconceptions I held about what would happen entirely failed to anticipate what did happen. It is from this context that I reflect back upon what did happen and the powerful experience that unfolded at General Hospital. The case study is humbling and peels away any last remnants of my faith in the voracity of rational management methods unleashed upon organizations by remote all powerful top management. I am confident I cannot find the eloquence of expression to do justice to the experience that I think, it is safe to say, we (the authors and the reader) all went through side by side with the employees of General Hospital. It is, therefore, with humility that I provide a conclusion that, as I read in draft, would have been hard to imagine writing at the start of the work.

The case of General Hospital is perhaps, in many ways, so horrible, so filled with persecutory and depressive anxiety, so filled with potential countertransference that it can neither be looked upon nor overlooked. What happened is so distressing that it must be denied and rationalized but, in the end, there is no escape. It cannot be disposed of by any other means, because the events that occurred at General Hospital are all around us, filling our daily lives with anxiety, fear, shame, helplessness, and anger. Dr. Stein notes that, "No one is truly exempt, and everyone in some way becomes complicit." This realization is extraordinarily depressing. Where is the caretaking, listening, and love that we all hope for from the organizations we work for?

My three colleagues have struggled with how much the case contains elements similar to the Holocaust and its deep meaning for them as Jews. The dreadful comparison, as they note, provides insight and learning—dare we repeat it again. My own experience of the work reminded me of my fateful encounter with Vietnam, which contains for me, like many veterans, a sense of powerful subordination, no escape or fighting back, and useless suffering accompanied by no recognition of the sacrifices made. The experience was ultimately so painful for Americans that it is better that we, the soldiers, are forgotten. In fact, as I wrote the last sentence in the preceding paragraph, I was reminded of the Vietnam-era song that has the refrain, "Where have all the soldiers gone?"

General Hospital contains within it the incredible duplicity of Vietnam that we are currently and painfully being reminded of by Robert McNamara, twenty years after the extraordinary chaotic images of the last-minute evacuation of Saigon. McNamara, like his counterparts at General Hospital, pursued rational management strategies (like downsizing, restructuring, and reengineering) bolstered by soothing statistics (kill and infiltration ratios and trends) not unlike those produced by the consulting companies at General Hospital. How comforting it must have been for those at the top to know that we were killing them faster than they were killing us. The question posed by the case is whether the collective psychic wound of Vietnam (or the Holocaust) and the wounds imposed by America's internal war to downsize, restructure, and reengineer our organizations are ultimately similar. Doing it by the numbers is not necessarily so logical or right, and might we not, as a nation, look back to find that we have not merely alienated a generation in the 1960s and 1970s, but also our entire workforce in the 1980s and 1990s? One is left to wonder.

Perhaps the culture of narcissism described by Christopher Lasch (1979), and the results of recent research that point to young people being more self-absorbed and more interested in promoting their career rather than being loyal to an organization, are, in part, accounted for by the American culture of downsizing, restructuring, and reengineering. Who would be foolish enough to think that he or she is not expendable today?

Finding any meaningful way to conclude this book that does justice to the events at General Hospital just does not seem possible. In much the same way as the horrors of Nazi Germany and Vietnam defy easy comprehension or passage from awareness, I think it must be the same for Americans who have their jobs downsized, restructured, and reengineered out of existence and themselves escorted to the door by security guards. The comparisons are hard to ignore, as is the tendency to deny and forget horrible events.

The only question that remains is, "Who will build the monument to celebrate the loss of a loyal workforce?" It is on this note that I too take leave of General Hospital and the suffering of its employees. There can be no hope to end the self-inflicted war on Americans, other than all of us assuming personal responsibility for our complicity. Doing it by the numbers cannot be accepted as good-enough management anymore. Organizational change must move beyond the use of downsizing, restructuring, reengineering, and numbers in the form of benchmarks, best practice, and ratios in order to avoid killing our organizations from within by laying waste to the self-esteem, dreams, and fantasies of the people who create them every day when they come to work.

» «

References

Ablon, Joan. "Reactions of Samoan Burn Patients and Families to Severe Burns." *Social Science and Medicine* 7 (3; 1973): 167–178.

Allcorn, Seth. *Anger in the Workplace*. Westport, Conn.: Quorum Books, 1994.

Armstrong-Stassen, Marjorie. "Survivors' Reactions to a Workforce Reduction: A Comparison of Blue-Collar Workers and Their Supervisors." *Canadian Journal of Administrative Sciences* 10 (4; 1993): 334–343.

Balint, Michael. *The Basic Fault*. London: Tavistock, 1968.

Baum, Howell. *The Invisible Bureaucracy*. New York: Oxford University Press, 1987.

Baum, Howell. "Transference in Organizational Research." *Administration and Society* 26 (2; 1994): 135–157.

Bell, Clark. "Advice for Easing the Pain of Layoffs." *Modern Healthcare* 25 (3; 1995): 27.

Bion, Wilfred. *Experiences in Groups*. New York: Ballantine, 1959.

Boyer, L. Bryce. "Introduction: Countertransference—Brief History and Clinical Issues with Regressed Patients." In *Master Clinicians on Treating the Regressed Patient*. Volume 2. Edited by L. Bryce Boyer and Peter L. Giovacchini. Northvale, N.J.: Jason Aronson, 1993, 1–22.

Byrne, John. "The Pain of Downsizing." *Business Week* 3370 (1994): 60–68.

Caldwell, Bruce. "Missteps, Miscues." *Informationweek* 480 (1994): 50–52.

Cameron, Kim. "Strategies for Successful Organizational Downsizing." *Human Resource Management* 33 (2; 1994): 189–211.

Clark, Walter Van Tilburg. *The Ox-Bow Incident*. New York: Random House, 1940.

Davis, Madeleine, and David Wallbridge. *Boundary and Space: An Introduction to the Work of D. W. Winnicott*. Harmondsworth, England: Penguin, 1983.

De Board, Robert. *The Psychoanalysis of Organizations*. London: Tavistock, 1978.

Devereux, George. "Charismatic Leadership and Crisis." In *Psychoanalysis and the Social Sciences*, Volume 4. Edited by Geza Roheim. New York: International Universities Press, 1955, 145–157.

Diamond, Michael. *The Unconscious Life of Organizations: Interpreting Organizational Identity.* Westport, Conn.: Quorum, 1993.

Erikson, Erik. *Identity, Youth, and Crisis.* New York: Norton, 1968.

Erikson, Kai. *Everything in Its Path: Destruction of Community in the Buffalo Creek Flood.* New York: Simon and Schuster, 1976.

Fairbairn, W. R. D. *An Object-Relations Theory of the Personality.* New York: Basic Books, 1954.

Farrell, John. "A Practical Guide for Implementing Reengineering." *Planning Review* 22 (2; 1994): 40–45.

Filipowski, Diane. "Downsizing Isn't Always Rightsizing." *Personnel Journal* 72 (11; 1993): 71.

Freud, Sigmund. *Group Psychology and the Analysis of the Ego.* Volume 18. London: Hogarth Press, 1955 [1921], 69–143.

Freud, Sigmund. *Civilization and Its Discontents.* Volume 21. London: Hogarth Press, 1961 [1930], 64–145.

Furey, Timothy. "A Six-Step Guide to Process Reengineering." *Planning Review* 21 (2; 1993): 20.

Goffman, Erving. *Asylums.* Garden City, N.Y.: Doubleday, 1961.

Goldwasser, Charles. "The Initial Reengineering Project at Southern California Gas." *Planning and Review* 22 (3; 1994): 34–37.

Greengard, Samuel. "Don't Rush Downsizing: Plan, Plan, Plan." *Personnel Journal* 72 (11; 1993): 64–70.

Grotstein, James S. *Splitting and Projective Identification.* New York: Jason Aronson, 1981.

Guntrip, Harry. *Schizoid Phenomena, Object Relations, and the Self.* New York: International Universities Press, 1969.

Hall, Gene, Jim Rosenthal, and Judy Wade. "How to Make Reengineering Really Work." *Harvard Business Review* 71 (6; 1993): 119–131.

Hartmann, Heinz. *Ego Psychology and the Problem of Adaptation.* New York: International Universities Press, 1958 [1939].

Heenan, David. "The Right Way to Downsize." *The Journal of Business Strategy* 12 (5; 1991): 4–7.

Hockenos, Paul. *Free to Hate: The Rise of the Right in Post-Communist Eastern Europe.* New York: Routledge, 1993.

Horney, Karen. *Neurosis and Human Growth.* New York: Norton, 1950.

Janis, Irving. *Groupthink.* Boston: Houghton Mifflin, 1982.

Jaques, Elliot. "Social Systems as a Defense against Persecutory and Defensive Anxiety." In *New Directions in Psychoanalysis.* Edited by M. Klein, P. Heimann, and R. E. Money-Kyrle. New York: Basic Books, 1955.

Kets de Vries, Manfred, and Danny Miller. *The Neurotic Organization.* San Francisco: Jossey-Bass, 1984.

Klein, Mark. "The Most Fatal Reengineering Mistakes." *Information Strategy: The Executive's Journal* 10 (4; 1994): 21–28.

Klein, Melanie. "Notes on Some Schizoid Mechanisms." *International Journal of Psycho-Analysis* 27 (3 & 4; 1946): 99–110.

Kluckhohn, Florence, and Fred Strodtbeck. *Variations in Value Orientations.* Evanston, Ill.: Row-Peterson, 1961.

Koestler, Arthur. *Darkness at Noon.* New York: The New American Library, 1961.

Kohut, Heinz. *The Analysis of the Self.* New York: International Universities Press, 1971.

Kohut, Heinz. *The Restoration of the Self.* New York: International Universities Press, 1977.

Krystal, Henry. *Mass Psychic Trauma.* New York: International Universities Press, 1968.

Krystal, Henry. "Integration and Self-Healing in Posttraumatic States." In *Psychoanalytic Reflections on the Holocaust: Selected Essays.* Edited by Steven A. Luel and Paul Marcus. Denver: Holocaust Awareness Institute Center for Judaic Studies, University of Denver; and New York: KTAV Publishing House, 1984, 113–133.

La Barre, Weston. *The Human Animal.* Chicago: University of Chicago Press, 1954.

La Barre, Weston. *The Ghost Dance: The Origins of Religion.* New York: Dell, 1972.

Langer, Susanne. *Philosophy in a New Key.* Boston: Harvard University Press, 1957.

Lasch, Christopher. *The Culture of Narcissism.* New York: Warner Books, 1979.

Levinson, Harry. *Psychological Man.* Cambridge, Mass.: The Levinson Institute, 1976.

Lifton, Robert. *The Nazi Doctors.* New York: Basic Books, 1986.

Lowenthal, Jeffrey. "Reengineering the Organization: A Step-by-Step Approach to Corporate Revitalization: Part 2." *Quality Progress* 27 (2; 1994): 61–63.

Luel, Steven A., and Paul Marcus, Editors. *Psychoanalytic Reflections on the Holocaust: Selected Essays.* Denver: Holocaust Awareness Institute Center for Judaic Studies, University of Denver; and New York: KTAV Publishing House, 1984.

Mahler, Margaret, and Manuel Furer. *On Human Symbiosis and the Vicissitudes of Individuation.* New York: International Universities Press, 1968.

Margulis, Stephen. "Bad News, Good News about Downsizing." *Managing Office Technology* 39 (4; 1994): 23–24.

McDermott, John. *Corporate Society.* Boulder, Colo.: Westview Press, 1991.

Meissner, William. *The Paranoid Process.* New York: Jason Aronson, 1978.

Menzies, Isabel. "A Case-Study on the Functioning of Social Systems as a Defense against Anxiety." *Human Relations* 13 (2; 1960): 95–121.

Mishra, Aneil, and Karen Mishra. "The Role of Mutual Trust in Effective Downsizing Strategies." *Human Resource Management* 33 (2; 1994): 261–279.

Mitscherlisch, Alexander, and Margarete Mitscherlisch. *The Inability to Mourn.* New York: Grove Press, 1975.

Moad, Jeff. "Reengineering: Report from the Trenches." *Datamation* 40 (6; 1994): 36–40.

Moore-Ede, Martin. *The Twenty Four Hour Society.* Reading, Mass.: Addison-Wesley, 1993.

Nedelmann, Carl. "A Psychoanalytical View of the Nuclear Threat—From the Angle of the German Sense of Political Inferiority." *Psychoanalytic Inquiry* 6 (2; 1986): 287–302.

Niederland, William. "Clinical Observations on the 'Survivor Syndrome.'" *International Journal of Psycho-Analysis* 49 (2; 1968): 313–315.

Noer, David. "Leadership in an Age of Layoffs." *Issues & Observations* 13 (3; 1993): 1–5.

Ogden, Thomas. *The Primitive Edge of Experience.* Northvale, N.J.: Jason Aronson, 1989.

Owen, Wilfred. "Preface." In *The Collected Poems of Wilfred Owen.* Edited by C. Day Lewis. New York: New Directions Publishing Co., 1964 [1920].

Parin, Paul. "The Ego and the Mechanism of Adaptation." In *The Psychoanalytic Study of Society.* Volume 12. Edited by L. Bryce Boyer and Simon A. Grolnick. Hillsdale, N.J.: Analytic Press, 1988, 97–130.

Pinola, Richard. "Building a Winning Team after Downsizing." *Compensation & Benefits Management* 10 (1; 1994): 54–59.

Preston, Paul. "Downsizing: The Aftermath." *Administrative Radiology* 11 (9; 1992): 21–25.

Rangell, Leo. "Discussion of the Buffalo Creek Disaster: The Course of Psychic Trauma." *American Journal of Psychiatry* 133 (3; 1976): 313–316.

Rapaport, David. "A Historical Survey of Psychoanalytic Ego Psychology." Introduction to Erik H. Erikson, *Identity and the Life Cycle, Selected Papers by Erik H. Erikson. Psychological Issues* 1 (1; 1959): 5–17. New York: International Universities Press.

Reich, Robert. "Of Butchers and Bakers: Is Downsizing Good for the Company." *Vital Speeches of the Day* 60 (40; 1993): 100–102.

Rigby, Darrell. "The Secret History of Process Reengineering." *Planning Review* 21 (2; 1993): 24–27.

Roth, William. "The Dangerous Ploy of Downsizing." *Business Forum* 18 (4; 1993): 5–7.

Sartre, Jean-Paul. *No Exit and Three Other Plays.* New York: Vintage Books, 1956.

Schwartz, Howard. *Narcissistic Process and Corporate Decay: The Theory of the Organization Ideal.* New York: New York University Press, 1990.

Searles, Harold. *Collected Papers on Schizophrenia and Other Subjects.* New York: International Universities Press, 1965.

Spiegel, John. *Transactions: The Interplay Between Individual, Family, and Society.* New York: Science House, 1971.

Stamm, Ira. *Countertransference in Hospital Treatment: Basic Concepts and Paradigms.* Paper Series No. 2. Topeka, Kan.: The Menninger Foundation, 1987.

Stein, Howard. *The Culture of Oklahoma.* Norman: University of Oklahoma Press, 1993.

Stein, Howard. "'The Eternal Jew': Resurgent Anti-Semitism in the Post–Cold War World." *The Journal of Psychohistory* 22 (1; 1994a): 39–57.

Stein, Howard. *Listening Deeply: An Approach to Understanding and Consulting with Organizational Cultures.* Boulder, Colo.: Westview Press, 1994b.

Stein, Howard. "Domestic Wars and the Militarization of Medicine." *The Journal of Psychohistory* 22 (4; 1995): 406–445.

Stein, Howard, and Robert Hill. *The Ethnic Imperative: Exploring the New White Ethnic Movement.* University Park: Pennsylvania State University Press, 1977.

Sullivan, Harry. *The Interpersonal Theory of Psychiatry.* New York: W. W. Norton, 1953.

Vaill, Peter. *Managing as a Performing Art: New Ideas for a World of Chaotic Change.* San Francisco: Jossey-Bass, 1989.

Volkan, Vamik D. *Linking Objects and Linking Phenomena: A Study of the Forms, Symptoms, Metapsychology, and Therapy of Complicated Mourning.* New York: International Universities Press, 1980.

Winnicott, Donald. *The Maturational Processes and the Facilitating Environment.* New York: International Universities Press, 1965.

Winnicott, Donald. *Playing and Reality.* London: Tavistock, 1971.

Zdrodowski, Paul. "Downsizing with Dignity." *Chemical Business* 15 (9; 1993): 5–7.

» «
=====

Index

ABOUT THE AUTHORS

SETH ALLCORN is a principal of DyAD, a consulting company that supports change in organizations. He has worked twenty years as an academic health-science-center executive and is a member of the Medical Group Management Association and the International Society for the Psychoanalytic Study of Organizations. He is the author of 6 books, 3 chapters, and more than 50 papers.

HOWELL S. BAUM is a Professor of Urban Studies and Planning at the University of Maryland. He is the author of 3 books, 9 chapters, and more than 40 papers. He is a member of the International Society for the Psychoanalytic Study of Organizations.

MICHAEL A. DIAMOND is a Professor in the Department of Public Administration, University of Missouri—Columbia. He is the author of 1 book, 2 chapters, and more than 25 papers. He was awarded the American Psychological Association 1994 Harry Levinson Award for Excellence in Consulting Psychology. He is a principal of DyAD, a consulting company that support change in organizations. He is a member of the International Society for the Psychoanalytic Study of Organizations as well as a number of other associations.

HOWARD F. STEIN is a Professor in the Department of Family Medicine at the University of Oklahoma Health Sciences Center. He is the author of 16 books, 31 chapters, and more than 160 papers. He also frequently publishes poetry. He is a member of the International Society for the Psychoanalytic Study of Organizations as well as a number of other associations and societies.